SOMETHING
TO BELIEVE IN

SOMETHING TO BELIEVE IN

Is Kurt Vonnegut the Exorcist of Jesus Christ Superstar?

Robert Short

Published in San Francisco by
HARPER & ROW, PUBLISHERS
New York, Hagerstown, San Francisco, London

FIRST EDITION

Designed by Donna Davis

Library of Congress Cataloging in Publication Data

Short, Robert L
    Something to believe in.

    Includes bibliographical references.
    1. Theology—20th century.   2. Christianity and
culture.   3. Vonnegut, Kurt—Religion and ethics.
4. United States—Popular culture.   5. Blatty, William
Peter.   The exorcist.   6. Jesus Christ superstar
[Motion picture]   I. Title.
BR115.C8S53   230'.09'04   75-36754
ISBN 0-06-067381-8

The text of this book is printed on 100% recycled paper.

78 79 80 81 82   10 9 8 7 6 5 4 3 2 1

Contents

Prelude and Dedication

—Garry Trudeau, Doonesbury

Think of all our knowledge! Think of all the wisdom and awareness that we've arrived at through tears and misery. It's magnificent. Fantastic. We've discovered ourselves. . . . It's unheard-of, Marianne. Analysis is total, knowledge is boundless. But I can't stand it. . . . Because I refuse to accept the complete meaninglessness behind the complete awareness. I can't live with that cold light over all my endeavors. If you only knew how I struggle with my meaninglessness. Over and over again I try to cheer myself up by saying that life has the value that you yourself ascribe to it. But that sort of talk is no help to me. I want something to long for. I want something to believe in.

—Ingmar Bergman, Scenes from a Marriage[1]

Paul reflected that the big trouble, really, was finding something to believe in.

—Kurt Vonnegut, Player Piano[2]

Drawing by W. Miller; ©1975. The New Yorker Magazine, Inc.

*For my sweet little daughter SARAH ELIZABETH
—whose given names, unlike so many meaningless
names in an age of meaninglessness, mean that there is
indeed something to believe in. She is, as her names
say, "a princess consecrated to God."*

1

The Popular Arts and the Unpopular God

I deliberately started this conversation as stupidly as I could . . . because the more stupidly we talk about these things, the closer we come to the point. The stupider the clearer. Stupidity is brief and straightforward, while intelligence is tortuous and sneaky. Intelligence is crooked, while stupidity is honest. I've carried my argument to the point of despair, and the more stupidly I present it, the more to my advantage that will be.
     —Dostoevsky, *The Brothers Karamazov* [1]

Make the reader laugh and he will think you a trivial fellow, but bore him in the right way and your reputation is assured.
    —Somerset Maugham, *The Gentleman in the Parlour* [2]

A man may take to drink because he feels himself to be a failure, and then fail all the more completely because he drinks. It is rather the same thing that is happening to the English language. It becomes ugly and inaccurate because our thoughts are foolish, but the slovenliness of our language makes it easier for us to have foolish thoughts. . . . So . . . the fight against bad English is not frivolous and it is not the exclusive concern of professional writers.
    —George Orwell, "Politics and the English Language" [3]

If incisiveness, exactness, conscientiousness and responsibility matter anywhere in our talk, then most of all in our talk of God. Here it is well to be silent before we open our mouth, to inquire before we make assertions, to test each word before we let it pass our lips. . . .
For how can we speak of God today without facing the fact that a considerable section of our contemporaries must honestly confess

*that they have really no idea what we are talking about when we
talk of God? Could the reason for that possibly be, that God is
spoken of thoughtlessly?—with a supposed self-evidence that can
only hinder understanding the evidence, with such lack of awareness of our own questionableness that no genuine questions arise
and we therefore also lose the power to arouse genuine questions?
The man who ventures to speak of God today and does not wish to
be without conscience and love, must venture to face with a wake-
ful heart the questionableness of speaking of God. . . .*

Worldly talk of God is therefore clear talk of God. *. . . There is
no place here for unclear, pious jargon, evasion of problems, ob-
scuring of facts. One might say that the tone itself betrays the man
who shies in clarity in his talk of God. For where there is in the true
sense a spiritual approach, there is freedom to be natural and to
face the world uninhibited.*

—Gerhard Ebeling, *Word and Faith* [4]

*Who [writes] as simply as you? . . . You say that you had to
wrestle very hard for simplicity; that I can believe. Simplicity is an
intellectual achievement, one of the greatest.*
—Dietrich Bonhoeffer, *Letters and Papers from Prison* [5]

The aim and object of this command is the love which springs
from a clean heart, from a good conscience, and from faith that is
genuine. Through falling short of these, some people have gone
astray into a wilderness of words.
—1 Timothy 1:5−6, NEB

When people are not anchored in the world by the humanity of God in Christ, their lives will vacillate between two extremes: an overemphasis on the intellect
or an emphasis on the body and an increasing "earth-
iness." This vacillation quickly shows up in the ways
they talk and write. In the church this situation shows
up as wavering between seemingly deep speech that
is actually an empty abstraction, and the speech of a
flashy but shallow "relevance." For language, like all
other aspects of life, will wander between these two
extremes, looking for its lost referent. "The world,
like all created things, is created through Christ and
with Christ as its end, and consists in Christ alone
(John 1:10; Col. 1:16). To speak of the world without
speaking of Christ is empty and abstract. The world is
relative to Christ, no matter whether it knows it or
not" (Dietrich Bonhoeffer).[6]

1. Mr. Newman and How You Talk

TV newsman Edwin Newman is disturbed by the awful things all of
us are doing to the language; so in order to help us face a sick situation, he has written a couple of funny and clever books (an interesting technique). In one of them, *A Civil Tongue,* newsman Newman
has this to say:

> There has to be some explanation for the fact that, as we
> become more and more open about ourselves, speak ever
> more freely about sex . . . and—men and women alike—use
> language in what once would have been called polite society
> that no polite society would tolerate, our language in other
> parts of our lives becomes less and less frank, more and more
> covered and obscure.[7]

Newman never gets around to speculating very seriously about
why this is true. Therefore, with all due respect, Mr. Newman, I'd
like to suggest my above thesis as a possible answer. In other
words, I think Christ has something (the lion's share) to do with it.

This is because I am a *systematic theologian.* A systematic theologian is an academic pedant trained to see all sorts of connections between bad thinking or no thinking about Christ and bad thinking or no thinking about everything else. This is a frightening thing to see, even for an academic pedant.

I also know from frightening *personal* experiences how bad thinking or no thinking about Christ leads to a lot of garbled thinking about everything else. This is because other people's garbled thinking about Christ, not to mention my own, has frequently garbled me. So I think there is a place for systematic theologians—those who try to do a better job of thinking about Christ and all his "connections." So be it.

But we surely need more Edwin Newmans too—those who can describe so effectively what the situation is today: that all our speech tends to be divided into only two parts: the highfalutin or the lowfalutin, with a vast no man's language in between. And the language of the churches, in keeping with the times, also goes on at one extreme or the other of what Karl Barth called "silly or too subtle speech."

Try it out. Go into the best religious bookstore you can find. You will easily be able to classify 90 percent of the books in there in one of two categories: cultivated claptrap by Theobore Theologian or homegrown ignorance by Pat Popcorn. Theobore's stuff is indigestible theological scholarship; Pat's is religious junk food.

A plague on both these houses!

2. Life Is Never Pointless When You Stick to the Point

The only thing that can finally keep life and language from sliding off one deep end or the other is to "stick to the point." However, this is difficult as long as people consciously or unconsciously think of life as ultimately "pointless." If there is finally no point to life, then anything goes . . . and goes . . . and goes . . . and doesn't know where to stop. . . . So it goes.

So *they* go. Life and language together:

*" . . . to have and to hold in counterproductive as well as productive time frames,
so long as you are bilaterally capable of maintaining a viable life-style. . . ."*

Reprinted from *Saturday Review* by permission of artist, Donald Reilly.

Christians, though, are a people persuaded that life is not pointless. They are "the dogs of God." They stick to the point with
doglike devotion and humility. Like dogs, it is their joy faithfully to
serve and obey their Master. What kind of dogs are they? *Pointers.*
Pointing sums up everything they do and are commanded to do.
Here is how Saint Martin Luther summed up the Christian's entire
responsibility:

To this man [Jesus] thou shalt point and say, Here is God.[8]

The Christian believes that in the man Jesus, God revealed himself to people once and for all. To put it another way, in Jesus, God
has revealed decisively, normatively, and pointedly the meaning, or
"the point," of all life and death. Christians—otherwise why call
them by this peculiar name?—are only different from other people
because they believe that Christ and Christ alone is God's "man-to-
man talk" with the world, that Christ alone is "the still point of the
turning world." Therefore, all the Christian's saying and doing and
sticking to the point has this single direction and purpose: to point to
this point (X) and say, "Here is God." Yet like characters in a
Kilgore Trout story (Trout is himself one of Kurt Vonnegut's fictional characters), our efforts are often marked by a "tragic failure
to communicate."

Drawing by Stevenson; ©1976. The New Yorker Magazine, Inc.

3. Woe to You, Theobore Theologian —God's Holy Prig

When it comes to communicating, the church has this problem: its theologians (or "thinkers") aren't good popularizers, and its popularizers aren't good theologians. It's like a person having creaking arthritis and Saint Vitus's dance at the same time: These two only get in each other's way.

First, the theologians. Here is one of the things I liked best about Mr. Newman's book *A Civil Tongue:* When he starts rummaging around for good examples of the current use of unintelligible gobbledygook and jargon, he knows instinctively where to look. He chooses some of our "best" American theologians. For instance, he quotes a long, murky passage by theologian Paul Lehmann (who is actually a very find theologian as theologians go) and concludes that the point Lehmann is trying to make is this: "The Biable is viable."

As one trained in theology, I have examined the Lehmann passage carefully, and I'll be flipped if Newman isn't an improvement. (Mr. Newman, would you be interested in teaching a few courses?)

4. Can the Germans Be Germane? *or* "Deutschland über Alles"

But because Newman limits himself to American speech, the best examples of the worst academic pomposity are unavailable to him. These are found in German theology. It is generally admitted that the Germans write the best theology. They certainly write most of it, but also, with a few exceptions, they do the best job of botching it up. They are like what Vonnegut's Eliot Rosewater says of Kilgore Trout:

> "Jesus—if Kilgore Trout could only *write!*" Rosewater exclaimed. He had a point: Kilgore Trout's unpopularity was deserved. His prose was frightful. Only his ideas were good.[9]

One of the funniest things Mark Twain ever wrote, I think, is his essay "The Awful German Language." Actually, I don't think Twain ever knew just how awful it could be, for when he gave us examples of how the Germans have trouble ending their sentences and compound words, he only mentioned their newspapers. "An average sentence, in a German newspaper," Twain said,

> is a sublime and impressive curiosity; it occupies a quarter of a column; it contains all the ten parts of speech—not in regular order, but mixed; it is built mainly of compound words constructed by the writer on the spot, and not to be found in any dictionary—six or seven words compacted into one, without joint or seam . . .[10]

So much for everyday German journalism. Had Twain taken a look at their everyday theology, he could have *really* had fun, after recovering from the shock.

Over a period of many years and after thousands of pages, I have developed a foolproof method for piecing together books and articles written by German theologians and more or less translated into English: With each new sentence you must imagine you are going for a roller coaster ride. Get a firm grip on the first word of each sentence, and then hang on with wide-eyed attention until that sentence is finished some two to four pages later. If your attention wavers for one millisecond during any of the author's parenthetical dives or subordinate swerves, you will either fall off or have to return to the beginning of that sentence to start over. Usually I fall off and don't wake up until half an hour later to have another go at it.

The other day I came across a run-on sentence in Wolfhart Pannenberg, that, as far as I know, is still running. I never did finish that sentence. But then it didn't look as if Pannenberg planned to finish it either.

5. The Blessed Martin Luther

But lest anyone think that theologians, especially the Germans, have always been a bunch of incomprehensible bores, he or she should go back and read something from the blunt, plain-spoken Martin Luther. This can be a hair-raising experience. For Luther was a bull in the theological china shop. Much of his vocabulary came fresh from the barnyard, if not the gutter. He could cuss the air blue when he wasn't even mad. When he *was* angry (and he often was), I have no doubt that the atmospheric conditions included all the terrifying sounds and flashing displays of a spring storm in the Black Forest.

Pious types, like Beetle Bailey's "Chaplain Staneglass," are usually scandalized by this kind of talk from Luther, and they go to great lengths to make excuses for him. But Luther, the great, rotund top sergeant of the Reformation, knew well enough what he was doing.

©King Features Syndicate, Inc. 1969.

6. Two New Laws for Theobore Theologian

Someone once asked Luther why he used such language. He replied: "Our Lord God must precede a heavy shower with thunder and then let it rain in a very gentle fashion. . . . To put it differently, I can cut through a willow branch with a knife, but to cut through tough oak requires an axe and wedge . . ."[11]

And it is true that Luther was a master of gentle, sweet talk as well as of the verbal thunderstorm. A good example of his gentle sweetness is the short catechism he took great pains in writing for small children. It is a model of the powerful and complex mind stooping to charming simplicity. His *Small Catechism* is still widely used and is considered one of the greatest documents of the Reformation. Luther himself never stopped teaching and preaching from it. But where are the great theologians of today who will "come off it"—come down from their ivory towers—for such an effort? Childlike brevity and directness are apparently beneath the dignity of today's great theological geniuses. And what is a genius?

genius: n   a mistaken attribute usually applied to a master of vagueness.

B.C. by permission of Johnny Hart and Field Enterprises, Inc.

Therefore, I propose the following law: As soon as any theologian has written more than he or she can lift (a drop in their verbal bucket), he or she shall not be allowed to publish anything more until he or she has written a five-page catechism for children six years old and up. Then, for every subsequent twenty-five pounds the theologian publishes, he or she will be allowed to add two sentences to their catechism.

Think what this would mean! No longer would there be the confusing proliferation of thick books, written by other theologians whose interpretations never agree, on "The Theology of Professor

So-and-So." We would just have "The Children's Catechism of Professor So-and-So" and that would be that.

Think of all who would benefit from this law! Everyone six and over would be able to understand what the great theologian was saying and to come to some conclusion about it—the great theologian included. For then these geniuses would have to say what this man has just said:

THE NOW SOCIETY

"That's it, in a nutshell!"

Franz Kafka formulated another law for all Theobore Theologians, and it should be enshrined in the depths of their hearts. Here is "Kafka's Law":

When the plain truth is in question, great minds discard the niceties of refinement.[12]

What a wonderful statement! There isn't a theologian in all Christendom who doesn't consider himself or herself a "great mind." Therefore, when theologians sit down to write their books or articles or sermons, if "Kafka's Law" is not already engraved on their hearts, as it should be, then it should be stitched with steel wool on the inside of their underpants. At least this way it would still have a chance to shake their foundations.

For Kafka is absolutely right. When the plain truth is in question, "the niceties of refinement" are the last things "great minds"—or even someone as horrible as Hägar—should think about.

7. What Theobore Theologian Needs to Learn

God's academic drudges have something important to learn about themselves. Here is what it is:

"Harrington, I have just learned, quite inadvertently, that we are considered insufferable."

Or, as expressed in another *New Yorker* cartoon, where one worried old boy says to another at their club: "Times are changing, Whittleby. Being a pompous ass is no longer enough."

But such ego-shattering lessons are hard to learn. Egos, like oaks, are tough. And so it goes with theologians. Even if they should be bluntly and unambiguously told that they are pompous bores, they have an effective way of quashing such an unflattering judgment: They can simply drown it in more pomposity.

B.C. by permission of Johnny Hart and Field Enterprises, Inc.

8. Crap

Here is a question Kurt Vonnegut addresses to all Christian scholars:

> Who has time to read all the boring crap you write and listen to all the boring things you say?[13]

I especially like Vonnegut's use of the word "crap" here, for I never will forget the day I came face-to-crap with some crap I was manufacturing. I was in the library of the local theological seminary, standing at the card catalogue and looking for some footnotes to add to a paper I was writing. Two carpenters slowly wandered by. I wasn't surprised to see them because I knew the library was planning some renovations. But these fellows were looking around in wide-eyed amazement.

"Aha!" I thinks to my learned self. "Two blue-collar types overwhelmed by the sheer magnitude of theological scholarship!" Then one of them says to the other, "How do you suppose they got all this crap in here?"

That's when I called it a day at the library and went home to play with the kids.

But back to Vonnegut's question: Who has time to read the theologians' crap or listen to what they say? Why, only other theologians of course! That's their job. And so we have what can be called "the rhetorical captivity of the church." In Christ, God humbled himself in order to speak to the world with directness and clarity. But Theobore Theologian only speaks to other theologians and in a sort of impenetrable code. This makes it even easier for the world to ignore Theobore's monologue and to go on to more interesting conversations.

"I'm afraid Coggleston sometimes gets a bit caught up in his own rhetoric."

Drawing by Stan Hunt; ©1976. The New Yorker Magazine, Inc.

9. God Bless You, Herr Zahrnt

Heinz Zahrnt, a German theologian who nevertheless seems to live in the real world, has this to say:

> We cannot imagine that the question of God is as complicated as theologians sometimes make it. . . . The complication of our theology is in flat contradiction to divine revelation. It thereby contradicts the clear will of God to which every page of the Bible bears witness, that God wishes to seek men out, then reveal himself, impart himself and make himself known to men. God has left his concealment and entered the manifold variety of life, and has revealed himself in *one* human life, in the man Jesus of Nazareth. Through this revelation the concealed and manifold God has become "simple" on our behalf. The incarnation of God in Jesus Christ implies both the simplification of God and simplification of theology.

Just as Switzerland possesses only a small professional army, whose task it is to set up a large territorial army, so theologians, too, ought to form only a small professional army with the sole task of building up a large territorial army. And therefore Christian dogmas and doctrines must be brought down from heaven to earth for Adam and Eve, on the same earth on which Jesus of Nazareth and the whole Bible stand. What we say about God can no longer be uttered "from above," in an authoritarian fashion and in the form of a monologue. We must now speak about him "here below," at ground level, on the level of those who listen to us—that is, we must speak of him democratically in the form of a dialogue. This is in accordance with God's own coming down from heaven.[14]

I believe you are right, Herr Zahrnt. Theologians *are* in a sense the generals responsible for building up the church's army. But then, as the fellow says, "If the trumpet-call is not clear, who will prepare for battle?" (1 Cor. 14:8, NEB).

BEETLE BAILEY   ©King Features Syndicate, Inc. 1974.

10. And the Word Became Words . . . and Words . . . and Words . . . Etc.

But isn't what Zahrnt is saying fairly obvious? A recent book-jacket blurb by an American theologian describes a book by Karl Barth as being "Daringly down-to-earth!" Good grief, Mr. American theologian, why shouldn't a theologian, even a great one, dare to be down to earth!? As Zahrnt points out, since God has "dared," in Christ and in the Bible, to *be* down-to-earth, isn't this the first thing any Christian scholar should be? Precisely because God became flesh—particular, concrete, and specific flesh—theologians, of all people, should know better than to inappropriately envelop themselves in ethereal metaphysical clouds.

If theologians really believe that what they are saying is important, and if as a group they are presumably concerned with "love," is it an act of Christian love *not* to bother to make themselves clear? If theologians really are those "doctors of the soul" who are basically concerned about the real person, then why should what they say sound so forbiddingly impersonal and technical?

MISS PEACH by Mell Lazarus. Courtesy of Mell Lazarus and Field Newspaper Syndicate.

But theologians tend to be "clear" only in the sense of being invisible. They are absolute masters at hiding their light, God's Word, under bushels of scholarly words. For instance, in George Orwell's famous 1946 essay "Politics and the English Language," there is an often-quoted example of how *not* to write English. And where does Orwell go for his example? He begins by quoting a beautiful and well-known verse from the Bible's book of Ecclesiastes:

> I returned, and saw under the sun, that the race is not to the swift, nor the battle to the strong, neither yet bread to the wise, nor yet riches to men of understanding, nor yet favour to men of skill; but time and chance happeneth to them all (Eccles. 9:11, KJV).

Then Orwell shows us how Theobore Theologian would say the same thing:

Objective considerations of contemporary phenomena compels the conclusion that success or failure in competitive activities exhibits no tendency to be commensurate with innate capacity, but that a considerable element of the unpredictable must invariably be taken into account.[15]

"A parody," says Orwell, "but not a very gross one."

So, as a group concerned with "the plain truth," theologians obviously should shun words and ways of speaking that aren't plain. They should, as they would say, "eschew obfuscation." But they don't. Therefore, there must be a more practical reason why theologians, who at least know better in theory, have a genius for taking anything any good Christian already knows and making it sound confusing. Here is the best statement I have found to explain what they are up to:

It's gratifying that so many people are becoming aware of, and offended by, bad writing and speaking. Most of us have been taught that it is *our* fault, not the writer's, if we can't understand some unfathomable piece of prose. There is good reason for this. If the academic, governmental and corporate elites can make us believe their illiterate cant is in some way profound but beyond our intellectual reach, they can keep us respectful and subservient. . . .

Whole academic disciplines, including most of the social sciences, owe their existence to their ability to make commonplace thoughts sound profound.[16]

In other words, if you want to be an expert and enjoy an expert's paychecks and prestige, then there have to be a lot of folks around who don't know as much as you do. Or at least they mustn't *think* they know as much as you. So if they start learning too much or if they begin to suspect how little you really know, then you must disguise your "commonplace thoughts" in an intimidating form of theoretical double talk. "The great enemy of clear language is insincerity," said Orwell. "When there is a gap between one's real and one's declared aims, one turns as it were instinctively to long words and exhausted idioms, like a cuttlefish squirting out ink." This cut-tlefish game is called "Keeping Nonexperts in Their Place," and it works like this:

"In theory, yes, Mrs. Wilkins. But also in theory, no."

Thus also the frowning humorlessness of most present-day theo-logical writing and speaking. "Wear a frown," says Andy Capp, "and you'll get credit for thinking."

In 1972 Kurt Vonnegut worked as a magazine reporter at the Republican National Convention. As part of his job he interviewed a real, live American theologian and tried to get him to say some-thing intelligible. Failing this, however, he went on to talk to a group of real, live American Indians who had come to the convention "to beg . . . that their religions be recognized as respectable religions under law. As the law now stands," Vonnegut reports the Indians told him,

. . . their religions are negligible superstitions deserving no respect.

I'll say this: Their religions couldn't possibly be more chaotic than the Christianity reinvented every day by Dr. D. Elton Trueblood, Professor at Large.[17]

I mention this incident not to single out Trueblood, but because I think Vonnegut's experience is fairly typical nowadays. Most Christian theology is not rejected because it is considered wrong. Few people get far enough into it to form this kind of opinion. It's simply rejected because it seems incomprehensible and boring.

©King Features Syndicate, Inc. 1976.

According to Vonnegut, the late Irving Langmuir, a Nobel Prize chemist, once said: "Any person who can't explain his work to a fourteen-year-old is a charlatan."[18]

If Langmuir was right, there sure are a lot of theological charlatans around.

11. Woe to You, Pat Popcorn —God's Harebrained Popularizer

Both Theobore Theologian and Pat Popcorn use a lot of words, words, words. But while Theobore uses a mystifying academic jargon, Pat Popcorn prefers a "with it" gibberish and slang. We have all met Pat Popcorns. They sound more or less like—

"Like, man, you know. I mean, like, you know, wow!"

You will note that both Theobore Theologian and Pat Popcorn like to hold forth at friendly gatherings or anywhere they can give dumbfounded audiences the benefit of their wondrous words. Both believe the mouth is quicker than the eye.

This is too bad because the very first commandment of Jesus and/or God[19] is to "love him [God] with all your heart, all your understanding, and all your strength" (Mark 12:33, NEB). This means means to love God with all your *heart,* all your *head,* and all your *hand.* But Theobore Theologian tends to overdo it with his or her head, and Pat Popcorn is all heart. Neither is very handy.

Pat Popcorn has a close cousin, René Relevant. These two have decided to be relevant at all costs, even at the cost of thinking or of any other kind of work that requires silence. Usually they believe that if you love God with all your heart, jump for joy, smile a lot, and just keep praising the Lord (relevantly), that should just about do it.

For Pat Popcorn, the church is one of the few places left where you can say what you think without even thinking. Pat recognizes no distinction between free speech and cheap talk. In about the same way that Theobore Theologian makes my head ache, Pat

Popcorn makes my stomach turn. This of course is because Pat only feeds me spiritual popcorn. It is *pop* in the sense of wanting to be popular, but it is also *corn* because it is corny and shallow. Like popcorn, it is noisy and can be fun to eat in small amounts, but it is hardly nourishing, and more than a little of it will soon make you sick.

I do not think that Pat Popcorn and René Relevant should be dismissed as a couple of harmless phonies simply because they are such intellectual lightweights. Even though their phoniness is usually easily spotted, in the meantime it casts the suspicion of phoniness over everything genuine in the church.

Copyright, 1972, G. B. Trudeau/Distributed by Universal Press Syndicate.

No one denies the need of the church to be popular and relevant. It is part of the church's very nature to try to make its message strongly worded and meaningful to all people, but any relevance that loses sight of what it is supposed to be *related to* is itself irrelevant. Any relevance in the church that sacrifices truth for an intellectually shallow popularity or for the latest cultural fads and trends, is irrelevance itself. As Bonhoeffer said of modern American Christianity, but in a statement that should be a warning to the church anywhere, "The almost frantic propagation of modern methods betrays the dwindling of the content." [20]

MISS PEACH by Mell Lazarus. Courtesy of Mell Lazarus and Field Newspaper Syndicate.

12. New Law for Pat Popcorn

Just as Kafka formulated a new law for Theobore Theologian, Gerhard Ebeling has come up with one for Pat Popcorn. Here is "Ebeling's Law":

> The man who in thinking about faith is not as scrupulous as his thinking capacity will allow, incurs at least the suspicion of not being scrupulous about faith itself. And such a man ought not to appeal to faith. . . . The faith that is afraid to think is unbelief in the mask of piety.[21]

13. How Visual Aids You and Me

I like to use pictures, especially cartoons, to illustrate what I write. I want my manuscripts to be illuminating by being illuminated. This is no "modern method," but a method the church has always used and one that has played an important part in its history. The two best examples of this importance are probably the parables—or "word pictures"—of Jesus and the use of cartoons during the Protestant Reformation. As Roland Bainton says of the Reformation's rapid spread through Germany: "This success was achieved through a wave of propaganda unequaled hitherto and in its precise form never repeated. The primary tools were the tract and the cartoon."[22] Luther also used other types of pictures to great advantage. For instance, his *Small Catechism,* which I mentioned above, was "enlivened with quaint woodcuts of episodes from the Bible suitable to each point."[23]

I like to use pictures "suitable to each point" for two general reason: First, from a strictly practical point of view, pictures know *how* to say things effectively. Like the parables of Jesus (*parable* means "a placing beside," that is, to *place* an illustrating figure or picture *beside* what is said), pictures can get our attention, hold it, and tell us more that we will understand and remember than can words alone. "Show and tell" is always more effective than "only tell." This is because showing appeals to our eyes and hearts as well as to our heads. When the eyes and the head vie for our attention, actions will always speak louder than words

CAPITOL GAMES

Reprinted by permission of JAMES STEVENSON. Copyright ©1976 by JAMES STEVENSON.

Pictures are not only better at getting our attention, but also *what* they then tell us is usually better understood and remembered. Simple images are the basic units of thinking. We learn to "see car" before we can say car. Therefore, like international highway signs, images speak a more universally understandable language. Also, when pictures do resort to actual verbal messages, the words must be carefully chosen and few if they are not to crowd out the picture. In this way pictures are forced to give only the verbal essentials. Cartoonists, for instance, must reduce what their characters say to the utmost brevity—"the soul of wit."

And because most pictures contain something visibly human, they can speak more directly than mere words to our hearts or emotions or human interest. Here is how Kurt Vonnegut puts it:

Most people are mainly interested in people. . . . Or that has been my experience in the writing game. That's why it was so intelligent of us to send human beings to the moon instead of instruments. One of the things that I tell beginning writers is this: "If you describe a landscape, or a cityscape, or a sea-scape, always be sure to put a human figure somewhere in the scene. Why? Because readers are human beings, mostly interested in human beings." [24]

This is why a story, which is a picture that has movement and recognizable characters in it, has always been the most successful way of getting people to listen. It appeals to our human interest as well as to our "image-ination."

BEETLE BAILEY

©King Features Syndicate, Inc. 1976.

And on a strictly practical level, there should be no mystery why *funny* pictures appeal to us. "A good laugh is a mighty good thing," said Melville, "and rather too scarce a good thing; the more's the pity." [25]

HI AND LOIS

©King Features Syndicate, Inc. 1975.

This unique ability to furnish a funny, popular, and brief abstract for our eyes, heads, and hearts makes cartoons for us today what plays were in Shakespeare's day: "They are the abstract and brief chronicles of the time," said Hamlet.[26] One example of this truth is a remark President Gerald Ford recently made about Garry Trudeau's popular comic strip, *Doonesbury:*

> There are only three major vehicles to keep us informed as to what is going on in Washington: the electronic media, the print media, and *Doonesbury,* not necessarily in that order.[27]

But the cartoon is an extremely effective teacher, not only of what's "going on in Washington," but in the rest of the world as well. It "refines material until only the . . . essence remains. Circumstances impossible in the real world are staged upon the cartoonist's proscenium."[28]

14. Visual Theology

Second general reason why I like to use pictures: From a theological standpoint, pictures, especially those containing humor, are by their very nature close to *what* the Christian faith says. For at the very center of Christian faith is the *visible.*

God's becoming visible in Christ was a condescension or a concession to the fact that all people are by nature originally people of "sight" rather than of "faith" (2 Cor. 5:7). Therefore, to change our natures God met us in Christ on our own home ground—in the world of *visible* flesh and blood. Throughout his ministry Jesus pointed to *himself* as the visible flesh-and-blood point upon which all Christian faith and work hang—the single point at which God himself became a particular, historical, and concretely visible man. "He who has seen me has seen the Father" (John 14:9).

But Jesus was not only the *visible* man. He was also the *visual* man, teaching in *words* filled with visual imagery (the parables, for instance) and in *deeds* of striking visual significance (for instance, the crucifixion). For pictures, verbal or otherwise, give life to bloodless words in the same way that deeds do. In much the same way that "One act of obedience is better than a hundred sermons" (Bonhoeffer),[29] "one picture is worth more than ten thousand words" (a Chinese proverb). To people of sight, both the picture and the deed lend authority to what is *said* by what is *shown*. Therefore, when the church uses the picture and the deed, "then you will have something to say to those whose pride is all in outward show and not in inward worth" (2 Cor. 5:12, NEB).

When Christians try to communicate in ways that overlook the visual, they are inconsistent with God's own condescension in visibility for people of sight. This is especially true now that technology easily puts pictures anywhere, making us more and more a people of sight and less and less a people of words.

MOTLEY'S CREW

©1976 Chicago Tribune—New York News Syndicate, Inc.

15. Theology—The Science of the Last Laugh

Humor, like the pictorial, is also by nature close to the Christian faith. Faith sees "the fall of man" as the cosmic version of the old banana peel pratfall. Humor involves a "fall" or "error" that is painful and humiliating but that is recognized by the onlooker as not being ultimately serious. We know that the person who has slipped on the banana peel will rise to walk again. Therefore, this person's situation strikes us as funny rather than tragic.

The Christian faith looks upon the entire human race as being in this same "humorous" situation: Humankind has fallen away from faith in God, a separation that causes pain and humiliation. But this faith has additional "inside information": that *finally* there can never be for *any* person "any created thing, [that] can ever come between us and the love of God made visible in Christ Jesus our Lord" (Rom. 8:39, JB). Christian faith has been "let in on" the end of the story of humankind: *All* humankind is *already* loved, saved, and redeemed, and *all* will finally be raised again to be with God where *all* will recognize and enjoy his love endlessly. Anything less than this makes God's universe a meaningless tragedy rather than a divine comedy. This is why the only truly *joyful* laughter can come from knowing that there is a happy ending for all people. If we believe our ending will be adverse, or fear that it is somehow still up for grabs, how can we laugh at that?

MISS PEACH by Mell Lazarus. Courtesy of Mell Lazarus and Field Newspaper Syndicate.

16. Who the Last Laugh Is On

The dispute between unbelief and Christian belief is basically about who is the more *foolish* of the two. Because all believers were originally unbelievers themselves (hence the doctrine of "origin-al sin"), they know how foolish their faith looks in the eyes of the world. As St. Paul could say, "We preach Christ crucified, a stumbling block to Jews and folly to Gentiles" (1 Cor. 1:23, RSV). We must admit that the kingdom of God is pretty funny-looking. Its king is a clown-like nobody from the countryside, and the foolish themselves are the first to enter his kingdom.

When one adds the admitted foolishness of the Christian faith to all the foolish mistakes historically associated with this faith, then we can easily understand why the church often comes in for some severe ribbing—and ought to!—like the kind we find in Mark Twain and Kurt Vonnegut, for instance. But whether they know it or not, those who poke fun at the church are among its best and most helpful friends. Their laughter can only help clean off from the church what needs to be cleaned off. They can never harm the real thing. For this reason, those who think they are the church's "detractors" are often closer to the kingdom of God than those who think they are the church's "defenders."

On the other hand, believers have their fun too. They know they look foolish, but they also know, to continue with St. Paul, that

the foolishness of God is wiser than men, . . . God chose what is foolish in the world to shame the wise, God chose what is weak in the world to shame the strong, God chose what is low and despised in the world, even things that are not, to bring to nothing things that are, so that no human being might boast in the presence of God (1 Cor. 1:25, 27–29, RSV).

For this reason Christians tend to be absolutely shameless in their confident shaming of the wise and strong, in their laughter at the foolishness of the world, in their gleeful tipping over false gods and poking holes in worldly presumptions and pomposities. "We may as well admit it," said Karl Barth of the Christian, "he has got something to laugh at, and he just cannot help laughing." But then Barth added this important point: "His laughter is not bad, but good, not a mockery, but an open and relaxing laughter, not a diplomatic gesture . . . but honest and sincere laughter, coming from the bottom of man's heart." [30]

If there's anything in this world more incongruous than a Christian without a sense of humor, it is a Christian without *good* humor. As Barth pointed out, the Christian's humor can never be sardonic, hateful, or joyless. This kind of humor is really more appropriate to the fundamental sadness of the world as it attempts to live without God's self-revelation in Christ. As long as Christians are consistent with what they claim is true, their humor will always be *good* humor.

Good humor should come easily to Christians since they've been let in on the knowledge of who really has the last laugh. Who has it? God and *all* God's humanity. In Christ we learn that God is *for* us—*all* of us. And "if God is for us, who is against us?" (Rom. 8:31, RSV). Therefore the Christian has indeed "got something to laugh at, and he just cannot help laughing."

17. The Popular Arts

The arts—all forms of art—can usually be used effectively and appropriately in communicating the Christian message. This is because the arts, when they do what they're supposed to, are sensitive to all things human. And so is the Christian faith.

The cartoons and photographs I have used in my books are called *popular arts.* This term, along with *popularizer,* is sometimes used abusively by academic snobs. But I like it because I believe the church, in trying to get its message across, should especially make good use of the "lowly" popular arts. The more popular the better. For *popular* simply refers to something a lot of people like and probably understand. Trying to communicate a message through something people don't like or don't understand doesn't make a lot of sense to me.

In other words, using the popular arts is simply an attempt to use "laymen's language"—laymen, as Vonnegut puts it, "in their anguished need for simple clues as to what is *really* going on." [31]

Putting the popular arts in a Christian context helps put Christ in a popular context. Therefore, it seems to me that the church should always be fluent in the language of the popular arts.

"I can't put it into layman's language for you. I don't know any layman's language."

Drawing by Dana Fradon; ©1975. The New Yorker Magazine, Inc.

18. Is Kurt Vonnegut the Exorcist of Jesus Christ Superstar?

In this book, while again using cartoons, I also want to focus on three other popular "arts": Kurt Vonnegut, a very popular American writer; *The Exorcist,* a novel by William Peter Blatty; and *Jesus Christ Superstar,* a rock opera based on Christ's passion—the events just before his death.

That these three are popular there can be no doubt. But here's something else: They are also important. They are important because they are popular and because they are *representative.* And they are representative because they are accurate present-day expressions of something basic and important now going on in our lives, something that has gone on in the past, and something that will probably continue to go on for a long time.

19. Kurt Funnygood

I am aware, of course, that Kurt Vonnegut is generally considered a popular artist rather than a popular art. But I have met the man, and I am happy to report that he is also a genuine work of art. He is, as they say, a beautiful person.

I address Kurt Vonnegut personally in this book. This is because I like to think of him as a friend. I think almost anyone would. Most of Vonnegut's readers seem to agree that he comes across as a gentle and kind uncle or distant relative who likes to tell you stories and make you laugh, likes to teach you some things and make you think, and generally has nothing but other people's best interest at heart. At least that's the way he comes across to me, both personally and in his writings.

Kurt Vonnegut and I recently had a conversation that was recorded on magnetic tape. A transcript of that conversation is in the back of this book.

I also want to address Kurt Vonnegut personally in this book because I think that the church's "dialogue with the world," whenever possible, should be just that.

Hello again, Kurt.

20. The Good Doctors Barth and Bonhoeffer—and Dostoevsky Too!

I would no more think of making a move without my theological heroes than I would think of leaving the house in the morning without my pants. Although I never had the great good fortune of meeting either Karl Barth or Dietrich Bonhoeffer—nor Dostoevsky either, of course—I consider the three of them about the best friends I have. They are my favorites among the few first magnitude stars of Christian thought. In heaven if I do not attend a seminar in which these three are together teaching a course on "Nineteenth- and Twentieth-Century Christian Thought," I will consider eternity something less than advertised.

I bring them along with me, not only because *what* they say is wonderful, but also because all three of them knew *how* to write, in spite of the fact that both Barth and Bonhoeffer are usually regarded as "theologians' theologians." Reading Barth's many words is for me like being caught up in a spiritual jet stream: It is graceful, swift, powerful, and exhilarating. And although Bonhoeffer (himself a "Barthian")[32] is sometimes typically German in his complexity, his writings are like finely tooled steel in their stylistic precision and concreteness. And Dostoevsky has always been widely read, even in Russia, just for the fun of it.

Therefore I say to Sarah, my precious little daughter to whom this book is dedicated: Sarah, darling, in addition to your Bible, of course, please read *The Brother's Karamazov* by about the time you are a senior in high school. Then read it again every seven or eight years, for I don't believe a greater one-volume "defense" of the Christian faith has ever been written.

Then read Dr. Karl Barth's *The Faith of the Church*. Dr. Barth was a famous university professor and the author of many fat books about Christian doctrine. But in this little book he sounds more like your daddy when he's drinking a can of beer and has his feet up on his desk.

Then read Dr. Bonhoeffer's *Ethics* and also an account of his life. For the good doctors Barth and Bonhoeffer were also brave "comrades in arms" who backed up their words with their lives, and this makes their wonderful words even more believable and exciting.

And so on.

2
Hell—The Monstrous Misunderstanding

*The thing that more than anything else profoundly determines
the way we feel about life is the way life is related to death.*
—Wilhelm Dilthey[1]

*Whence does it draw its sustenance, this non-Christianity, if not
from the offense that has been given to it by the fragility of Orthodox, of Roman and of Protestant Christianity?*
—Karl Barth, *Against the Stream*[2]

*It is not only out of kindness, out of good nature, that the [Apos-
tles'] Creed does not mention hell and eternal death. But the Creed
discusses only the things which are the object of faith. We do not
have to believe in hell and in eternal death. I may only believe in
the resurrection and the judgment of Christ, the judge and the ad-
vocate, who has loved me and defended my cause.*

*The Creed discusses the things to be believed. To believe. . . .
We cannot "believe" in sin, in the devil, in our death sentence. We
can only believe in the Christ who has overcome the devil, borne
sin and removed eternal death . . .*

*And let us not add: "Yes, but sin is a grievous thing"—as though
hell and so many horrors were not on earth already! If one does really believe, one cannot say: "But!" this terrible and pitiful "but." I
fear that much of the weakness of our Christian witness comes from
this fact that we dare not frankly confess the grandeur of God, the
victory of Christ, the superiority of the Spirit. Wretched as we are,
we always relapse into contemplation of ourselves and of mankind,
and, naturally, eternal death comes up no sooner than we have
looked on it. The world without redemption becomes again a
power and a threatening force, and our message of victory ceases*

to be believable. But as it is written: "The victory that triumphs over the world, this is our faith" (I John 5:4).
— Karl Barth, *The Faith of the Church*[3]

There is only a limited number of possible ways of eliminating eternal torment. The simplest is to deny personal immortality.
— D. P. Walker, *The Decline of Hell*[4]

The life of the world as well as the lives of individuals tend to go around in a bumpy, vicious circle. The contours of this circle can be described as follows:

Atheism→ Nihilism→ Religion→ Jesus→
Atheism→ Nihilism→ Religion→ Jesus→
Atheism→ . . . . etc.

This circle got its start and is encouraged to continue because it has rarely been made clear to people that in Jesus Christ, God has given us his Word that he has destined *all* people for "the life everlasting" in heaven.

Almost since its beginning, the church has been the victim of a monstrous misunderstanding—the idea that there is after death "an eternal damnation for the wicked." In short, the idea that there is a literal "hell."

It is almost impossible for anyone to conceive of the trouble this idea has wreaked on the world. Within the church itself, it has fathered countless other heresies. And at the root of Christendom's turning away from Christ lies the teaching of "eternal torment." Therefore, "hell" is not only the cause of most of the world's unbelief, but also the cause of most of the widespread and deep miseries that unbelief and false belief leave in their wake.

More than any other single factor, the teaching of a "hell" to come later causes a hell on earth now. So how did such a monstrous misunderstanding come into being in the first place?

Jesus didn't "invent" the idea of hell, as Mark Twain thought.[5] Scholars have shown that the Israelites imported the idea from the Zoroastrian religion about two centuries before Christ.[6] But like so

many other ready-made ideas that Jesus came into contact with, he
picked up this idea and used it. He used it in two ways.

1. What Is Hell? Stewing in Your Own Juice
Where Is Hell? Low and Inside
When Is Hell? Hell Comes When False Gods Go

First, because the people in Jesus' time thought of hell as unendurable suffering, Jesus used this concept to describe the unendurable *despair* people will experience when the false gods they worship
finally bite the dust.

The entire New Testament assumes that *everyone* has a god or a
master or a center to his or her life, some one thing that a person
"worships," or trusts, without questioning, some one thing that is
this person's "joy above the rest." It also assumes that, at any one
time, "no one can serve *two* masters" (Matt. 6:24, RSV) or gods or
"joys above the rest." It also assumes that no person starts out in
life serving the *true* God. At the beginning of a person's life, "he
does not know the true God, but this is not the whole of it, he
worships an idol as God" (Kierkegaard).[7] This is what is meant by
"original sin": No one starts out—or "originates"—in life believing in
the only true God or master or center of life. Originally, at the
center of our lives, there is not the true God but only a false god, a
wretched little god that, whatever it might be, is not capable of fulfilling our hearts. Here is how St. Augustine described this problem:
"Our hearts are formed for thee, O Lord, but remain empty until
they are fulfilled by Thee."

ZIGGY

YOUR PROBLEM, ZiGGY,
IS THAT YOUR LiFe CeNTeRS
AROUND A VOID....

The false gods we all orginally serve are put together with cellophane tape, and we know it. Our conscious awareness that they are only taped together can go from vague to painfully vivid. But to one degree or another we are all aware that these taped-up idols can come unstuck at any time. And this tends to make us anxious. And unhappy. And full of hate. In any case this situation, which exists from the very day of our birth, puts all of us under considerable strain.

"Well, yes, actually, I have been under considerable strain. Since October 23rd, 1908, if you must know."

Drawing by Weber; ©1973. The New Yorker Magazine, Inc.

As long as we remain idolators (and all "sin" is nothing more than idolatry), our entire lives are anxious, unhappy attempts to tape up our false gods more securely. This is the kind of "life" the Bible is alluding to when it says, "The man who does not love is still in the realm of death" (1 John 3:14, NEB). So when St. Paul said, "The wages of sin is death" (Rom. 6:23, RSV), this is what he meant: "The results of living for a god held together with cellophane tape is a living death." This is why a continuation of life can lose its appeal for many of us.

B.C. by permission of Johnny Hart and Field Enterprises, Inc.

Now here is something else: Whenever one of our taped-up gods *does* become completely unstuck, this is an entirely *new* experience for us, and is generally what the New Testament means by "the hell of fire."

This experience is new because now, for the first time in our lives, we have absolutely nothing we can trust or depend on or believe in or hang on to. Previously we always had at least some one thing, some little taped-up god, we could finally fall back on. Now there is nothing.

This experience is "hell" for the same reason. The New Testament descriptions of "hell" are actually apt and accurate, for the inward experience of losing one's god is seemingly bottomless, endless, and escapeproof. When our taped-up god comes unstuck, our heart comes unstuck with it. Therefore, the *place* of hell is actually like the ball that is so difficult for batters to hit: It is "low and inside." It's tightly locked up inside us so it can't get out. This, however, is the kind of control over it we'd rather not have, and it makes for the worst of all possible prisons: Instead of being *in* "hell," the hell is in us.

MISS PEACH

MISS PEACH by Mell Lazarus. Courtesy of Mell Lazarus and Field Newspaper Syndicate.

This experience is often appropriately described as *fire* because it involves the total destruction of the very foundation of our lives, the very thing we have worshiped and lived for. Our false god has "gone up in smoke." So this is what the "fire of hell" really is: the unendurable "internal combustion" that comes with the destruction of our false gods. Hell comes when our false gods go. It works about like this:

©1966 United Feature Syndicate, Inc.

And so *hell,* the *real* hell, is a reality that exists in *this* lifetime. The New Testament obviously says the same thing about the Holy Spirit. This explains why the New Testament uses "fire" to represent both. For hell and the Holy Spirit are two aspects of the same reality: the power of God guiding us by both *negative* (hell) and *positive* (the Holy Spirit) reinforcement.

The "fire of baptism," the Holy Spirit, is the same fire burning in the "hell of fire." The fire that consumes our false, original god ("Our God is a consuming fire," Heb. 12:29, RSV) is the same fire that can then introduce us to the true God (Jesus "will baptize you with the Holy Spirit and with fire," Luke 3:16, RSV). That is, this fire can introduce us to the true God if we begin to understand what is happening. For this same fire of God, which first painfully purifies us (1 Cor. 3:11–15), can then warm our hearts and, with this warmth, guide us in the knowledge of God (Luke 34:32).

Thus the fire of hell and the fire of the Holy Spirit are two sides of the same coin. We experience them as fear and as absence of fear. In reality, however, they are God's wrath and his compassion, compassion being much closer to God's attitude behind *all* that happens—love:

> For a brief moment I forsook you,
>   but with great compassion I will gather you.
> In overflowing wrath for a moment
>   I hid my face from you,
> but with everlasting love I will have compassion on you,
>   says the Lord, your Redeemer.
>
> For the mountains may depart and the hills be removed,
> but my steadfast love shall not depart from you,
>   and my covenant of peace shall not be removed,
> says the Lord, who has compassion on you
> (Isa. 54:7–8, 10, RSV).

These two elements, the wrath and compassion of God, work together to guide us inwardly to belief in him and to keep us in this belief. They guide us in much the same way that Billy Pilgrim was guided in Vonnegut's *Slaughterhouse-Five:*

> Billy was guided by dread and the lack of dread. Dread told him when to stop. Lack of it told him when to move again.[8]

This, then, is the major way that Jesus used the idea of hell in his teaching and preaching. He did not use it to describe a dreadful existence we will have after death. Rather he used it to describe an experience that occurs in *this* lifetime, the same experience St. Paul described when he said, "For we see [present tense] divine retribution revealed from heaven and falling upon all the godless wickedness of men" (Rom. 1:18, NEB). Hell, then, is a terrifying experience designed to make believers of us *now*.

2. The Threat of a Hell after Death = A Dark Background to Help Us See the Light

Jesus also used the idea of "hell" in a second powerful way. Because some people in Jesus' time thought of "hell" as a reality that existed after death, Jesus used this concept to stress the question mark at the end of this sentence: What happens to us after death? The Sadducees didn't believe in any kind of afterlife. Other people believed in the existence of heaven and hell. Others believed in other things. And by pointing to the *possibility* of a literal hell existing after death, Jesus forced his hearers to ask themselves seriously, "Who knows?" "Fear him who can destroy both soul and body in hell," Jesus commanded (Matt. 10:28, RSV). Obviously God *can* do this. Will he?

Who knows?

This was Hamlet's famous question, and it is the question that Jesus even now forces on all modern-day Sadducees, such as Kurt Vonnegut, who look forward to only "sleep" after death. "For in that sleep of death," Kurt, "what dream may come?" as Hamlet asked.

Who knows?

Jesus' answer to this question was, in essence, this: "Only I know. And therefore only by trusting in me can anyone else know." Death is that undiscovered country from whose boundaries only one traveler, Jesus, has returned. And it was precisely for this reason that the New Testament writers could face death, "the last enemy," with such boundless hope and confidence. "But we see Jesus, . . . crowned with glory and honor because of the suffering of death, so that by the grace of God he might taste death for every one" (Heb. 2:9, RSV).

This then is the second way Jesus used the idea of "hell": He undercut or called into question all false certainties people had about the mystery of death, and therefore he also undercut all false certainties they had about life. For the way we live life is based on the way we think about death.

Jesus didn't raise the gloomy specter of "hell" to promise that people would go there. Instead, he wanted to provide a dark backdrop against which *he*—as the true "light of the world" (John 8:12, 9:5, and so on)—could be more clearly seen and recognized and then trusted as the only true certainty about all of life and death. "Hell" is a dark uncertainty against which the only unconquerable certainty, Jesus—as the conqueror of hell and "the Savior of the world" (John 4:42, RSV)—is more starkly set in relief and appreciated for what he really is. Without Jesus, life is a hell of uncertainty. And Luther was right: "Uncertainty is the most miserable thing in the world." [9] Without Jesus, life is the hell Pascal described:

> Not only do we know God by Jesus Christ alone, but we know ourselves only by Jesus Christ. We know life and death only through Jesus Christ. Apart from Jesus Christ, we do not know what is our life, nor our death, nor God, nor ourselves.
>
> Thus without the Scripture, which has Jesus Christ alone for its object, we know nothing and see only darkness and confusion in the nature of God, and in our own nature. [10]

And thus the question of a "hell" *later* has a way of bringing out in the open the only real hell there actually is—the hell of a deep, "these days" uncertainty *now;* a hell caused by not knowing the answer *everybody* is looking for, Jesus Christ; and yet a hell that is necessary in order to make us look.

"These days, everybody is looking for answers."

Drawing by Geo. Price; ©1975. The New Yorker Magazine, Inc.

Without Jesus, who knows? But with Jesus, it is as Barth said: "We now know that Jesus Christ has destroyed the power of hell, however great it may be." [11]

The only basic difference between Christians and non-Christians is that Christians *now know*. They now have this happy certainty. What difference does this make, especially since all people are going to heaven anyway!? It makes a *hell* of a difference in "the meantime." There is literally a "hell of a difference" between those who now know this and those who don't. Therefore the writer of Proverbs was absolutely right: "Be assured, an evil man will not go unpunished" (Prov. 11:21, RSV). How will he be punished? In hell. In this lifetime. Like this:

"Nothing for him, thanks. He's going to stew in his own juice."

Drawing by Richter; ©1974. The New Yorker Magazine, Inc.

The above understanding of hell makes it possible for us to see how the Bible can talk about hell, and yet at the same time clearly and unmistakably proclaim God's "plan for the fulness of time, to unite all things in him, things in heaven and things on earth" (Eph. 1:10, RSV). For biblical literalists can't have it both ways: They can't believe that the Bible means what it says *literally* when it speaks of hell, and then inconsistently interpret *metaphorically* its many doom-busting passages like these:

Then as one man's trespass led to condemnation for all men, so one man's act of righteousness leads to acquittal and life for all men (Rom. 5:18, RSV).

For God has consigned all men to disobedience, that he may have mercy on all. . . . For from him and through him and to him are all things (Rom. 11:32, 36, RSV).

God was in Christ reconciling the world to himself, no longer holding men's misdeeds against them (2 Cor. 5:19, NEB).

Through him [Christ] God chose to reconcile the whole universe to himself, making peace through the shedding of his blood on the cross—to reconcile all things, whether on earth or in heaven, through him alone (Col. 1:20, NEB).

Such prayer [for all men] is right, and approved by God our Saviour, whose will it is that all men should find salvation and come to know the truth. For there is one God, and also one mediator between God and men, Christ Jesus, himself man, who sacrificed himself to win freedom for all mankind, so providing, at the fitting time, proof of the divine purpose (1 Tim. 2:3–, NEB).

3. The Scriptures and the Power of God

If the above understanding of "hell" really is the New Testament's understanding of the matter, then how did it happen that a hell occurring *after* death has been the church's more traditional understanding? How did this "traditional" understanding originate? How did this monstrous *misunderstanding* become "orthodox" Christian teaching?

The answer lies in what Jesus said to the Sadducees when they, like the believers in a literal hell, also displayed a misunderstanding about "the resurrection of the dead" (Matt. 22; Mark 12). "Jesus said to them, 'You are mistaken, and surely this is the reason: you do not know either the scriptures or the power of God.'" (Mark 12:24, NEB).

In this passage one of the things Jesus meant by "the power of God" is God's power to "convert" a person even in opposition to this person's own desires—which is the only way a person is ever converted. As I have said, we all originate in life with a false god, and a *god,* by definition, means everything to us. We will love this god and cling to it for all we're worth until there is absolutely nothing left of it we can hang on to. We will never let go of this false god by our own power, or "free will." How could we? It's all we have. As Linus says of his precious "security blanket": "Only one yard of outing flannel stands between me and a nervous breakdown." Or as Vonnegut says in *The Sirens of Titan:* "Nobody thinks or notices anything as long as his luck is good. Why should he?"[12]

Therefore, if we are to be re-created into radically new people, the boom has to be lowered on us from outside outselves, for who's going to lower the boom on himself or herself? Who's going to toss away his or her own security blanket? Or, as Jesus could ask, "How can Satan cast out Satan?" (Mark 3:23, RSV).

B.C. by permission of Johnny Hart and Field Enterprises, Inc.

This is how God wakes up all of us. Only when God's power, against our own inclinations and wills, violently dispels the dream of our false god can we be "free" or open to serving the true God. Only then can we really begin to think or notice anything. God first meets us "like a boxer's closed fist" (Barth),[13] like a consuming fire that totally destroys our false gods.

I am describing, of course, the experience of *conversion*. No one can understand the Scriptures (the Bible) without it. "The unspiritual [natural] man does not receive the gifts of the Spirit of God, for they are folly to him, and he is not able to understand them because they are spiritually discerned" (1 Cor. 2:14, RSV).

Many people know the Scriptures without knowing the power of God. But, as Jesus said, if God is truly to be known, two things must be present: *knowledge* of the Scriptures and *the experience* of the power of God. In the following cartoon, Beetle Bailey at first knows his "father" only in the sense that we "know" Scripture— we know its words. But by the time this little scene is over, Beetle has also learned of his father's *power*. And this power "converts" Beetle's understanding of his father's words, as we can see by his willingness to obey.

BEETLE BAILEY

In this same way, "The fear of the Lord" [or experiencing the "power of God," or "going to hell"] "is the beginning of wisdom" (Ps. 111:10, RSV). Tarzan couldn't swim worth a hoot until he saw his first crocodile.

In Christ's parable of the rich man and poor Lazarus (Luke 16:19–31), the rich man would not believe in God's truth until he himself became a poor wretch in "hell." And this is what this parable teaches us: that no one can believe or understand the Christian message without first "going to hell," without first experiencing the negative aspect of God's power.

4. Trying to Understand Hell Without Having Been There

When a person who hasn't experienced the power of God reads about hell in the New Testament, he or she is like a four-year-old trying to make sense out of an adult conversation about sex. It's bound to be misunderstood. Since this "hell" is not a part of my own experience, this person will reason, then obviously it's got to mean something that takes place in the future. Furthermore, it must be an experience that occurs after death, for it would be frightening and humiliating to think of it as an unpleasant experience that I myself now need—but haven't had.

Also, hell must occur only to some people and not to others, since this is what the New Testament seems to be saying and also because I don't want it occurring to me. Therefore, there must be a way to avoid hell, and this way must be within a person's own power, since it certainly wouldn't be fair of God to toss people in an everlasting bonfire for reasons beyond their own control. Therefore,

I will do whatever I must to earn my way to heaven. The dummies will get the hell they deserve.

Get the picture? It's a complete misunderstanding of God caused by not knowing "the power of God." Nevertheless, this is a fair account of the way most people even today think of hell—if they think of it at all.

Abraham Lincoln was a "biblical Christian" who believed in Christ's universal salvation of *all* people.[14] But Lincoln's proverbial honesty would not allow him to join a church. Why? Because where could he find a branch of Christendom that doesn't *officially* subscribe—even to this day—to something about like this:

FUNKY WINKERBEAN

FUNKY WINKERBEAN by Tom Batiuk. ©Field Enterprises, Inc., 1975. Courtesy of Field Newspaper Syndicate.

In any case, this is certainly the way the church, early in its history, began to think of hell when, for whatever reason, it began to fail to experience God's power. Scripture then *had* to be interpreted in this way.

5. "You Are My Church, and I Will Give You the Cosmic Fire Insurance Monopoly"

As soon as people began relegating hell to a nether world existing after death, and as soon as they also began thinking that it was within their own power to avoid such a horror, then the "institutional church" really came into its own. For just as soon as we seriously believe "Heaven or eternal damnation! It's up to you!"

then the first thing we will scurry around looking for is an elite company of experts who can tell us exactly and infallibly what we must and must not do in order to avoid this everlasting torment. Once we have swallowed this misunderstanding of hell, the need for an infallible and monolithic church is as logical and makes as much sense as anything else in this world. Gradually the power all of us think we have, the power to save ourselves from "hell," is handed over to a group of "professionals." They know more about these things than we do. Gradually the ultimate norm of truth—the Holy Spirit, the "power of God," or "the Spirit of truth [who] . . . will guide you into all the truth" (John 16:13, RSV)—is supplanted by the power of the church.

But this is just the way we want it! After all, the Holy Spirit is notoriously unmanageable, as Jesus himself admitted:

> You ought not to be astonished, then, when I tell you that you must be born over again. The wind blows where it wills; you hear the sound of it, but you do not know where it comes from, or where it is going. So with everyone who is born from spirit (John 3:−8, NEB).

The church, on the other hand, is like a rock: It doesn't go anywhere. It just sits there and one always knows where one stands in relation to it. This is the way it ought to be, because when one's eternal destiny is at stake one doesn't want to fool around with something as shifty and unreliable as the Holy Spirit. The fire of the Holy Spirit may be a fine thing for a bunch of loony mystics or charismatics to play around with. Admittedly something called the Holy Spirit is mentioned in Scripture and all. But serious people concerned about the flames of "hell" aren't going to base a church on any flighty bird like this! No, sirree, Bob!

Therefore we will capture the Holy Spirit and let it have its exercise only at the end of a tightly held rope.

Think of the power this idea of "hell" then gave to the church! This world is only a brief prelude for deciding our ultimate and everlasting destiny: "hell" or the kingdom of heaven. Therefore the church is now in possession of our souls by being sole possessor of "the keys of the kingdom" (Matt. 16:19; this is how this historically important passage has actually been interpreted).

No wonder the medieval church became one of the greatest powers in all history. The entire sacramental structure of this church became a means of distributing or withholding the commodity it had absolute control over—cosmic fire insurance.

No wonder the emperor and other heads of state could stand in line (one stood barefoot in the snow!) [15] to beg for the church's favor. For a while the church virtually *was* the government. Later, as government became a more independent power, it still was—and often still is!—deathly afraid to make a move without the power of the institutional church behind it.

Whenever a church—any church—claims to have a monopoly on cosmic fire insurance, and people seriously believe such a claim, this church can easily go into business for itself and swing just about any kind of ridiculous deal it might want.

Tank McNamara

Copyright, 1975, Universal Press Syndicate.

6. The Blessed Martin Luther Blows His Stack

It's an old story: Power corrupts and absolute power corrupts absolutely. So it was inevitable that the powerful medieval church would become more and more corrupt and that there would be a protest and a call for reform—a "Protestant Reformation." And what tiny spark ignited the keg of Reformation dynamite? Ah, yes! The Dominican monk Tetzel and his cheap cosmic fire insurance policies for the Germans. (Rome had need of new revenues.) He was innocently selling "indulgences" at the time. Even had a little poem to help push them:

> As soon as the coin in the coffer rings,
> The soul from purgatory springs.[16]

Luther exploded, and we're still feeling the fallout.

But when the church finally stumbled into the Protestant Reformation, its understanding of hell wasn't reformed as much as we might hope. The Protestants correctly saw that faith was a matter of the heart's disposition and fulfillment, rather than the fulfillment of a manipulatable set of rules. But for the most part they failed to see that when the New Testament speaks of hell, it is usually describing the heart's experience of becoming dreadfully conscious of the *need* for faith.

Therefore, the Protestants still assumed that all eternity was divided into two parts, heaven and hell. They just wanted to renegotiate the means of getting to the one and avoiding the other.

The medieval church had said that everything depended on people's own "free decision" to obey the dictates of the church. The Protestants now said everything depended on *God's* free decision (or "grace") to relate a person personally, or subjectively (or "spiritually"), to Christ. In this way, the Holy Spirit was reinstated, and the power to damn or save was taken out of the weak, corruptible hands of people and church and placed squarely where it belongs: in the hands of God and/or Christ. The Protestants correctly believed that in this way our futures were in much more competent hands.

MISS PEACH by Mell Lazarus. Courtesy of Mell Lazarus and Field Newspaper Syndicate.

Here is how Luther said almost the same thing:

> *Of the comfort of knowing that salvation does not depend on "free will"*

I frankly confess that, for myself, even if it could be, I should not want "free-will" to be given me, nor anything to be left in my own hands to enable me to endeavour after salvation; not merely because in face of so many dangers, and adversities, and assaults of devils, I could not stand my ground and hold fast my "free-will" (for one devil is stronger than all men, and on these terms no man could be saved); but because, even were there no dangers, adversities, or devils, I should still be forced to labour with no guarantee of success, and to beat my fists at the air. If I lived and worked to all eternity, my conscience would never reach comfortable certainty as to how much it must do to satisfy God. Whatever work I had done, there would still be a nagging doubt as to whether it pleased God, or whether He required something more. The experience of all who seek righteousness by works proves that; and I learned it well enough myself over a period of many years, to my own great hurt. But now that God has taken my salvation out of the control of my own will, and put it under the control of His, and promised to save me, not according to my working or running, but according to His own grace and mercy, I have the comfortable certainty that He is faithful and will not lie to me, and that He is also great and powerful, so that no devils or opposition can break Him or pluck me from Him. . . . Thus it is that, if not all, yet some, indeed many, are saved; whereas, by the power of "free-will" none at all could be saved, but every one of us would perish.[17]

But here is another reason why the Protestants were correct to emphasize strongly that the only ability to save people lay solely in *God's* hands: Any ability we think we have to save ourselves really amounts to—and grows out of our desire for—*self*-trust or *self*-righteousness or idolatry of one's *self*.

Therefore, said the Protestants, we can do absolutely nothing to work our way into heaven or to deserve in any way its blessing. It is *solely* the work of God's grace to save whomever he chooses by putting faith in Christ inside his chosen ones. And this faith carries with it the presence of God's Holy Spirit, which comforts the believers and assures them that they are destined for heaven and not for hell.

Sola fides, sola gratia, sola Christus! as the Protestant battle cries went. And of course, all this was carefully backed up solely by Scripture. *Sola scriptura!*

7. The Dreadful Decree—Double Predestination

And so by and by, when the theological dust from the Reformation began to settle, there stood Luther and Calvin, and Lutheranism and Calvinism, with the horrible grimace of *double predestination* on their faces.

What the devil is *double predestination?* This teaching says that God decided long before people were even born ("pre-") who would go to heaven and who would go to hell ("double destination"), and there's absolutely nothing anyone can do to change this "absolute decree."

Now, this view of things hardly seems fair. Even crusty old John Calvin could admit, "The decree is dreadful indeed, I confess." [18] So there should be no mystery why the doctrine of double predestination wasn't predestined to remain popular for long

©1957 United Feature Syndicate, Inc.

8. Two New Large Streams of Thought

Nevertheless, by the end of the Protestant Reformation the doctrine of double predestination had been plopped like a huge, forbidding rock smack in the mainstream of Protestant thinking. And it was largely because of its rock's obvious hardness and dreadfulness, that most Protestant thought then flowed around both its sides to create two new separate streams of thought: Neo-Protestantism and the Enlightenment.

In both these developments we can see how the "humanless godism" of "hell" leads to "godless humanism." Or to put it another way, we can see how belief in a literal "hell" forces people to become their own gods and hence leads to a denial of both heaven *and* "hell."

9. Neo-Protestantism or Protestant Do-It-Yourselfism

Neo-Protestantism is the stream of thought that went around the rock of double predestination on the *double* side. That is, Neo-Protestantism wanted to keep God around, and with him, the "double" of heaven and hell. And in order to do this, it was more than happy to sacrifice God's control over human destiny.

Here are a couple of examples of many similar biblical statements that got the goats of the Neo-Protestants:

Jesus answered them, ". . . No one can come to me unless the Father who sent me draws him; . . . no one can come to me unless it is granted him by the Father" (John 6:43–44, 65, RSV).

For he [God] says to Moses, "I will have mercy on whom I have mercy, and I will have compassion on whom I have compassion." So it depends not upon man's will or exertion, but upon God's mercy. . . . he has mercy upon whomever he wills, and he hardens the heart of whomever he wills (Rom. 9:15—16, 18,RSV).

Statements like this would seem to confirm the view of double predestination, as long as God's "hardening" and "not granting" is interpreted to mean that the hardened and not-granted folks are sent to "hell." Therefore, here in effect is what the Neo-Protestants then said:

"To hell with this nonsense! Our hands may be incompetent, but whether we end up in heaven or hell is far too important to leave in the hands of such an outrageously capricious, arbitrary, and inscrutable God. Therefore, please stand aside, God. In this little matter of where we're going to spend eternity, we'll decide ourselves with our own 'free wills,' thank you! But please don't go too far away, God, in case something else comes up. In the meantime, God, don't call us—we'll call you!"

And in this way most of Protestantism reverted to the same kind of "do-it-yourself salvation" they had fought so hard against in the Reformation. The only major difference now was that the Protestants were no longer going to let any church tell them how to do this. Instead, they would—when convenient!—look only to the Bible for their authority.

Karl Barth called this development Neo-Protestantism, or Protestant "religion." For Barth, *religion* was usually a derogatory word meaning "do-it-yourself salvation." Only Christianity is "the true religion," Barth said.[19] And one reason it is this is that it doesn't believe one whit in the power of people to save themselves. Only God can save people, and people are in no way God. All do-it-yourself salvation schemes are actually either unconscious or disguised atheism. These do-it-yourselfers do not believe that God is the only master, but instead believe that "I am the master of my fate, I am the captain of my soul." This means they finally trust themselves rather than God, and self-trust or self-worship is not at all the same as God-trust or God-worship. And the result of self-worship is the same hell that comes from worshiping any other false god.

"Frankly, I have days when I wish to hell somebody else was master of my fate and captain of my soul."

Drawing by Stevenson; ©1974. The New Yorker Magazine, Inc.

Because of Protestant do-it-yourselfism, Dostoevsky took one good look at the European liberal Protestantism of his time and said, "Protestantism with gigantic strides is being converted into atheism and into vacillating . . . (and not eternal) ethics." And when a Billy Graham says that "you yourself" must make your own "free decision" to decide your salvation, he also is actually promoting the same human *self*-confidence that most atheists possess.

Protestant do-it-yourselfers can be liberals *or* conservatives.

Nevertheless, as long as Protestantism considered the dreadful decree of double predestination to be the only real alternative to do-it-yourself religion, we can easily understand why most Protestants returned to some form of the Pelagian self-righteousness they had knocked themselves out rejecting during the Reformation.

But all such schemes of salvation-by-my-own-decision, however subtle or from whatever church, are at best only one step away from the self-confidence of "man's" outright deification and of atheistic humanism. Said Barth:

Obviously, we can have faith only in a God who is present in His decision and election, who is actually the electing and deciding God. If he is not that, and we cannot have faith in Him, it is only a short step to the denial of the existence of God. Or, to put it better, if we do not have faith in God, if we do not know Him as actually the electing and deciding God, His existence is, in fact, already denied.[20]

Protestants may have succeeded in extricating themselves from dependence on the church to save them from "hell," but insofar as they have only replaced this dependence with self-dependence, they still haven't changed much. They've only replaced one idol with another.

B.C. by permission of Johnny Hart and Field Enterprises, Inc.

10. The Enlightenment

Putting the power for salvation back in our own hands is one way of dealing with the threat of eternal damnation. But as D. P. Walker says in the quote I used at the beginning of this chapter, the *simplest* way "of eliminating eternal torment . . . is to deny personal immortality."

This method of dealing with the threat of doom and damnation is certainly simpler than Neo-Protestantism, for it's based on the same humanistic *self*-trust as Neo-Protestantism, but lacks Neo-Protestantism's delusion that it trusts in God.

In other words, self-righteous Christians can continue to try to control God's salvation by their own power and remain ordinary losers. Or they can go on into the Enlightenment, forget about God altogether, try to control everything else, and become complete incompetents.

This latter course was taken by the Christians who "went on" to produce the Enlightenment and its results. The Enlightenment is as easy to understand as Neo-Protestantism. All we have to do is think of the gloomy, dark doctrines of "hell" and double predestination, and we can readily see why a lot of people couldn't get themselves "enlightened" fast enough. As in the case of any great historical movement, many forces converged to bring about the Enlightenment, but among these forces none was greater than this: These Enlightenment folks were tired as hell of being tyrannized by all the different churches and their threats of "hell." Since "hell" was God's invention, he was a hell of a God. And they were willing to scrap him and personal immortality to boot if they could just get away from such a monstrous absurdity and all the other miserable absurdities stemming from it.

In this same way, the Enlightenment rejected the *double* of double predestination, the question about whether our afterlives would be spent in heaven or hell. Instead, Enlightenment said (over on Elm Street)—

"To life as we know it!"

11. Secularization—or Rendering to the World the Things That Are the World's

Thus the Enlightenment flowed around the rock of double predestination on the *predestination* side. For the Enlightenment's appreciation of nature's intricate network of causes and effects, in life as we know it, is a secularization of predestination. Predestination said that all things are causally related to God. The Enlightenment left off the God part.

As a matter of fact, the entire Enlightenment can be seen as a kind of secularized Protestantism brought on by Protestantism itself. Therefore, Kurt, those who are proud of their ideological roots in the Enlightenment, as I know you are, should also give due respect to their deeper Christian roots from which the Enlightenment sprang.

In a nutshell, here are a few of the positive ways in which the Christian faith helped to bring about the Enlightenment:

The entire process of secularization, the appreciation of nature or "life as we know it," was made possible largely by the Protestant reemphasis of an important Old Testament theme: the *goodness* of God's creation, a creation given to people to be used and enjoyed.

The secularization of *creation* into *nature* and the secularization of *predestination* into *determinism* laid the foundation for modern science and technology. As Reinhold Niebuhr said:

> Modern science required an attitude toward nature which could be furnished only by the Christian idea of creation. For that idea made it possible to view nature as neither divine nor corrupt; and therefore as subject to analysis without the danger of impiety on the one hand and as worthy of analysis on the other.[21]

Just as capitalism can be seen as a secularization of the Protestant work ethic, the Enlightenment emphasis on tolerance and human rights can be seen as a secularization of Protestant social ethics.

Because Protestantism believed that the correct relationship to God was an extremely personal faith, rather than mere obedience to an outward rule, this faith could never be *forced* on people by other people. Therefore, true faith would thrive best in a context of freedom from enforced belief. The only kind of persuasion permissible should be the "friendly persuasion" of beliefs freely discussed, which is certainly a more appropriate way of "proving" God's love shown in Christ. These ideas, along with the Protestant emphasis on Original Sin, which distrusted any centralization of human power, were combined with the general thrust of the Enlightenment to produce more democratic forms of government.

12. No Hell! No Hell! No Hell!

But it was primarily because of a literal hell that Enlightenment atheism could itself become a gospel—a good news. It was the good news that the bad news of "hell" was done for. Just as it was the all-pervading threat of "hell" that made the Dark Ages so dark, it was getting rid of this hell that made the Enlightenment so light. The Enlightenment was a joyful liberation from the Monster God. It was the greening of hell. It was like the experience of the futuristic Rev. C. Horner Redwine in Vonnegut's *The Sirens of Titan* (Redwine is a minister in "the Church of God the Utterly Indifferent." Better an "utterly indifferent"—or deistic—God than a vindictive one who may throw you into "hell"):

> Redwine cried out for joy. He ran back into his church and jerked and swung on the bell rope like a drunken chimpanzee. In the clanging bedlam of the bells, Redwine heard the words that the Master of Newport said all bells spoke.
> "NO HELL! whang-clanged the bell—
> "NO HELL,
> "NO HELL,
> "NO HELL!" [22]

And this is where Kurt Vonnegut comes in.
Welcome, Kurt!

3

Kurt Vonnegut—Pilgrim's Progress Today
—or—
Atheism's Downward Path into Meaninglessness and Nihilism

Thus the philosophy of enlightenment finally led to the Europe of the black-out.

—Albert Camus, *The Rebel* [1]

When faith is spoken of, the non-believer is the most appropriate listener. He is at all events a salutary criterion, which compels us not to speak too glibly of faith. . . .

For faith and unbelief must be in conflict with each other. They must therefore know each other, and lie hard upon each other. . . . In practice, however, those who champion the cause of faith have often very little idea of those who deny faith, and only a completely distorted picture of them. . . .

The same is true vice versa of the picture the so-called non-believer has of faith. To a great extent we can only admit that he is right in his rejection of faith. For if faith were really what he considers it to be, we should have to be ashamed to be believers. But even if it is a miserable caricature of faith, the believer has cause to be ashamed of it. For it is somehow a charge on the believers after all, if the non-believers have no idea of faith. And indeed this dreadful ignorance about faith on the part of non-believers corresponds only too closely with the dreadful ignorance about faith on the part of believers. What sort of knowledge and understanding of faith does the normal Christian today really have? No wonder the non-believer feels himself confirmed in his attitude, though of

*course without guessing that he is a dupe who has let a muddled
faith drive him into muddled unbelief and keep him there—save
that the "muddled faith," just like the "muddled unbelief," probably is actually unbelief.*

—Gerhard Ebeling, *Word and Faith* [2]

*The fateful issues of the Christian faith are often wrestled with
more profoundly outside the church than within.*

—Amos Wilder, *Modern Poetry and the Christian Tradition* [3]

*Though raised in a family of atheists, Vonnegut quarrels with
God like a parochial-school dropout.*

—John Updike [4]

*A doctrine of God today . . . is abstract speculation if it does not
have the phenomenon of modern atheism before it from the
start. . . .*

*If we would begin to sense the depth of the problem, then we
must not stop at the phenomenon of common atheism, which is a
changing mixture of rightly rejecting false ideas, and of
simple-mindedness, presumption and volitional impulses of various
kinds. Rather we must think of that basic experience which bursts
upon a man with primeval force and in which nihilism is learned to
be the dire truth of atheism.*

—Gerhard Ebeling, *Word and Faith* [5]

I hold all evil to be grounded upon disbelief.

—Fyodor Dostoevsky, *Letters* [6]

**At first it would seem to be better to be an atheist and
believe that "When you're dead you're dead" (Vonnegut) than to believe in the Monster God of eternal
damnation—"a God who," as Mark Twain described
him,**

> **could make good children as easily as bad, yet
> preferred to make bad ones; who could have
> made every one of them happy, yet never made a**

single happy one; who made them prize their bitter life, yet stingily cut it short; who gave his angels eternal happiness unearned, yet required his other children to earn it; who gave his angels painless lives, yet cursed his other children with biting miseries and maladies of mind and body; who mouths justice and invented hell—mouths mercy and invented hell—mouths Golden Rules, and forgiveness multiplied by seventy times seven, and invented hell; who mouths morals to other people and has none himself; who frowns upon crimes, yet commits them all; who created man without invitation, then tries to shuffle the responsibility for man's acts upon man, instead of honorably placing it where it belongs, upon himself; and finally, with altogether divine obtuseness, invites this poor, abused slave to worship him! [7]

However, because the atheist believes that all of life is ultimately defeated by death, the atheist's life—without God's final victory over death—is ultimately meaningless. Atheism, then, is finally as unsatisfactory as belief in the Monster of God of "traditional" Christianity.

1. Kurt Vonnegut—Most Popular Boy

Kurt Vonnegut is probably the widest known, best-selling contemporary American author, especially among young people. On a CBS "60 Minutes" TV program, Harry Reasoner called Vonnegut

the current idol of the country's sensitive and intelligent young people. . . . Young people snap up his books as fast as they are reissued. . . . He is suddenly a star, a luminary, a guru to youth. His gentle fantasies of peace and his dark humor are as current among the young as was J. D. Salinger's work in the 1950's and Tolkien's in the 60's. [8]

Nowadays most young people are constantly on the lookout for something more to life, something to believe in. But while they're looking, Vonnegut helps make their lives worth living. If they read at all, they usually read Vonnegut:

BEETLE BAILEY

THERE MUST BE MORE TO LIFE THAN JUST WORKING

AND HIKING BACK AND FORTH TO CAMP

AND WATCHING THE SOX ON TV AND PLAYING SCRABBLE

AND LISTENING TO SCOTT JOPLIN RECORDS AND TAKING BUNNY TO THE MOLE HOLE

AND READING KURT VONNEGUT AND GOING TO TRAVERSE CITY ON FURLOUGHS

AND SEEING WOODY ALLEN MOVIES AND GOLFING AT MILBROOK

AND SAVING FOR A NEW SLR AND LEARNING TO PAINT WITH ACRYLICS

AND RAPPING WITH THE GUYS AT THE COFFEE HOUSE OR HELPING OUT WITH THE HEAD START KIDS

OR WRITING A SHUT-IN OR STUDYING MIND-CONTROL

OR LEARNING CHESS OR COLLECTING FOR THE RED CROSS

OR FIXING MY DUNE BUGGY, OR...

THERE MUST BE MORE TO LIFE THAN KEEPING THOSE GUYS WORKING

MORT WALKER

5-27

©King Features Syndicate, Inc. 1973.

"On balance," writes Benjamin DeMott, "the kids' lighting on Kurt Vonnegut is an undeservedly good break for the age."[9] Whenever our age puts its first things first, these things—at least for today's young people—will surely include "a little Vonnegut."

2. Representative Vonnegut

But Vonnegut is not representative of the age just because he's popular. It's more the other way around: He's popular because he's so representative. What he thinks and can express in appealing ways is what most of us think. In our conversation, Vonnegut explained his popularity this way:

> What people feel . . . is the shock of recognition and not of discovery. "Christ, this guy is thinking what I've always thought!" And the nature of my mail is mostly that. People don't write and say . . . "You really gave me a whole bunch of new ideas—my head's all awhirl." They seem to see the same things I'm thinking.[10]

3. Kurt Vonnegut—Pilgrim's Progress Today

This is also why Vonnegut is important. He is important because he is a popular, accurate representation of what most of us think and feel nowadays. He has given hilarious and fascinating artistic expression to something most of us feel strongly but have only dimly been able to understand. "The case is," says DeMott, "that Vonnegut is loved . . . for a congeries of opinions, prejudices, and assumptions perfectly tuned to the mind of the emergent generation."[11]

And this is why Vonnegut, more than any other personality I know of, represents today's new "Pilgrim" and his progress. Vonnegut *is* us. In many typical ways Vonnegut, in his experience and thinking, has come from where most of us have come and has gone through what most of us—in one way or another—have gone through. And his perception of the future is generally only a more sensitized version of our own. "I have the canary-bird-in-the-coal-mine theory of the arts," he says. "You know, coal miners used to take birds down into the mines with them to detect gas before men got sick. . . . I continue to think that artists—all artists—should be treasured as alarm systems." [12]

Among the many famous figures in modern literature, Vonnegut's Billy Pilgrim and his "progress" is probably the most fitting *fictional* representative for us pilgrims and our progress today.

4. Vonnegut—An American Camus?

In order to understand what Vonnegut is telling us about ourselves and our world, it's helpful to know first that he's a person of *ideas*. He has definite "theories" in his head and, as he says of his own fictional Kilgore Trout, he has "advanced his theories disguised as . . . fiction." [13]

What are these theories? They are not so easy to track down and label, especially when they come from a mind as complex and deep as Vonnegut's. But if we can point to other well-known writers who have represented the same ideas more openly and without fictional disguises, we'll have a clearer view of Vonnegut's own theories.

Vonnegut is a sort of Julian Huxley and Albert Camus rolled into one. This combination isn't surprising when we think of Vonnegut's strong background in the sciences. University trained in chemistry and anthropology, and also a humanist from a family of humanists, Vonnegut has an understandable affinity for Huxley's brand of "scientific humanism." Huxley's influence can easily be seen in his writings and Vonnegut openly admits it's there. [14] Like Huxley, Vonnegut believes we humans should be "aggressively rational" in solutions to our problems. Both agree that even our religions should be based on reason and not on revelation. A religion can be useful as long as it is finally ruled by our heads and not by our hearts.

And yet Vonnegut's writing also includes the kind of "existentialist humanism" more typical of Camus. All three of these men are atheists and "aggressively rational." But like Camus and unlike Huxley, Vonnegut is preoccupied with the atheist's problem of the *heart*—the ultimate meaninglessness of life when there is no God. Both Camus and Vonnegut see how this meaninglessness tends to make people mean. And, as humanists, both are therefore committed to finding a basis for human kindness and morality that can stand without support from God and ultimate meaning in life.

All of this results in making Vonnegut a sort of *American* Camus—a more *technology-oriented* Camus; a more *Protestant* Camus, because of Vonnegut's more pessimistic estimate of human nature; and also the possessor of one important ingredient so typically American and so conspicuously lacking in both Englishman Huxley and Frenchman Camus: a *sense of humor.*

5. Mark Twain Lives!

And yet I don't think Vonnegut as "an American Camus" brings him into focus as clearly as possible. On the contrary, if I believed in reincarnation I would point to Vonnegut and say, "Here is Mark Twain!" As a matter of fact, I think I'll say it anyway: *Here is Mark Twain!—*

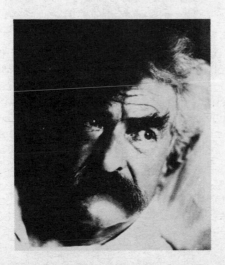

Here really is Mark Twain of course, easily recognized with his wild hair, wild mustache, wild eyes, etc. And now, in a picture I took of him in 1976, *here is Kurt Vonnegut!*—with his wild hair, wild mustache, wild eyes, etc.

Both grew up in the American Midwest, and both received the most formative parts of their boyhood educations from black slaves or servants. Both were taught to write by newspaper people, and both have strong backgrounds in science and technology.

Both are humorists who use their humor to create "tragedy traps," as Twain put it, or "black humor," as Vonnegut refers to the same method in his madness. Both write in a vernacular, come-as-you-are style, and both have occasionally illustrated their writings with their own drawings.

Both have made good use of the lecture platform to popularize their writings and opinions, and both tend toward pacifism and political liberalism.

Both obviously are deeply distressed by human suffering, stupidity, and greed; and both are obviously out to do something about it. And as a footnote, Vonnegut tells me his son Mark was named after Mark Twain.[15]

6. Kurt Vonnegut—A Space Age Mark Twain

So there are a lot of superficial resemblances. So what? So this: These surface resemblances are nothing when compared with the way these two men *think*. Vonnegut & Twain are virtually in intellectual and philosophical lock step. The only difference is that Vonnegut, because of living later, has had the chance to move farther down the path that both he and Twain have taken. Vonnegut takes up where Twain leaves off. But even with this advantage, Vonnegut has never gone very far beyond Mark Twain. In American literature Twain is the nineteenth century's Tweedledum to Vonnegut's twentieth century Tweedledee. Therefore as we follow pilgrim Vonnegut and the progress he has made, I'll try to show all along the way how pilgrim Twain has already blazed the trail.

I may as well begin now. I have said that Kurt Vonnegut and his famous Billy Pilgrim represent "Pilgrim's Progress Today." And the book by Mark Twain that secured *his* fame, *The Innocents Abroad,* has this subtitle: "The New Pilgrim's Progress."

7. The Good Pilgrims Vonnegut & Twain —and Dostoevsky too!

So Vonnegut & Twain provide excellent commentaries on each other. But the single personality who provides the best commentary on them both is Dostoevsky. This is because early in his life Dostoevsky was the same type of atheistic humanist as Vonnegut & Twain. But Dostoevsky's mind was so powerful and prophetic that he soon began to anticipate—and experience—the weaknesses and disastrous consequences of this position. Thus Dostoevsky outgrew the humanism of his youth and went beyond it to find something infinitely stronger to believe in. He then spent the rest of his life fighting humanism's "lie" and "struggling against the seductions of *atheistic love of mankind.*" [16]

For these reasons Dostoevsky is one of the strongest antidotes around for "mere humanism," which is represented so well by Vonnegut & Twain. Most good humanists know this and are quick to duck when they see Dostoevsky coming. He stands like a huge roadblock in the atheistic humanist's path. Camus had "a lifelong struggle against the compelling logic of Dostoevsky's world" [17] and never did overcome it. Twain evidently never read Dostoevsky. But Vonnegut has, and Vonnegut knows a dangerous opponent when he sees one. Therefore in a single paragraph in *Slaughterhouse-Five,* Vonnegut cleverly tries to defuse Dostoevsky by first paying him a compliment:

> Rosewater said an interesting thing to Billy one time about a book that wasn't science fiction. He said that everything there was to know about life was in *The Brothers Karamazov,* by Feodor Dostoevsky. "But that isn't *enough* any more," said Rosewater. [18]

If I had any criticism of Dostoevsky as a champion of the Christian faith for curing the follies of the present age, it wouldn't be that Dostoevsky "isn't enough." If anything, he's too much. He's overkill. The double-barreled gun of Dostoevsky's mind and faith is so powerful that anyone it hits may never really know or understand what hit them. The sword of Dostoevsky's pen is so sharp that his opponents often don't realize they've already been dismembered. "Ha! You missed me!" snarls one knife-fighter at the other. "Oh, did I?" replies his opponent. "Just wait 'til you try to turn your head!"

It may be that we are only now beginning to realize this about Dostoevsky. Maybe we are only now trying to turn our heads and learning how incisively he has cut to the heart of what ails us. German theologian Jürgen Moltmann may be right in this recent statement:

> I believe that we [in Europe and America] are standing before a new "hour of Dostoevsky," for many people are becoming inwardly disappointed over short-lived protests and mere technocratic reforms. They are struck by the ultimate

questions and are sensing that the answers may be in religious dimensions. Hopefully, they will find a religion that will carry on the revolution of man for which they were yearning.

The "hour of Dostoevsky" can also break into the Soviet Union so that the unfinished, unrealized hopes of the 1917 revolution of the Russian people may be renewed.[19]

For my part I am persuaded that in Dostoevsky there is more than enough nourishing bread for today's hungry pilgrim, who is exactly the person Dostoevsky prophetically baked it for.

Billy Pilgrim, Rosewater gave you a bum steer! The only problem to watch out for in reading *The Brothers Karamazov* can easily be solved:

©1966 United Feature Syndicate, Inc.

8. Vonnegut & Twain Belong to All of Us

Vonnegut & Twain are both fools in this positive sense: They use their humor to communicate their "theories." They are like the wise fool in Shakespeare's *As You Like It:* "He uses his folly like a stalking-horse, and under the presentation of that he shoots his wit" (act 5, sc. 4).

But they are also fools in this negative biblical sense: "The fool says in his heart, 'There is no God' " (Ps. 14:1,RSV).

They are "nobody's fools" in the sense of being worldly wise and shrewd, but they are also "nobody's fools" because they belong to all of us—they represent the way all of us tend to think and live nowadays.

B.C. by permission of Johnny Hart and Field Enterprises, Inc.

I have said that Vonnegut & Twain are atheistic humanists. Probably not many of us consciously think of ourselves as atheistic humanitsts. Nevertheless, that's what most of us are nowadays, whether we realize it or not. And those who aren't, are constantly tempted to convert. Atheistic humanism, says Paul Schilling, "is without doubt the working presupposition or practical mood of multitudes of persons in Europe and America today, whatever beliefs they may verbally profess." [20] Whenever the modern church thinks that atheism is only one of the minor problems it has to face, it has another think coming. As Gerhard Ebeling can say:

> We must not indulge in any illusions as to the fact that the full measure of the results of modern atheism is doubtless still ahead of us. But I am not concerned with statistics, or with forecasts either. I am concerned with the inner grasp of something which is far more complex than short-winded apologists suspect, and which does not . . . threaten Christianity only from without, but has already also penetrated . . . through the walls of the heart into our inmost being as a sort of atmosphere whose influence no one can evade. [21]

I find Vonnegut, and before him Mark Twain, to be almost perfect literary representations of the atmosphere of atheism that is today permeating the church and the world. As such, they can be extremely useful in helping us understand the nature of modern atheism, where it comes from, its deep and widespread results, and how its challenge is to be met.

This is why Vonnegut-Twain are *wrang-wrangs* of atheism.

9. Vonnegut-Twain—They Furnish "Wrang-Wrangs" for God

True, Vonnegut & Twain are like Tweedledee and Tweedledum. But it would probably be more accurate to say they are like "wrang and wrang." Because according to Vonnegut in *Cat's Cradle,*

> A *wrang-wrang* . . . is a person who steers people away from a line of speculation by reducing that line, with the example of the *wrang-wrang's* own life, to an absurdity.[22]

In other words *wrang-wrangs* are "bad examples." But this makes *wrang-wrangs* important and helpful. We need bad examples just like we need good ones:

ANDY CAPP

©1973 Daily Mirror Newspapers Ltd. ANDY CAPP Dist. Field Newspaper Syndicate.

Somebody's got to be the bad example. As Vonnegut says in *Player Piano* of one of his characters, who refuses to be tranquilized by psychiatry, "Somebody's just *got* to be maladjusted . . . somebody's got to be uncomfortable enough to wonder where people are, where they're going, and why they're going there."[23]

In their lives and in their writings, Vonnegut & Twain intentionally and unintentionally furnish us with excellent *wrang-wrangs*. They laugh to scorn many false gods and stupid ideas in the world and in the church that should be ridiculed and scorned. They give us first-rate intentional *wrang-wrangs* when they give the baby a bath with the strong soap of their hilarious but hard *questions*.

But Vonnegut & Twain become unintentional *wrang-wrangs* when they begin throwing out the baby along with the tepid bath water of their own weak *answers*. Their answers are superficial and inadequate for meeting the depths and strengths of their own questions. Their *answers* work about like this:

©1969 United Feature Syndicate, Inc.

10. Oh, This I Will Say of Vonnegut & Twain: They Are Strong in the "No Shit" Department but Weak in the "No Pain"

Both Vonnegut & Twain think of their work as having a double-edged purpose: to afflict the comfortable and to comfort the afflicted. (They no doubt picked up this attitude from God, who also "sets his face against the arrogant but favours the humble"[1 Pet. 5:5, NEB].) In his preface to *Welcome to the Monkey House,* this is how Vonnegut expresses this dual purpose in his work:

> My only brother, eight years older than I, is a successful scientist. His special field is physics as it relates to clouds. His name is Bernard, and he is funnier than I am. I remember a letter he wrote after his first child, Peter, was born and brought home. "Here I am," that letter began, "cleaning shit off practically everything."
>
> My only sister, five years older than I, died when she was forty. . . . Her dying words were, "No pain." Those are good dying words. It was cancer that killed her.
>
> And I realize now that the two main themes of my novels were stated by my siblings: "Here I am cleaning shit off practically everything" and "No pain."[24]

But Vonnegut & Twain are much better at affliciting the comfortable than at comforting the afflicted. Their answers are no match for their questions. The feeble balms they put on our wounds for helping us feel "no pain" are not nearly so effective as the strong antiseptics they use for cleaning these wounds. But they seem to know this. They both seem resigned to their primary—but very important!—function of providing *wrang-wrangs,* of furnishing "canary-bird-in-the-coal-mine alarm systems." They give us effective warning sirens. As a matter of fact, like the huge fire-siren Eliot Rosewater buys for the little town of Rosewater, Indiana, Vonnegut's works may constitute one of "the loudest alarms in the Western Hemisphere" today.[25]

Twain certainly knew *he* was better at clearing away the old weak answers than coming up with new strong ones. As he could say of his wife: "I took Livy's religion away from her, and gave her nothing—worse than nothing—in return. I gave her alarm."[26]

Vonnegut also struggles to find answers strong enough to satisfy his own questions, but in the meantime he sees clearly that there is no chance of finding the right answers unless the right questions have first been asked. As he says in *The Sirens of Titan:*

> The questions are important, I have thought harder about them than I have about the answers I already have. That is

the first thing I know for sure: (1.) If the questions don't make sense, neither will the answers.[27]

This is a lesson the church needs to learn. Wherever it fails to suit the depth of its answer to the depth of human questioning, it falsifies and cheapens this answer. By answering what has not been asked, it throws pearls before swine. The church's answer is then only a meaningless puzzle to those who pass it by:

Copyright, 1973, Universal Press Syndicate.

11. Vonnegut & Twain—Promising Godlessness

Thomas Hardy once wrote, "If way to the Better there be, it exacts a full look at the Worst."[28] This is precisely what Vonnegut & Twain help us do: to seek the Better by facing the Worst. For this reason the following statement by Peter Reed is equally true of both men:

> It would be wrong to approach Vonnegut as a philosopher with final answers to the meaning and nature of our world. In fact, his greatest service in terms of workaday philosophy may be his insistence on facing the anxieties of the inexplicable and the incongruous.[29]

And so Vonnegut & Twain, like the Old Testament prophets in helping us see the Worst and look for the Better, are "full of promise." They are much closer to the kingdom of God than the hopeless godlessness of most so-called Christian piety, the pious godlessness which hides behind an idol as God—the Monster God of "eternal damnation." Therefore, to know Vonnegut & Twain is to know what Bonhoeffer meant by "promising godlessness":

> It would be quite wrong simply to identify western godlessness with enmity towards the Church. There is the godlessness in religious and Christian clothing, which we have called a hopeless godlessness, but there is also a godlessness which is full of promise, a godlessness which speaks against religion and against the Church. It is the protest against pious godlessness in so far as this has corrupted the Churches, and thus in a certain sense, if only negatively, it defends the heritage of a genuine faith in God and of a genuine Church. There is relevance here in Luther's saying that perhaps God would rather hear the curses of the ungodly than the alleluia of the pious.[30]

12. Is Kurt Vonnegut the Exorcist of Jesus Christ Superstar?

This question is also the subtitle of this book. And now is a good time to try to answer it.

If by "Jesus Christ Superstar" we mean anything less than Jesus Christ himself, then, yes, Kurt Vonnegut is probably the exorcist of Jesus Christ Superstar and just about everything else connected with the church that isn't 100 percent pure. Vonnegut, with his "purifying laughter . . . has advanced from diagnostician to exorcist," says author Richard Schickel.[31] This means that Vonnegut is not only an expert in cleaning the shit off—but also in exorcising!—practically everything.

And I can say from painful personal experience that Vonnegut has exorcised and cleaned *me* off more times than I care to admit. But in the process he has also forced me to learn more good theology than most of the professional theological teachers I've had. Thank you, Kurt!

On the other hand, if by "Jesus Christ Superstar" we mean Jesus Christ himself, then Kurt Vonnegut is not an exorcist. For only Jesus Christ himself is the *real* exorcist. Only Christ can cleanse us from our real demons and at the same time really give us "no pain" but real peace and joy, a peace "not as the world gives" but a joy that "no one will take . . . from you" (John 14:27; 16:22, RSN). In this sense "Jesus Christ Superstar" is the exorcist of Kurt Vonnegut and of all the rest of us as well.

13. Vonnegut & Twain—Children of the Enlightenment

Most of the basic ideals of Vonnegut & Twain come straight out of the Enlightenment. To arrive at these ideas, Twain had to rebel against the gloomy form of Presbyterianism in which he was raised. But Vonnegut comes from a long line of well-educated Germans who had quickly embraced the ideas of the Enlightenment. His ancestors then immigrated to the United States, where the social ideas of Protestant Puritanism and the Englightenment had converged to form the American Constitution. "So I'm not rebelling against organized religion," says Vonnegut. "I never had any. I learned my outrageous opinions about organized religion at my mother's knee. My family has always had those. They came here absolutely crazy about the United States Constitution and about the possibility of . . . the brotherhood of man here. . . . and they were atheists." [32]

Vonnegut & Twain both stand in the literary and ideological tradition of Voltaire, the hilariously irreverent eighteenth-century champion of the Enlightenment. And both have read, marked, and inwardly digested Voltaire. But this doesn't make the ideas of Vonnegut & Twain passé. The Enlightenment is still very much with us. The ideas most of us live by every day "can, by and large, trace their beginnings to the intellectual effervescence of the eighteenth-century Enlightenment." [33]

For instance, all of Vonnegut's fiction is set in either the gruesome here and now or in the even more gruesome future. And yet in this fiction two "nutshells" perfectly describe two different "Gods" that are still raising a lot of real hell in the world today: the "God" (if it can be called that) that the Enlightenment fled from, and the "God" (if it can be called that) that the Enlightenment then fled to.

The nutshell describing the "God" *fled from* is found in *God Bless You, Mr. Rosewater.* It is in the form of an oath that a little orphan girl, Selena Deal, is required to repeat at her orphanage once a week before Sunday supper. This oath, "which Selena had taken six hundred times, before six hundred very plain suppers," goes like this:

> I do solemnly swear that I will respect the sacred private property of others, and that I will be content with whatever station in life God Almighty may assign me to. I will be grateful to those who employ me, and will never complain about wages and hours, but will ask myself instead, "What more can I do for my employer, my republic, and my God?" I understand that I have not been placed on Earth to be happy. I am here to be tested. If I am to pass the test, I must be always unselfish, always sober, always truthful, always chaste in mind, body, and deed, and always respectful to those to whom God has, in His Wisdom, placed above me. If I pass the test, I will go to joy everlasting in Heaven when I die. If I fail, I shall roast in hell while the Devil laughs and Jesus weeps.[34]

Large numbers of people are still fleeing from this "God."
Small wonder.

The second nutshell describes the "God" the Enlightenment *fled to.* It is from Vonnegut's futuristic *The Sirens of Titan,* and it is in the form of a prayer by a character I've already mentioned, The Reverend C. Horner Redwine, a minister of "the Church of God the Utterly Indifferent." Here is his prayer-nutshell:

> O Lord Most High, Creator of the Cosmos, Spinner of Galaxies, Soul of Electromagnetic Waves, Inhaler and Exhaler of Inconceivable Volumes of Vacuum, Spitter of Fire and Rock, Trifler with Millennia—what could we do for Thee that Thou couldst not do for Thyself one octillion times better? Nothing. What could we do or say that could possibly interest Thee? Nothing. Oh, Mankind, rejoice in the apathy of our Creator, for it makes us free and truthful and dignified at last.

No longer can a fool . . . point to a ridiculous accident of good luck and say, "Somebody up there likes me." And no longer can a tyrant say, "God wants this or that to happen, and anybody who doesn't help this or that to happen is against God." O Lord Most High, what a glorious weapon is Thy Apathy, for we have unsheathed it, have thrust and slashed mightily with it, and the claptrap that has so often enslaved us or driven us into the madhouse lies slain![35]

This is a good description of the apathetic God of *deism,* a God that was typical of most Enlightenment thinking, and yet a God that is still hanging around in our heads today. It is the God who creates a clocklike universe, winds it up, and then walks off and forgets it. And of course when anyone believes in a God like this, denial of any God—complete atheism—is inevitable and only an easy step away.

Nevertheless, the Enlightenment was overjoyed to ease the "traditional" Christian God out of the picture for reasons that these two nutshells clearly show. And all of these reasons can be reduced to two:

(1.) The traditional Christian God with his "hell" is a Monster God.

(2). A Monster God produces monstrous Christians.

14. Why Do Christians Find It so Easy to Be Cruel?

In Chapter 2 we discussed how the Enlightenment was fed up with the Monster God and his "hell." I now want to turn to the second reason the Enlightenment dropped this God like a brimstone potato: The Enlightenment saw that this cruel Monster God produces cruel, monstrous Christians.

In *Slaughterhouse-Five* Kilgore Trout has written a book called *The Gospel From Outer Space.* In it a "visitor from outer space made a serious study of Christianity, to learn, if he could, why Christians found it so easy to be cruel."[36] This question, based on obvious facts of history, is one that Vonnegut constantly shoves in our faces. But—

> *As long as we keep the Monster God and his "hell" in mind,*
> *The reasons for "Christian cruelty" are not hard to find.*

Here are four types of cruel "Christianity" caused by belief in the cruel Monster God:

A. *The Cruel "Christianity" of Enforceable Deeds*

One of the "Christian cruelties" that Vonnegut & Twain often mention is the Inquisition. And of course the Inquisition is only representative of a whole bunch of other dumb stuff that has constantly gone on. For instance "The Children's Crusade," another beautiful page in Christian history, is Vonnegut's subtitle for *Slaughterhouse-Five.*

But if we look at such atrocious behavior in the light of a serious belief in "hell," then this behavior makes complete sense and can even seem humane. For example, the "heretics" roasted by the Inquisition held beliefs that were a dangerous temptation to those who were weak in faith. And therefore if the number of souls who were to burn in everlasting torment could be reduced by *now* burning to death a few hundred thousand heretics (hardened heretics who were obviously already doomed to "hell" anyway), then what could be more rational? By stoking up the flames of "hell" for a few heretics just a little bit sooner, many souls might thereby be saved from "hell's" eternal flames later.

Obviously the Inquisition was only doing what it had to do. It was only doing its job. It was "murder with a heart"—something about like this, only a little more so:

©King Features Syndicate, Inc. 1976.

As for the Crusades, there were all kinds of wonderful motives behind them—the pleasures of plunder, the love of looting, the raptures of raping, "see the world," and so on. But the only "religious" motive behind these disasters was to save one's soul from "hell," and to force the infidels into saving theirs too. All you had to do was go on a crusade and the church would issue you a one-way, guaranteed ticket to eternal bliss.

Otherwise you could go to "hell."

If I'd been born in Europe during the Crusades, I suppose I would have been a crusader too, bopping Moslems and other enemies of the faith, "leaving boots sticking out of snowbanks, warming myself with my secretly virtuous insides," as Vonnegut says in *Mother Night.* [37]

For in all of this I would *think* I was escaping "hell," never dreaming I was already *in* it.

And it in me.

B. *The Cruel "Christianity" of Self-Righteous Belief*

The Protestants, as we have seen, tried to avoid this mistake of enforceable belief by making faith strictly a matter of *inward* decision. Protestants were going to be saved from "hell" by saving themselves. They would make their very own decisions for Jesus. However, when faith is thought of as the *right* decision made by our very own *selves,* this causes the flames of "hell" to backfire in another direction: *self-righteousness.*

For no one can be more righteously vengeful than the *self*-righteous. No indignation can be so totally destructive as *righteous* indignation. This is because self-righteousness is simply a person's natural meanness encouraged by what they think is their own rightness. Self-righteousness has all of the unrestrained power of sin wearing a halo. Luther, that great foe of all self-righteousness (or the righteousness of "works"), probably said it best: "No one judges and thinks so harshly of others as do those who are devoted to human exertions and works." [38]

For if I am free to get mine, then you are too. And if you haven't gotten yours, as I have mine, then this is only a result of your own freely chosen meanness and laziness. Therefore I am quite justified in treating you as a deliberately mean and irresponsible person. Self-righteousness, like the "Enlightened Self-interest" of Vonnegut's *God Bless You, Mr. Rosewater,* gives people a flag, which they adore on sight. It is essentially the black and white Jolly Roger, with these words written beneath the skull and crossbones, "The hell with you, Jack, I've got mine!" [39]

At heart all self-righteousness is simply smug hatefulness—the same kind of smug hatefulness that is written across this man's face:

Drawing by McCallister; ©1974. The New Yorker Magazine, Inc.

The demonic cruelty of self-righteousness—the cruelty "that wants to hate with God on its side," as Vonnegut can say, [40] can be considerable, as we can easily see in war. But more of this later when we get to a little incident called "the fire-bombing of Dresden."

In the meantime there are countless other ways self-righteous belief can do its cruel work. Here, for instance, is a news item that showed up recently in *Playboy*. It was entitled *"HATE THY NEIGHBOR"*:

Berkeley, California—*Further evidence has been found supporting the view that there is a strong correlation between churchgoing and . . . prejudice. . . .*

Commenting on a five-year study of the subject, research
sociologist Rodney Stark . . . . attributed the connection between church membership and bias to the Western Christian
"radical free-will image of man": If a man believes everyone
controls his own destiny, he is likely to be intolerant of the
weaknesses of others and to blame the disadvantaged for
their own misery. The result is resistance to the civil rights
movement and to large-scale attempts to improve the lot of
minority groups.[41]

But as long as there's belief in "hell," there will also have to be
belief in "free-will," which is the basis for most self-righteousness.
Otherwise how can we save ourselves from "hell"? And how could
we possibly justify God's sending anyone there?

C. The Cruel "Christianity" of God's Special Messengers

God's once and for all revelation of himself in Christ will always
be insufficient for those who believe in "hell." For even though the
knowledge of our salvation in general may be complete in Christ,
what about my future in particular? Here I need more information.
Here I need something more than the Christ of the New Testament.

As long as there is belief in a real "hell" after death, there's going
to be real questions like this. And as long as these questions exist,
people are going to be desperately looking for special signs and
messages from God—signs and messages that will assure them that
they are indeed among those chosen by God to escape the flames
of "hell."

They will want detailed information about this escape: the "future
schlock" of "biblical prophecy," guidebooks for helping them escape the imminent doom of our late, great planet, and so on.

In this way "hell" cracks the door open to countless special de-
livery signs, messages, portents and revelations from God. And as
soon as this door is opened just this much, it is then flung completely open not only to every kind of crackpot conceivable, but
also to every crook who can convince people that they have special
information from God.

And so, as Vonnegut puts it, any tyrant can "say, 'God wants
this or that to happen, and anybody who doesn't help this or that to
happen is against God'." But all such tyrants had better watch their
step. Anyone can play this game:

*"Let me get this straight. According to the
stars, I should abdicate and crown you king?"*

Drawing by Joseph Farris ©1969, Saturday Review, Inc.

And so it goes that special messages from God, to the discredit of
the Christian faith, become the specialty of kooks or crooks or both.
And all of this because of belief in "hell"—a hell of a belief.

For when the gospel of Jesus Christ is correctly understood as
being as *completely* good and *all*-encompassing as it actually is, as-
suring *all* people of their future with God, then there is no need to
look for other messages or messengers from God. As Karl Barth
said:

> The prophet is the man who is the messenger and sover-
> eign ambassador of God, his father, commissioned to ex-
> pound plainly God's will to the world. Jesus is this messenger
> and this ambassador. He declares the will of God. No man
> declares the will of God, except in terms of Christ, who is the
> only real prophet. The point is, therefore, that we must not
> fancy ourselves as "private" prophets; no, we do not need
> any new discoveries in the realm of the divine. All we need
> has been said and we have just to repeat it. To take part in
> the prophecy means for us to be pupils in the House of God.

> Such a wealth of riches is there that we should not regret that
> we are not, that we cannot be, prophets. . . .[42]

With such a wealth of riches, there is *every* reason for mankind *really* to rejoice, not in bitter-sweet "rejoicing" for "the apathy of our Creator," but in real rejoicing for God's unconditional and everlasting love for "*all* the people."

For this is what the rich gospel of Christ—the "good news"—actually is: "Be not afraid; for behold, I bring you good news of a great joy which will come to all the people. For to you"—to *all the people*—"is born this day . . . a Savior who is Christ the Lord" (Lk. 2:10–11).

D. *The Cruel "Christianity" of Fear of the Body and Neglect of the Body Politic*

Whenever "hell" is understood literally, our own bodies will become our enemies. They become a source of constant temptation that can easily cause our fall into the bottomless pit of eternal night. Therefore we hate and fear our bodies, and treat them with cruel contempt. *Any* bodily pleasure must be seriously feared as "sin," because any bodily pleasure can lead to our turning away from God, and therefore to our "roasting in hell while the Devil laughs and Jesus weeps."

©King Features Syndicate, Inc. 1976.

The church has called this hatred and fear of the body the heresy of "Manicheism." Manicheism is the belief that the spirit is good but the flesh isn't. But the church has rarely realized that behind this heresy is the heresy of a literal "hell." Therefore as long as this monstrous misunderstanding of hell persists, Manicheism will too.

People who believe in a literal hell will also have the same contempt for the "body politic" that they have for the body. "I understand that I have not been placed on Earth to be happy. I am here to be tested." Therefore it is not my job to make the testing ground any easier. To hell with the testing ground! My job is simply to pass the test. For "if I pass the test I will go to joy everlasting in Heaven when I die. If I fail I shall roast in hell. . . ."

And therefore folks who believe in "hell" are quite willing to let the world go there while they are busy "saving souls"—their own and others'.

What a vacuum of social responsibility this attitude has left in the world! And into this vacuum, guess who stepped! People like Selena Deal's "employers," who said if the meek didn't want the world, they would take it. Or people like Marx, Engels, Stalin, etc.—people who were not so willing to let the world go to hell or to fall into the hands of greedy "robber baron" employers and such.

This is why unscrupulous tyrants often show respect for religion and like to have it in the lands they rule: Because religion—the only religion they know, the religion of the Monster God and his "hell"—makes people such contented and compliant sheep and so easy to rule. Because these sheep are so preoccupied with what they consider the only *really* important problem, getting to Heaven and avoiding "hell," they are willing to go along with just about anything that happens here and now on earth. The sheep concerned only with "how to get to Heaven," are the easiest type to fleece.

ZIGGY

This is also why Communist leaders show contempt for religion and do not like to have this "opiate" in the lands they rule: Because religion—the only religion they know, the religion of the Monster God and his "hell"—leads to such neglectful indifference to this world and its possibilities here and now. The Marxists were not guilty of the heresy that denies the goodness of God's creation. They wanted to "hear it for the flesh." Therefore they have very little use for the Rev. John Goodbodys and their cruel God.

THE COLONIALS

Reprinted by permission of artist, Joseph J. Escourido

As Karl Barth tells us, it was the Monster God who "was the occasion of so many fatal developments to the right hand or to the left, and was even pushed on one side as a kind of offense—to the great detriment of thinking upon the basis of the Christian faith. . . ."[43]

It was the Monster God and his "hell" that made inevitable—along with so many other "fatal developments"—modern Fascism and Communism.

Hi ho.

15. The Atheistic Humanism of Vonnegut & Twain

Meanwhile, back to Vonnegut & Twain, our excellent examples of how and why the modern Western world began turning its back on Christ. The tragedy was that this world felt it had only three alternatives:

1. To follow the cruel "Christian" Monster God and his cruel Christians.
2. To follow the hopelessly backward gods of non-Christian religions and superstitions. _____
3. No God at all.

For the most part, Western civilization chose number 3. It scarcely dreamed of how good the good news of the gospel actually is. The only "good news" it knew was the bad news of damnation and "hell." This is the good news for which, as Mark Twain put it,

> . . . the missionaries braved a thousand privations to come and make [the natives] permanently miserable by telling them how beautiful and how blissful a place heaven is, and how nearly impossible it is to get there; and showed the poor native how dreary a place perdition is and what unnecessarily liberal facilities there are for going to it.[44]

Some good news.

These words of Twain's are the most fitting commentary I can imagine on the following saying of Jesus:

> Woe to you, scribes and Pharisees, hypocrites! because you shut the kingdom of heaven against men; for you neither enter yourselves, nor allow those who would enter to go in. . . . you traverse sea and land to make a single proselyte, and when he becomes a proselyte, you make him twice as much a child of hell as yourselves (Matt. 23:13, 15, RSV).

But all people must have some god or master or ultimate concern. So after disposing of the gods of religion, what god would the Western world put in their place? "Man. . . . That's all. Just man."

This is the way Vonnegut describes the humanism of Bokononism in *Cat's Cradle*. It is also a fair description of the atheistic humanism the Western world turned to after ditching the Monster God and his "hell".

> "What *is* sacred to Bokononists?" I asked. . . .
> "Not even God, as near as I can tell."

"Nothing?"

"Just one thing."

I made some guesses. "The ocean? The Sun?"

"Man," said Frank. "That's all. Just man." [45]

Modern atheistic humanism was born out of the *in*humaneness of the Monster God. If God is no more humane than this, it was reasoned, then we humans will depend only on ourselves for the foundation of humaneness in the world.

Modern civilization scarcely knew of *the humanity of God* in Christ; therefore it rejected the *humanless godism* of the Monster God and his "hell," almost the only God it did know, and replaced him with *godless humanism*.

The Western world now correctly saw that "hell" and the cruel Christians produced by "hell" were real "boners" committed by the church. Therefore the West was no longer willing to trust the church, or "Captain Boner," as its guide. If the church says "This way!" the world was now ready to head full speed "That way!"

©King Features Syndicate, Inc. 1976.

And this is how Vonnegut & Twain, just like most of the rest of us, began their hopeful pilgrimages into the modern world. So long, "Captain Boner"! Toodle-oo, God of "hell"! Good riddance of bad rubbish! As Twain could say:

The pulpit says God's ways are not our ways. Thanks. Let us try to get along with our own the best we can; we can't improve on them by experimenting with His. [46]

But then, after the first optimistic beginnings of godless humanism, a horrible thing started to happen. Another fatal development began to grow and spread everywhere. Let us call it—

16. "Godless Inhumanism" or Nihilism

Again, the experiences of Vonnegut & Twain are typical of what now began to happen. The experience of profound disillusionment that occurred late in Twain's life and early in Vonnegut's is typical of the disillusionment that soon occurred, in one form or another, throughout the world of "enlightened" atheistic humanism.

Vonnegut, in a speech to a 1970 graduating class, tells what happened to him.

> I use to be an optimist. This was during my boyhood in Indianapolis. . . .
>
> My brother Bernard was on his way to becoming an important scientist. . . . He made me very enthusiastic about science for a while. I thought scientists were going to find out exactly how everything worked, and then make it work better. I fully expected that by the time I was twenty-one, some scientist, maybe my brother, would have taken a color photograph of God Almighty—and sold it to *Popular Mechanics* magazine.
>
> Scientific truth was going to make us *so* happy and comfortable.
>
> What actually happened when I was twenty-one was that we dropped scientific truth on Hiroshima. We killed everybody there. And I had just come home from being a prisoner of war in Dresden, which I'd seen burned to the ground. And the world was just learning how ghastly the German extermination camps had been. So I had a heart-to-heart talk with myself.
>
> "Hey, Corporal Vonnegut," I said to myself, "maybe you were wrong to be an optimist. Maybe pessimism is the thing."
>
> I have been a consistent pessimist ever since, with a few exceptions. In order to persuade my wife to marry me, of

course, I had to promise her that the future would be heavenly. . . . And then I had to lie to her again every time she threatened to leave me because I was too pessimistic.

I saved our marriage many times by exclaiming, "Wait! Wait! I see light at the end of the tunnel at last!" And I wish I could bring light to *your* tunnels today. My wife begged me to bring you light, but there *is* no light. Everything is going to become unimaginably worse, and never get better again. If I lied to you about that, you would sense that I'd lied to you, and that would be another cause for gloom. We have enough causes for gloom.[47]

"There *is* no light." This is a good definition of *nihilism,* and here affirmed by a child of the Enlightenment!

The position of atheistic humanism began to fall apart when modern, "enlightened" humans didn't live up to their advance billing. In the beginning, atheistic humanism seemed like such a sound, healthy way of looking at things. Surely we had "come of age" as modern men and women. Surely it was time to forget about any god and start living for ourselves. Now we could be who we really are and look only to ourselves for our happiness. But somehow things didn't work out the way we expected.

MISS PEACH by Mell Lazarus. Courtesy of Mell Lazarus and Field Newspaper Syndicate.

Modern, enlightened people were now supposed to live *unselfishly.* But how they actually lived was closer to this:

We now believed that human beings were basically *rational* animals. Therefore we would no longer need to live irrationally and in fear. Nevertheless, this is how we continued to live:

MISS PEACH by Mell Lazarus. Courtesy of Mell Lazarus and Field Newspaper Syndicate.

We now believed that human beings were *basically good.* We no longer believed, as the church had taught us, that all people originate in life as "sinners"—as people originally dominated by petty and vain concerns, and blinded to this sin by the very pettiness and vanity of sin itself. No, humans were good by nature, and therefore needed no outside help to be good or to see clearly their own natures. Nevertheless—

Technological progress would now give us all such plenty that greed would soon be a thing of the past. However—

"The computer is only a tool. There will always be a place for unbridled avarice."

The light of *learning and education* would surely serve to bring peace to all humankind. But in fact it worked like this:

©King Features Syndicate, Inc. 1973.

Now we knew what life was all about: *love*. Just love. Plain, garden variety, human love. This was all that was essential. And because our hearts were by nature so full of love, we would all soon be drawn together in one great family of liberty, equality, fraternity—and love:

©1971 Chicago Tribune—New York News Syndicate, Inc.

More democratic forms of *justice* and *government* would now give all of us a chance to show what angels people actually are deep down inside.

B.C. by permission of Johnny Hart and Field Enterprises, Inc.

With *science* set to work on our problems, even the problem of human self-centeredness would soon be solved. Now we would all live for "MEN." In reality, however, we continue to fall a consonant short of that goal by living for—

Drawing by Ed Fisher; ©1968, Saturday Review, Inc.

Finally, we would look not to our sadly insufficient selves for all the answers to life. Instead we would look to the *future* and to the *unexplored* for our happiness and fulfillment and for greener grass. This was our dream. And this is the way it worked:

©1968 United Feature Syndicate, Inc.

Humankind's long march from the Dark Ages to the glorious dawn of our enlightenment was a struggle of immeasurable costs, but human *progress* is inevitable. It cannot be stopped. And now we have obviously arrived at the new day:

©King Features Syndicate, Inc. 1973.

Obviously the fly in the ointment of atheistic humanism is the "human problem." "Man," said Bonhoeffer, "has managed to deal with everything, only not with himself. He can insure against everything, only not against man. In the last resort it all turns on men."[48] Or, as scientist and atheistic humanist Albert Einstein sadly concluded late in his life: "The real problem is in the hearts of men. . . . It is easier to change the nature of plutonium than man's evil spirit." [49] It is easier for people to conquer the world than to master themselves. Plutonium and the world are only neutral, indifferent things, but man's evil spirit is a mean and tough customer.

©King Features Syndicate, Inc. 1977.

So now atheistic humanism has begun looking around for whatever it is that causes even enlightened, modern humans to act so toughly inhumane. And what many atheistic humanists are now finally beginning to realize is itself a startling development: The problem lies not in the *humanism* and its goals, but in the *atheism.* Because—

17. Atheism Makes Life Ultimately Meaningless and Ultimate Meaninglessness Makes People Mean

People go on living because they have something to live *for.* And whatever a person lives for—whatever is this person's center of value or ultimate concern—is also this person's "god" or "meaning giver." This means, of course, that almost anything can give *temporary* meaning to people's lives: material possessions, honors, fame, other people or another person, a dog, a cat, a theory about life, one's country, the pleasure of the present moment, and so on. It is impossible for anything—from the sublime to the ridiculous—to be that one thing, that single something, that a person lives for.

©1974 Daily Mirror Newspapers Ltd. ANDY CAPP Dist. Field Newspaper Syndicate.

But what about life itself, *all* of life? What does life itself live for? What meaning can life possible have if it all finally amounts to nothing, if all of life is finally defeated by death? What's the use of all our yesterdays, todays, and tomorrows if they only "light fools the way to dusty death"? All our careful "game plans" for tomorrow can give life a *provisional* meaning; but what about "tomorrow and tomorrow and tomorrow"—that is, what is life's *ultimate* meaning? What does it all mean—if anything!—"in the big game plan in the sky"?

BEETLE BAILEY

©King Features Syndicate, Inc. 1975.

Life, said Macbeth, is only a "brief candle," a "walking shadow," a "tale told by an idiot full of sound and fury signifying . . ." (that is, what *significance* does life finally have?) ". . . *nothing.*" And Macbeth is right if all life finally ends at nothingness, at death, at a literal dead end.

CONCHY by James Childress. ©Field Enterprises, Inc., 1974. Courtesy of Field Newspaper Syndicate.

By definition, a thing has meaning only when it points to something beyond itself. A thing has "sign-ificance" only when it is a sign of something outside itself. Therefore, if there is no God, life itself is ultimately pointless and meaningless and without significance. For without God, life finally only points to—or signifies—nothing, death, nonbeing. Without God, without something beyond life itself, all of life is ultimately pointless, purposeless, futile, and meaningless. For an atheist, everything *in* life can have a meaning or refer to something else in life. But this is not true of life itself. Ultimately life isn't going anywhere. It is only a crazy carousel ride to nowhere. "Where death is," says author Richard Coe, "there can be no optimism. What act or thought is *not* meaningless, when the end of all is annihilation?" [50]

"Kind of takes some of the fun out of being rich, eh, Hamilton?"

Drawing by Stan Hunt; ©1970. The New Yorker Magazine, Inc.

This experience of the meaninglessness of life is characteristic of the philosophy of nihilism. *Atheism* says there is no absolute being called God. *Nihilism* says there is no absolute at all. Nihilism (which comes from the Latin word *nihil,* or "nothing") is simply atheism that has finally reached its logical conclusion. There is *no* ultimate truth for nihilism. "Nothing means anything," as Vonnegut can say in *Mother Night.*[51] Any truth people think there is is just that: an arbitrary manmade "truth" or lie. People make up such lies in order to be able to live "as if" something were true, "as if" life had meaning.

But actually there can be no ultimate "truth" or meaning as long as death is the end of all things, as long as our mother is only the night. "The truth is death," says Vonnegut, quoting Céline and speaking like a "true" nihilist.[52] This world is finally only a slaughterhouse. For without God, nothing is ahead but plain old nothing.

CONCHY by James Childress. ©Field Enterprises, Inc., 1975. Courtesy of Field Newspaper Syndicate.

In case, dear Reader, you are thinking that nihilism must be a pretty far-out way of looking at things, a belief held only by a few "nuts," then please think again. There is an excellent chance that, deep down inside, *you* are a nihilist. This is because nihilism is the slow poison at the center of all atheism. And for a long time now, most of us have been, in one form or another, atheistic humanists. "No one with any insight," said philosopher Martin Heidegger, "will still deny today that nihilism is in the most varied and most hidden forms 'the normal state' of man."[53] Certainly Bonhoeffer had great insight into all of us today when he described "us" this way:

> For us the world has lost its gods; we no longer worship anything, we have experienced too clearly the frailty and invalidity of all things, of all men, and of ourselves for us still to be

able to deify them. We have lost too much confidence in the whole of existence for us still to be capable of having and worshiping gods. If we have an idol, perhaps it is nothingness, obliteration, meaninglessness.[54]

"In that respect," Bonhoeffer went on to say, "we are truly nihilists."[55]

18. Our Wealth of Means Reveals Little Meaning

The experience of the meaninglessness of life is brought about by two things: the belief that there is no God, and a strong sense of our own approaching death, our own mortality. In the recent past this experience was usually reserved for folks further along in life—folks who were drawing closer to "The End." Younger people, looking hopefully to the future, were happy they had no God to fear. But as they grew older and began running out of future, they came to realize that they also had no God to hope in. Youth only took *life* with deadly seriousness; they didn't show a lively seriousness about *death* until they got older. For it wasn't until then that they came face-to-face with the problem of the meaning of life. It worked about like this:

Copyright, 1975, G. B. Trudeau/Distributed by Universal Press Syndicate.

Garry Trudeau drew the above cartoon in 1975. At the time he was only twenty-six. I point this out to show how older people about the age of Zonker's dad no longer have a monopoly on the awareness of the need for meaning in life. People Trudeau's age and younger now cut their teeth on this painful awareness. How come?

The reason is simple: Our great progress in scientific, technological, and materialistic *means* has so cleared the road of life for us that we can now see very clearly what we are fast approaching at the end of that road: only scientific, technological, and materialistic—and therefore *meaningless*—death.

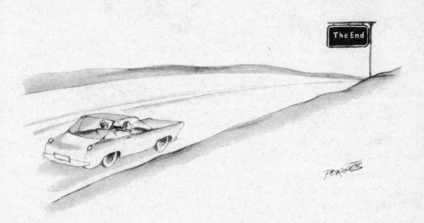

Drawing by Porges; ©1975. The New Yorker Magazine, Inc.

As he entered *his* later years, Albert Einstein, one of the great advancers of our scientific, technological, and materialistic means, came to this conclusion: "Perfections of means and confusion of goals seem—in my opinion—to characterize our age."[56] To put it another way, our lives are filled with plenty of means but little meaning. Our wealth of means, or "know-how," only heightens our awareness of our lack of meaning, or "know-why."

"They have the know-how, but do they have the know-why?"

Drawing by J. Mirachi; ©1972. The New Yorker Magazine, Inc.

On the one hand, we now live in a world of seemingly limitless possibilities. Almost any direction is open to us. But the great freedom we feel in which way to go through life, only raises a more perplexing set of questions: How do we know which is the best way to go? Is there a best way? How can we know anything for sure? And why bother to struggle at all for any of life's "swampy" goals?

BEETLE BAILEY

©King Features Syndicate, Inc. 1973.

On the other hand, the complex organizational and technical efficiency of modern life gives us the feeling that perhaps we are not really free at all. Perhaps we are only tiny, practically useless cogs in some enormous, meaningless, purposeless machine that is finally only the well-known "treadmill to oblivion." Or, to use an anlogy closer to Vonnegut, we feel like notes struck only once, and then heard no more, on some blind, chaotically discordant "player piano."

Drawing by Richter; ©1976. The New Yorker Magazine, Inc.

19. Life Without God Is Hell— the *Real* Hell

So the experience of the meaninglessness of life is the hell that most of us now live in—or, to be more precise, it is the hell that now lives in us. This is why most of the Western world is today in a tragically ironic situation. And that situation is this: Modern men and women were correct to reject the literal hell of a horrible burning that will take place after we die. But because they had been taught that this was also the hell that Christ had talked about, they have rejected Christ along with this "hell." As a result, their lives are godless and meaningless and filled only with the exact hell that Christ *did* talk about and indeed came into the world to defeat.

So now, having put out the fires of a literal hell, the *real* burning of the *real* hell goes on inside them, and they have little or no knowledge of its remedy—Christ. And in this way the original mistake about Christ is played out all over again: "He was in the world; but the world, though it owed its being to him, did not recognize him" (John 1:10, NEB).

In "the Now Society," the very hell that Christ came to save us from is simply called "life." And there is scarcely the slighest suspicion that life can be anything other than the hell it now is.

THE NOW SOCIETY

"I know you're going thru hell, darling, but that's life."

20. . . . and Ultimate Meaninglessness Makes People Mean

Meanwhile, back to the statement I made up the road at signpost #17: *Meaninglessness makes people mean.*

No one saw the truth of this principle with more clarity and foresight than Dostoevsky. Long before almost anyone else, Dostoevsky could see that atheistic humanism ("godless humanism") would necessarily lead to nihilism ("godless inhumanism") and that nihilism would soon cause all hell—the *real* hell—to break loose over the earth with a vengeance greater than ever before. This is one reason Dostoevsky was such a fan of Christ's final reconciliation of all men ("the humanity of God"), rather than a fan of the God of "hell" ("inhuman Godism"). Dostoevsky not only *believed* in the ultimate reconciliation of all men in God,[57] but he could also see that the God of a literal hell was an utter failure at winning friends and influencing people for a better life now.

In his fiction, Dostoevsky dramatized over and over atheism's downward path into nihilism. In his nonfiction, especially in his *Diary of a Writer,* he showed us how *history* is on its way down the same slippery slope. And history has since proven Dostoevsky right a thousand times over.

I don't know if you've ever read it, Kurt, but here is one of the passages from Dostoevsky's *Diary* that I alluded to in our conversation. Please take a close look at it, Kurt. It's good, strong stuff and close to Dostoevsky's heart. Atheism makes life meaningless, or futureless, and futurelessness makes people *despair* and *despise*. The quotation is a little on the long side. But, like Ira, I'm sure it can't be better expressed.

MISS PEACH by Mell Lazarus. Courtesy of Mell Lazarus and Field Newspaper Syndicate.

"Without faith in one's soul and its immortality," wrote Dostoevsky,

> . . . man's existence is unnatural, unthinkable, impossible. Now, it seems to me that I have clearly expressed the formula of a logical suicide. . . . In him there is no faith in immortality. . . . Little by little, the thought of his aimlessness and his

hatred of the muteness of the surrounding inertia lead him to the inevitable conviction of the utter absurdity of man's existence on earth. It becomes clear as daylight to him that only those men can consent to live who resemble the lower animals and who come nearest to the latter by reason of the limited development of their minds and their purely carnal wants. They agree to live specifically as animals, *i.e.*, in order "to eat, drink, sleep, build their nests and raise children." Indeed, eating, sleeping, polluting and sitting on soft cushions will long attract men to earth, but not the higher types. . . .

To me personally, one of the most dreaded apprehensions for our future—even our near future—is the fact that . . . there is spreading with ever-increasing rapidity complete disbelief in one's soul and in its immortality. And not only does this disbelief strengthen itself by a sort of conviction (as yet we have but few convictions of any kind) but also by some strange universal indifference—at times even scoffing at this loftiest idea of human existence. God knows by virtue of what law it spreads among us, and it is indifference not only toward this particular idea but toward everything that is vital—for the truth of life, for everything that generates and nourishes life, that brings health, that annihilates decomposition and fetidness. . . .

Neither man nor nation can exist without a sublime idea. And on earth there is *but one* sublime idea—namely, the idea of the immortality of man's soul—since all other "sublime" ideas of life, which give life to man, *are merely derived from this one idea*. On this point I may be contradicted (that is, on the question of this unity of the source of everything sublime on earth), but as yet I am not going to argue, and I am setting forth my idea arbitrarily. . . .

Irresistibly, there stand before [the "logical suicide"] the loftiest, the most pressing questions: "What is the use of living if he has already conceived the idea that for man to live like an animal is disgusting, abnormal and insufficient? And what, in this case, can retain him on earth?" He cannot solve these questions and he knows it. . . . it is this lucidity that finished him. Well, where is the trouble? Is what was he mistaken?—The trouble is solely in the loss of faith in immortality.

However, he himself ardently seeks . . . conciliation; he

meant to find it in "love for mankind"—"Not I but, perhaps, mankind will be happy and some day may attain harmony. This thought could retain me on earth." . . . And, of course, this is a magnanimous thought and one full of suffering. But the irresistible conviction that the life of mankind—just as his own—is, substantially, a fleeting moment, and that on the morrow of the realization of "harmony" (if one is to believe that this dream can be realized) mankind will be reduced to the same zero even as he, by the force of the inert laws of nature, and that—after so much suffering endured for the attainment of that dream—this thought completely stirs his spirit; this sets him in revolt precisely because of his love of mankind; it insults him on behalf of mankind as a whole. . . . it even kills in him love itself of mankind. Similarly it has been observed many a time that in a family dying from starvation, father and mother—when at length the suffering of their children grow intolerable—began to hate them, those hitherto beloved ones, precisely because of the *intolerableness* of their suffering. Moreover, I assert that the realization of one's utter impotence to help, to render some service, or to bring alleviation to suffering mankind—and at the same time when there is a firm conviction of the existence of that suffering,—*may convert in one's heart love for mankind into hatred of it.* Gentlemen of cast-iron ideas, of course, will not believe this and will be utterly unable to understand it: to them, love of mankind and its happiness are such cheap things; everything has been set and described so long ago that these things are not worth being given a thought to. But I intend to make them really laugh: I assert . . . that love of mankind is unthinkable, unintelligible and *altogether impossible without the accompanying faith in the immortality of man's soul.* Those who, having deprived man of the faith in his immortality, are seeking to substitute for it—as life's loftiest aim—"love of mankind," those, I maintain, are lifting their arms against themselves, since in lieu of love of mankind they are planting in the heart of him who has lost his faith seeds of hatred of mankind. Let pundits of cast-iron ideas shrug their shoulders at this assertion. But this thought is wiser than their wisdom, and unhesitatingly I believe that some day humankind will embrace it as an axiom. . . .

I even assert and venture to say that love of mankind *in general, as an idea,* is one of the most incomprehensible ideas for the human mind. Precisely as an idea. Sentiment alone can vindicate it. However, sentiment is possible precisely only in the presence of the accompanying conviction of the immortality of man's soul. . . .

It is clear, then, that suicide—when the idea of immortality has been lost—becomes an utter and inevitable necessity for any man who, by his mental development, has even slightly lifted himself above the level of cattle. On the contrary, immortality—promising eternal life—ties man all the more strongly to earth. Here is a seeming contradiction: if there is so much life—that is, if in addition to earthly existence there is an immortal one—why should one be treasuring so highly his earthly life? And yet, the contrary is true, since only with faith in his immortality does man comprehend the full meaning of his rational destination on earth. However, without the faith in his immortality, man's ties with earth are severed, they grow thinner and more putrescent, while the loss of the sublime meaning of life (felt at least in the form of unconscious anguish) inevitably leads to suicide. . . .

In a word, the idea of immortality is life itself—"live life," its ultimate formula, the mainspring of truth and just consciousness for humankind. . . .

. . . the whole sublime purpose and meaning of life, the desire and urge to live, emanate only from this faith.[58]

"Well, all this is logical." Anyway, Kurt, that's what you said when I attempted to "run off" the same "Dostoevskian argument" for you. And I think you're right. It makes complete sense, even to an atheist. As a matter of fact, in *The Brothers Karamazov,* when Dostoevsky later dramatized the whole argument and put it in a nutshell, it is repeated by Ivan, the brother who is an atheist. According to Ivan's friend, Muisov, Ivan "solemnly declared":

". . . that there was nothing on earth to force men to love their fellow men, that there was no law of nature that a man should love mankind, and that if there was love on earth it did not stem from any natural law but rather from man's belief in immortality. And . . . that if there was any natural law, it was precisely this: Destroy a man's belief in immortality and not only will his ability to love wither away within him but, along with it, the force that compels him to continue his existence on earth. Moreover, nothing would be immoral then, everything would be permitted. . . . He went even further, finally asserting that, for every individual—people like us now, for instance—who does not believe in God or immortality, the natural moral law immediately becomes the opposite of religious law and that absolute egotism, even carried to the extent of crime, must not only be tolerated but even recognized as the wisest and perhaps the noblest course. . . .

"Just a minute!" Dmitry shouted unexpectedly. "I want to get it straight: crime must be considered not only as admissible but even as the logical and inevitable consequence of an atheist's position. Did I get it right?"

"You've got it right," Father Paisii said.[59]

After Ivan owns up to producing this "Dostoevskian argument," Father Zossima tells him that he, Ivan, is "either blissfully happy" if he really believes it, "or desperately unhappy" if he doesn't. For if he doesn't believe in the truth of his "opinion," that there can be "no morality without immortality," then "within you, that problem has not been solved and yours is a great unhappiness, because the problem demands an answer." But, Zossima goes on to say, the problem can only be solved by belief in the immortality of the soul. Unbelief can never solve it.[60]

21. If There Is No God, Everything Is Permitted

Thus Dostoevsky's famous first principle is this: *Without immortality there will be no morality.* Or to put it another way: *If there is no God, then everything is permitted.* Anything goes. This principle is well illustrated in the following little scene. For what is true here of "TV programmers" can be just as true of anyone else:

INSIDE WOODY ALLEN

©King Features Syndicate, Inc. 1976.

If there is no God, there is no divine law to protect a person or a people from the whims of any other person or people. If there is no God, then all law is ultimately only an arbitrary manmade construct. If there is no God, then who is to say what is right and wrong? If there is no God, everyone must become his or her own judge of what is good and bad. Without God, all people are permitted—even forced—to become "a law unto themselves."

©1973 United Feature Syndicate, Inc.

"Rightly understood," wrote Bonhoeffer,

. . . the deification of man is the proclamation of nihilism. With the destruction of the biblical faith in God and of all divine commands and ordinances, man destroys himself. There remains an unrestrained vitalism which involves the dissolution of all values and achieves its goal only in final self-destruction, in the void.[61]

22. If There Is No God, Then What in Hell *Are* People?

If there is no God, then people are permitted to do anything. But what *are* people in this case? Kurt Vonnegut is a *naturalist*—he doesn't believe in God. I, on the other hand, am a *supernaturalist*—I believe in God. This difference in our views about God makes a lot of difference in what we think people are. Here is the way T. S. Eliot put it:

> Man is man because he can recognize supernatural realities, not because he can invent them. Either everything in man can be traced as a development from below, or something must come from above. There is no avoiding that dilemma: you must be either a naturalist or a supernaturalist. *If you remove from the word "human" all that the belief in the supernatural has given to man, you can view him finally as no more than an extremely clever, adaptable, and mischievous little animal.*[62]

Throughout his writings Vonnegut keeps asking, in one way or another, "What in hell are people *for?*"[63] He is seriously concerned with this question because logic tells him that "if we can't find reasons and methods for treasuring human beings because they are *human beings,* then we might as well, as has so often been suggested, rub them out."[64] And Vonnegut, I'm sure, doesn't want to see anyone rubbed out.

But before an answer can be given to What in hell are people *for?* we must first answer this more basic question: What in hell *are* people? Obviously, the way we answer this latter question will determine what we decide people are *for..*

Eliot (T. S., not Rosewater) says that, for the atheist, a person is "finally . . . no more than an extremely clever, adaptable, and mischievous little *animal."* And this is true for atheist Vonnegut. In

Breakfast of Champions he describes the ultimate, logical conclusion of "mere humanism," and also admits he was depressed by such a conclusion:

> I had come to the conclusion that there was nothing sacred about myself or about any human being, that we were all machines, doomed to collide and collide and collide. For want of anything better to do, we became fans of collisions. . . . I no more harbored sacredness than did a Pontiac, a mouse-trap, or a South Bend Lathe.[65]

That's depressing, all right. But in the same book Vonnegut says he is later "born again" when he overhears an interpretation of *The Temptation of Saint Anthony,* a painting consisting of a totally blank field of "Hawaiian Avocado" green transversed by a single vertical strip of day-glow orange. According to Vonnegut's drawing, the painting looked like this (Vonnegut's drawing's are so bad— they are obviously done with his toes—that I am made bold to try my own):

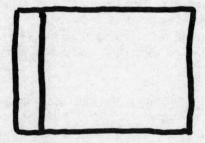

And here is the interpretation of this painting that "renewed" Vonnegut:

> It is a picture of the awareness of every animal. It is the immaterial core of every animal—the "I am" to which all messages are sent. It is all that is alive in any of us—in a mouse, in a deer, in a cocktail waitress. It is unwavering and pure, no matter what preposterous adventure may befall us. A sacred picture of Saint Anthony alone is one vertical, unwavering band

of light. If a cockroach were near him, or a cocktail waitress, the picture would show two such bands of light. Our awareness is all that is alive and maybe sacred in any of us. Everything else about us is dead machinery.[66]

What happy news! People have graduated from being mere machines and have now become mere animals. Like many atheistic humanists, Vonnegut is saying that since all we have is life we should learn to revere and cherish life. And he attempts to strengthen this reverence for life by calling all lives "unwavering bands of light."

This is the most optimistic answer the atheistic humanist can give to the question, "What *are* people?" But in this case we are still "finally no more than mischievous little animals." For in spite of the fact that we all may be "unwavering bands of light" while we live, we are still not "immortal." Vonnegut is very clear: He believes that "when you're dead you're dead." And this also means death to life's "awareness" or to the "unwavering band of light" in all us animals.

The problem with this point of view, of course, is that it places all us animals on the same level, the cockroach with the cocktail waitress. This may seem to be a benevolent attitude toward human beings as long as one is also kindly disposed toward cockroaches, but just as soon as one becomes for any reason *unkindly* disposed toward human beings, then logically the extermination of, say, six million human beings is no more unthinkable than the extermination of six million cockroaches. By this logic, the Nazi extermination of six million Jews can be seen as an "enlightened" form of pest control.

By Johnny Hart

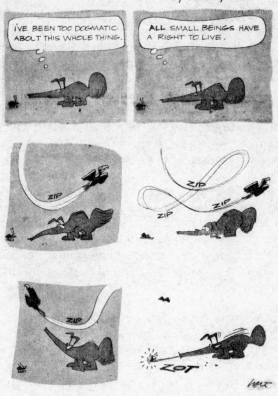

B.C. by permission of Johnny Hart and Field Enterprises, Inc.

To say that human beings are only animals, but that all animals are also "unwavering bands of light," may sound like a magnanimous thing to say about human beings when we first hear it. But how much weight is any such "light" idea going to carry among us animals as soon as it stands in the way of our *real* feelings?

Here is an interesting coincidence: In Vonnegut's *God Bless You, Mr. Rosewater,* Eliot Rosewater, a sort of "secular saint" who is Rockefeller rich but widely believed to be insane, sets up a Rosewater Foundation office in the wretched little town of Rosewater,

Indiana. Here he lives as simply as possible and devotes all his energies and resources to helping others in a totally unselfish way. Eliot's foundation has a motto, which he uses to answer the telephone and which is also painted on the windows of his shabby, second-floor office. Here is that motto: "ROSEWATER FOUNDATION—HOW CAN WE HELP YOU?" [67]

Meanwhile, at the very time Vonnegut was a prisoner of war incarcerated in a slaughterhouse in Dresden, Germany, Dietrich Bonhoeffer was a prisoner in Berlin. Bonhoeffer, a brilliant young German pastor and theologian, had been imprisoned when it was discovered that he, along with some German military officers, had attempted to assassinate Hitler. Shortly before the Nazis hanged him in 1945, Bonhoeffer composed an "Outline for a Book" that he wanted to write if he ever had the chance. In this book he was anxious to say some things "simply and clearly," and hoped the book would "be of some help for the church's future." Bonhoeffer had even selected a motto from the Gospels for this book he was never to write. Here is that motto: "Jesus said to him: 'What is it that you want me to do?' " [68]

I point this out to show how the Rosewater Foundation and Jesus can be seen as having the same basic "motto.": "How can we help you?" or "What is it that you want me to do?" In other words, the humanist and the Christian faith have identical goals in that both want lasting social change for the better. "Jesus wanted what you want," as Karl Barth once said to a group of European humanists. [69] The argument is over *the way* to achieve these goals. In *God Bless You, Mr. Rosewater,* Vonnegut formulated the problem this way:

> "The problem is this: How to love people who have no use?
> "In time, almost all men and women will become worthless as producers of goods, food, services, and more machines, as sources of practical ideas in the areas of economics, engineering, and probably medicine, too. So—if we can't find reasons and methods for treasuring human beings because they are *human beings,* then we might as well, as has so often been suggested, rub them out." [70]

Kurt. Dear Kurt. Please read this statement below. Your brother Dietrich has left an urgent message for you and others who hold similar views:

Precisely the socially valuable man makes no discrimination in assessing the rights of life. It is precisely this man who will be ready to risk his life for a lesser man, the strong for the weak and the sound for the sick. It is precisely the strong man who will not inquire about the usefulness to himself of the weak man. If anyone does this it will be the weak man. But the weak man's need will lead the strong man towards new tasks; it will lead him to develop his own social value. The strong man will see in the weak man not a diminution of his strength but a stimulus to loftier achievements. The idea of destroying a life which has lost its social usefulness is one which springs from weakness, not from strength.

But, above all, this idea springs from the false assumption that life consists only in its own usefulness to society. It is not perceived that life, created and preserved by God, possesses an inherent right which is wholly independent of its social utility. The right to live is a matter of the essence and not of any values. In the sight of God there is no life that is not worth living; for life itself is valued by God. The fact that God is the Creator, Preserver and Redeemer of life makes even the most wretched life worth living before God. The beggar Lazarus, a leper, lay at the rich man's gate and the dogs licked his sores; he was devoid of any social usefulness and a victim of those who judge life according to its social usefulness; yet God held him to be worthy of eternal life. And where if not in God should there lie the criterion for the ultimate value of a life? In the subjective will to live? On this rating many a genius is excelled by half-wits. In the judgement of society? If so it would soon be found that opinion as to which lives were socially valuable or valueless would be determined by the requirements of the moment and therefore by arbitrary decisions; one group of human beings after another would in this way be condemned to extermination. The distinction between life that is worth living and life that is not worth living must sooner or later destroy life itself.[71]

"And where if not in God should there lie the criterion for the ultimate value of a life?" As we saw above, Lucy was quite happy to nominate herself as the ultimate standard of "who is good and who is bad." If there is no God, then we ourselves must become this kind of arbitrary judge of one another. What other ultimate standard of judgment could there be? If there is no God, then we ourselves must also become the judges of "the ultimate value of a life." This is why Jesus could tell us to "judge not, that you be not judged" (Matt. 7:1, RSV). He knew that to judge in these matters was simply an attempt to be gods ourselves and that this attempt would result in disastrous here-and-now consequences, or judgment, upon ourselves.

If there is no God, everything is permitted. There is finally no ultimate law to restrain us. Nor are we restrained by what people are. Because for if there is no God, people are finally only animals, and they are *for* anything we may decide they are for.

23. If There Is No God, the Worst Is Permitted—and Encouraged!

Dostoevsky shows us over and over again that when we no longer believe in God we can believe only in ourselves. And when we have only ourselves to believe in, self-interest will corrupt the best intentions and encourage the worst.

This happens in several ways. As children of this world, we are by nature selfish just as children and just as animals are. We are not immediately concerned about the end of our lives but are only interested in self-gratification now. There is nothing particularly remarkable about this. It is simply nature's way of helping children and animals survive. It does, however, cause a lot of trouble for the other beings from whom this gratification must come. Other living beings must become food for animals, and a society must respond to the needs and demands of its children. But any society is in deep trouble if its children never "grow up." And if there is no God, people will tend to continue to live as animals or children. They will tend to live only for their own immediate *material* gratification. For if there is no God, people *are* finally animals. If there is no God, what finally is there to "grow up" to? If there is no God, it is the most natural thing in the world to live—to use Vonnegut's words again—like this: "The hell with you, Jack, I've got mine!"

HAGAR THE HORRIBLE

When we forget God, it is finally only the "law of the jungle" that is in effect—*or worse!*

Why worse? Because people have a problem that other animals don't have: People know they must die. The other animals don't know this. And this is usually what makes people so much meaner than other animals. People's natural selfishness is intensified by their knowledge that if they are ever going to get theirs they've got to get it *now* before it's too late! Sally Brown decided to be a "humanist" before one Christmas not so long ago.[72] She was going to be unselfish and not ask for any presents. But her experiment in mere humanism ended like this:

©1973 United Feature Syndicate, Inc.

As the guru says to Ziggy: "Grab all the kicks you can, Baby . . . You only make this scene once!!"

"You only go around once in life. So grab for all the gusto you can!" says the well-known beer ad. So perhaps Lucy was right after all when she stomped on that bug who "wasn't really living!" For if this life is finally all we really have, then this is the only thing "really living" can really mean:

"Sure enough, when winter came, the carefree, hedonistic grasshopper died. But the ant died, too, without ever really having lived at all."

Drawing by Ed Fisher; ©1971. The New Yorker Magazine, Inc.

Or as father figure Vonnegut expresses the two "morals" of *Mother Night* to his young readers, morals that are arranged in logical sequences:

When you're dead you're dead.
And . . . : Make love when you can. It's good for you.[73]

People usually use certain unobtrusive words that consciously or unconsciously reveal their deepest feelings. Such a word runs throughout Vonnegut's writings, a word which at the same time betrays the open secret of all atheism. That word is *bittersweet*. For instance, Dwayne Hoover in *Breakfast of Champions* "experienced a sort of bittersweet happiness as he told himself, 'Times change. Times change.' "[74] On many occasions Vonnegut can describe something as "heartbreakingly beautiful." In general, Vonnegut's view of life is well expressed in *The Sirens of Titan* when he says: "It was all so sad. But it was all so beautiful, too."[75] In short, life for Vonnegut is at best bittersweet.

But this is not surprising. For the atheist, the very sweetest that life has to offer will always be accompanied by the bitter knowledge that this too will soon pass away. All things finally come to nothing.

"All is vanity," as my other dear, bittersweet friend, Ecclesiastes, put it.[76] When death is the only certainty, as Vonnegut has said, then death is the barrier that "remains a barrier and does not become a place of exit. . . . Then is waiting not joyful but a bittersweet surrender to what is inevitable" (Karl Barth).[77]

This bitterness is the dark underside of even the sweetest portions of unbelievers' lives. For the greater the sweetness, the greater the bitterness that inevitably comes with it. The sweeter it comes, the bitterer it goes. Hell comes when our false gods go. But even before they are completely gone, false gods are *always* in the process of going. So it goes.

This is what makes even the best life hell for the unbeliever—the very same kind of hell Jesus was talking about. But the problem we are concerned with here is this: When people live in this hell, they tend to make life hell for everyone around them. *Meaninglessness makes people mean:*

"As the days dwindle down to a precious few,
I say to hell with everybody!"

Drawing by J. Mirachi; ©1975. The New Yorker Magazine, Inc.

In *Slaughterhouse-Five* when an American POW is suddenly beaten up by a German guard, he asks the guard, "Why me?" And the guard replies, "Vy, you? Vy anybody?"[78] Later on, when Billy

Pilgrim is captured by the Tralfamadorians and put aboard their flying saucer, Billy asks the same question: "Why me?" And they tell him:

> "That is a very Earthling question to ask, Mr. Pilgrim. Why *you?* Why *us* for that matter? Why *anything?* . . . There is no *why.*" [79]

As an atheist, this is what Vonnegut *must* believe—that there is no final meaning, that "thereis no *why.*" At the moment I am not disputing whether or not there is a *why.* I am just asking Vonnegut to see that the consequences of such a position are inevitably going to run about like this:

"Why? Why anything?"

Drawing by Ed Fisher; ©1970. The New Yorker Magazine, Inc.

This is the problem that preoccupies Vonnegut, and he knows it. It is the problem Dostoevsky shoves in his face: Without immortality there will be no morality. Without something ultimate to hope for, people's lives will necessarily be characterized by the two inevitable characteristics of hopelessness: People will *despair* and *despise.*

But Vonnegut doesn't want to see this happen. He is an extremely moral person. He wants to see people treat one another with the greatest possible respect and kindness. When Eliot Rose-water goes over to Mary Moody's shack to baptize her newborn twins, he finally tells them:

> "There's only one rule that I know of, babies—: " 'God damn it, you've got to be kind.' " [80]

Vonnegut has even painted this rule on a sign and placed it on a wall of his home. He wants the motto of all people to be closer to the motto of the Rosewater Foundation: "How can we help you?" But at the same time he knows that because life is made up of crises, changes, and shortages, including the crucial shortage in a life without God—namely, its "dwindling days"—then our mottoes will always tend to dwindle down to something like this:

Funky Winkerbean

FUNKY WINKERBEAN by Tom Batiuk. ©Field Enterprises, Inc., 1975. Courtesy of Field Newspaper Syndicate.

24. *All* False Gods Make People Mean

While it is true that meaninglessness—the result of atheism—makes people mean, *any* idolatry—even one that doesn't seem plagued by the despair of meaninglessness—will also make people mean. This is because, as Jesus put it, "Man cannot live on bread alone; he lives on every word that God utters" (Matt. 4:4, NEB). This is just the way we are made, the way we were created. And therefore any time we try to live on the foundation of any of this world's breads (like plain old bread or the bread of money, for instance), we are going to be left unsatisfied, and unhappy, and hungry. And unhappiness and hunger makes us irritable—and *mean*:

BEETLE BAILEY

©King Features Syndicate, Inc. 1975.

25. Even Humanism Makes People Inhumane

Strangely enough, idolatry of humanity itself, which is humanism's idolatry, often results in making humanists themselves the bitterest despisers of humanity. Vonnegut can scarcely keep his bitterness toward humanity in check. And Mark Twain, especially in his later years, gave full hateful vent to what he called "the damned human race." How does this happen?

The reason is simple: Humanists, not believing in God but preferring to believe in humanity as their god, have placed all their bets on this one race—the human race. And when humanists are disappointed in this race—as inevitably they must be—their high hopes are quickly reduced to the deepest disgust. Humanists tend to view humanity with a naïve sweetness that can easily become the most cynical bitterness when this sweetness is soured by *real* people.

Among the wide variety of people whose jobs involve alleviating the misery of others—physicians, psychiatrists, social workers, prison personnel, mental-health nurses, child-care workers, poverty lawyers, policemen, and so on—becoming *burnt-out* is a common malady. When they begin their work, people in these jobs are usually fired up with an idealistic and abstract, or humanistic, view of *people in general*. But this view is soon rudely disproved when they being to deal with real *people in particular*. They then begin to hate the very people they set out to help. Dostoevsky was pointing to this problem when he observed that human suffering "may convert in one's heart love for mankind into a hatred of it." And Bonhoeffer could see clearly that the humanistic philanthropist (or "lover of man") is close to being a despiser of man. He knew that "contempt for man and idolization of man are close neighbors":

> There is . . . an honestly intended philanthropism which amounts to the same thing as contempt for mankind. It consists in judging the man according to his latent values, according to his underlying soundness, reasonableness and goodness. This kind of philanthropism will generally arise in peaceful times. But even in great crises when these values shine out on particular occasions they may form the basis for a hard-won and well-meant love for humanity. With forced indulgence evil is interpreted as good. Baseness is overlooked and the reprehensible is excused. For one reason or another one is afraid to give a clear "no" for an answer, and one ends by acquiescing in everything. One's love is directed to a picture of man of one's own making, a picture which scarcely preserves any resemblance with the reality. And consequently one finishes once again by despising the real man whom God has loved and whose nature He has taken upon Himself.
>
> It is only through God's being made man that it is possible to know the real man and not to despise him. The real man can live before God, and we can allow the real man to live before God side by side with ourselves without either despising or deifying him. That is not to say that this is really a value on its own account. It is simply and solely because God has loved the real man and has taken him to Himself. The ground for God's love towards man does not lie in man but solely in God Himself. And again, the reason why we can live as real men and can love the real man at our side is to be found solely in the incarnation of God, in the unfathomable love of God for man.[81]

Human love can exist apart from Christ. But any love not based on God's love revealed in Christ, has no depth or staying power. It is like a house built on sand. And when that house proves shaky, disappointment will quickly convert all ill-founded love into the bitterest resentment. In other words, no one can end up with more hatred for people than those whose love is based on an ill-founded optimism about what people *are*. No one can be a greater hater than the disillusioned lover.

THE NOW SOCIETY

© Chronicle Publishing Co 1975   *10-23*

"I didn't turn out to be perfect and you didn't turn out to be a big deal."

26. "Unconscious Hell" Also Encourages the Worst

"There is no humanism without the Gospel," said Karl Barth.[82] Only in Jesus Christ do we learn who humans—all humans—really are. And it is only in Christ that we find a firm foundation for loving all humans as they really are. We are disobedient children of God whom God nevertheless loves—and will always love—with an unqualified, "unfathomable love." And we are given this knowledge in a single unifying, down-to-earth way: in belief in Jesus Christ and therefore in obedience to his command that we love others just as he has loved us. And Christ has loved us by revealing and "proving" this gospel to us.

A humanism based on anything else will sooner or later fail and will turn into the bitterest nihilism, or godless inhumanism. But even before this failure takes place so we can clearly see it, even before the nihilistic implications of our godlessness become excruciatingly apparent, they make trouble for us in the form of unconscious anguish or an unconscious hell. And this anguish invariably causes anguish for others. For even the unconscious assumption that we are only animals, and that time is quickly running out for us, takes a heavy toll on the entire race. A race of atheists will always be in a desperate race against time. And this of course creates the well-known "rat race," whose participants are actually members of this race:

B.C. by permission of Johnny Hart and Field Enterprises, Inc.

Remember the quote we discussed from *The Brothers Karamazov*, Kurt? The quote where Mitya tells Alexei: "Rakitin says that one can love humanity without God. Well, only a sniveling idiot can maintain that." [83]

Well, here is that quote in its immediate context and in a slightly different translation. I use it now because this speech of Mitya's starts out by showing now the "unconscious hell" of unbelief can backfire to cause hell for others as well. Mitya then proceeds to Dostoevsky's main theme: If there is no God, then everything—the worst—is allowed in theory and encouraged in fact:

"You see, I never had any doubts before, but they were all hidden inside me. And perhaps it was because all those ideas were raging within me without my even being aware of their existence that I drank, behaved wildly, and beat people up; without knowing it, I was trying to drown out and silence those doubts. . . . And what if there is no God? What if Rakitin is really right and God is just a fiction created by men? Then, if there is no God, man becomes master of the earth and of the universe. That's great. But then, how can a man be virtuous without God? That's the snag, and I always come back to it. For whom will man love then? Whom will he be grateful to? Whom will he praise in his hymns? Rakitin just laughs and says that one can love mankind without God. But I feel you have to be a piece of slime to say that. I can't see it at all. Solving the problem of existence is easy for Rakitin: 'If you wanted to do something useful today, you could, for instance fight for people's civil rights or even maintain the price of beef at a reasonable level; that would be a simpler and more direct way of manifesting your love for mankind than playing with all kinds of philosophical theories." So I said to him: 'But if there's no God, you'd jerk up the price of beef yourself if you knew how to, and if you had a chance, if you could, you'd fleece people to make a ruble of profit on each kopek.' That made him angry. But what's virtue then? You tell me, Alexei. We, for instance, may think that virtue is one thing while the Chinese may believe it's something quite different. Isn't virtue something relative then? . . . . You know, I'm surprised that some people can go through life without even wondering about these things. Ah, vanity! Well, Ivan has no God. . . .

"I said to him: 'Therefore everything is allowed, if that is so,' He frowned and said: 'Fyodor Karamazov, our dear papa, was a pig, but he reasoned correctly.' That was quite an answer, wasn't it?" [84]

So once again Ivan has admitted that without God even "correct reasoning" leads to the behavior of pigs. Or, as you once put it, Kurt, "Murder can easily become the most reasonable thing in the world." [85]

Here it is again, Kurt. Here it is in a nutshell. It's really as simple as Dostoevsky says it is: "It is so simple that one might hesitate to say it for fear that people might laugh, although it is the absolute truth! He who does not believe in God will not believe in God's people either." [86] And the reason behind his truth is simple also: "Immortality is in God," As Dostoevsky says. [87] And therefore if there is no God, and the end of all people is merely "dusty death," then this end, which finally makes our brief lives meaningless, will encourage and justify any meanness.

©1973 Daily Mirror Newspapers Ltd. ANDY CAPP Dist. Field Newspaper Syndicate.

27. Vonnegut & Twain & Many Others—Trying to Go Beyond the Hell of Nihilism

But Vonnegut & Twain are nobody's fools. They know that life is meaningless if there is no God, and that nothing demeans the human spirit so much as meaninglessness. Nevertheless, they both find it impossible to believe in God. But when I consider that for both of these men *God* always means the "Monster God" of eternal damnation, then I can't say I blame them. If that's who I really thought God was, I'm sure I'd still be an atheist too— meaninglessness or no meaninglessness.

Of course, this doesn't mean that I think atheists, or "outsiders," like Vonnegut, for example, will stop being atheists the moment they hear that the "God" of eternal damnation is a monstrous lie, an that the only God there really is is the God whose infinite power and love will finally be victorious over *all* things. However, I do agree with what Karl Barth said on this score in his book *The Humanity of God:*

> Thinking in terms of the humanity of God, we cannot at all reckon in a serious way with *real* "outsiders," with a "world come of age," but only with a world which *regards* itself as of age (and proves daily that it is precisely not that). Thus the so-called "outsiders" are really only "insiders" who have not yet understood and apprehended themselves as such. On the other hand, even the most persuaded Christian, in the final analysis, must and will recognize himself ever and again as an "outsider." So . . . what we have to say to them—and first to ourselves—is a strange piece of news in any case. Let us see to it that it really is the *great* piece of news—the message of the eternal love of God directed to us men as we at all times were, are, and shall be. Then we shall certainly be very well understood by them, whatever they may or may not do with it. He whose heart is really with God and therefore really with men may have faith that the Word of God, to which he seeks to bear witness, will not return to Him void.[88]

But in the mean time Vonnegut & Twain *don't* believe in God, and they *do* know what this means: that life is meaningless. And in this way, they are much better thinkers than most atheistic humanists.

Most atheistic humanists have all sorts of "virtues" hidden up their sleeves, which they have unconsciously imported from the Christian faith. They blissfully believe that these virtues are unquestionable "truths" that can stand on their own and need no support from God. They have not yet seen the logical necessity of Dostoevsky's conclusion: If there is no God, then anything is permitted, anything goes; there are no "truths," no "eternal verities;" all virtues are merely whatever people happen to think is good at the moment; tomorrow people may define something else as "good."

This is why most atheistic humanists find it easy to be "good"—at least for a while. They consciously reject the vine of religious faith, while unconsciously holding on to the branches of that same faith's moral implications. They have not yet realized that without the vine the branches have nothing to support them and will eventually wither and die. Therefore most atheistic humanists have a clear sense of what the world needs more of, but in rejecting the God of love, they have only the vaguest notions of how the world is going to find more of what it needs.

"More love!"

Drawing by Weber; ©1971. The New Yorker Magazine, Inc.

Most humanism is Christianity with its original center, Christ, removed. This means that mere humanism is empty at its center and will soon collapse unless it once more finds its origin, Christ, the only center that can really fulfill humanism and give it life and power. Like a chicken with its head cut off, humanism without Christ can be very lively and active for a short while, but it is already in the rapid process of death and decay. Jesus told the Samaritan woman at the well: "Everyone who drinks this water will be thirsty again, but whoever drinks the water that I shall give him will never suffer thirst any more. The water that I shall give him will be an inner spring always welling up for eternal life" (John 4:13–14, NEB). This is why humanism without Christ is goodwill disconnected from its power source. Most humanism, to use Bonhoeffer's words, is "the unconscious residue of a former attachment" to Christ. A humanist without Christ, Kurt, is this kind of "volunteer fireman":

Copyright, 1974, Universal Press Syndicate.

In 1952 Queen Elizabeth II of Great Britain had this to say:

I am sure that what is best in our countrymen comes from the habits and the wisdom bred in them by centuries of Christianity. But it may be that we are, in a sense, living on the moral capital which past generations have built up. Traditions which have no living basis soon become meaningless, and our children will suffer if we have no more to offer them than the virtues which we ourselves owe to an age of greater faith.[89]

This kind of message has not been lost on Vonnegut & Twain. Both men obviously have "habits and wisdom bred in them by centuries of Christianity." They know they have virtues that they owe to ages of greater faith, and they would like to see these same virtues spread more widely throughout humanity. Like so many people nowadays, Vonnegut & Twain are sincere fans of "the Christian virtues" of love and goodwill. Twain, for instance, could say: "All that is great and good in our civilization came from the hand of Jesus."[90] And Vonnegut can tell us, "I admire Christianity more than anything—Christianity as symbolized by gentle people sharing a common bowl."[91]

Therefore, Vonnegut & Twain can both see that without the input of a love from outside ourselves, our own innate, natural supply of love tends to be as obviously meager as this man's:

"Parker, you have exhausted my reservoir of good will."

Drawing by Lorenz; ©1975. The New Yorker Magazine, Inc.

Still, Vonnegut & Twain and many like them today, find they cannot believe in God. But because they see that human goodwill is indeed quickly exhausted by disbelief in God, they desperately try to find synthetic, manmade encouragements for morality and goodwill. As a matter of fact, Vonnegut told me that this is the central intention behind his entire work as an author. He doesn't believe his job is to convince people that God doesn't exist. No doubt he is right in feeling that most people today, when judged by how they actually live and not by what they say, are already convinced that there is no God. Therefore his job, as he puts it, is "to help people live ethically when there is no God." [92]

Camus, along with Vonnegut & Twain, is trying to do the same thing. Together they feel that a "superstitious" return to religious faith—even if this were desirable—is now impossible for most people who live in societies "enlightened" by science and technology. They believe we must honestly face two "facts": (1) There is no God (here they are mistaken); (2) Nihilism is the necessary outcome of atheism (here their own experience proves they are right).

They therefore believe that we must now find the means to go "beyond nihilism," to use Camus's phrase. We must find a way to escape from the nihilistic results of our own atheism. And the first step in going beyond nihilism, they think, is to recognize clearly that nihilism exists and is rapidly spreading. Says Camus:

> We cannot remain ignorant of nihilism and still achieve the moral code we need. No . . . we must first posit negation and absurdity because they are what our generation had encountered and what we must take into account.[93]

This is why Vonnegut, and a multitude of modern writers and philosophers like him, are so anxious for us all to face squarely the problem of nihilism. They feel it is only in a full, courageous look at this Worst that we can possibly arrive at the Better. Nihilism is the *wrang-wrang* that teaches us that we must find something better, that we must go *beyond* nihilism.

28. Meow

In Vonegut's *Cat's Cradle,* John, the story's narrator, tells us that while he was on an out-of-town trip he let "a poor poet named Sherman Krebbs" live in his New York City apartment. When John returns, he finds his apartment "wrecked by a nihilistic debauch" and his cat hanged. In the meantime he has been puzzled by stumbling across a gravestone with his own family's very unusual name on it. And here is what John concludes:

> I might have been vaguely inclined to dismiss the stone angel as meaningless, and to go from there to the meaninglessness of all. But after I saw what Krebbs had done, in particular what he had done to my sweet cat, nihilism was not for me.
> Somebody or something did not wish me to be a nihilist. It was Krebb's mission, whether he knew it or not, to disenchant me with that philosophy. Well, done, Mr. Krebbs, well done.[94]

In spite of the nihilistic implications of his atheism, Vonnegut doesn't want to be a nihilist. Nor does he want to see civilization as a whole go down the tube of a "nihilistic debauch." Therefore his mission, like that of many of the most sensitive writers and thinkers nowadays, is to find ways to "disenchant us with that philosophy." He feels the Western world would be foolish to give up the "enlightenment" of its atheism, for this is an enlightenment the West won only through a long and hard struggle for emancipation from the churches and their threat of "hell." But in accepting its atheism, the Western world must now also recognize that atheism's unforeseen result is the hell of meaninglessness and nihilism. For only in facing up to this "new" here-and-now hell (again, the kind of hell Jesus was talking about!) can we somehow find the means to go beyond it. Atheism cannot overcome its consequence of nihilism by pretending this consequence doesn't exist. Therefore, if we wish to go beyond the fires of nihilism, we can only go *through* them.

This, for example, is one reason Vonnegut uses the following verse from the Bible's Book of Job as a motto for *Breakfast of Champions:* "When he hath tried me, I shall come forth as gold" (Job 23:10, KJV).

In this, Vonnegut is in perfect harmony with Camus, who can tell us at the conclusion of *the Rebel:*

> All of us, among the ruins, are preparing a renaissance beyond the limits of nihilism. But few of us know it.[95]

29. Vonnegut & Twain & Many Others—Trying to Fill Nihilism's Bottomless Hole with Acorns —or— The Myth of the Blue Jay

Vonnegut & Twain are a couple of American writers who "know it": They know the horrors of nihilism in their own experiences—as different as those experiences have been—and therefore they are consciously trying to prepare "a renaissance beyond the limits of nihilism."

Theirs is a genuinely heroic effort—sometimes sad, sometimes funny—but always sincere and heroic. *Tragically heroic.* Tragic because without God, their efforts are always ultimately doomed to failure. Their efforts to overcome the meaninglessness of a godless life can finally only be the heartbreaking, bittersweet efforts of futility. And Vonnegut & Twain know this also. They know that outside the brackets that enclose all of humankind's heartbreakingly "sweet" efforts the bitter fact of death stands like a minus sign that finally nullifies all efforts. Nevertheless, Vonnegut & Twain persevere. They are like the atheist Dostoevsky described above: Against the futility of life they are set "in revolt precisely because of [their] love of mankind."

Camus used the ancient Myth of Sisyphus to represent humanity's rebellion against meaninglessness. It is Sisyphus' never-ending task to roll a huge stone to the top of a mountain, the stone always escaping him near the top and rolling down again. But Camus believed Sisyphus (humankind) should always defiantly wish to continue this task in spite of its ultimate futility.[96]

Vonnegut & Twain could never be quite so melodramatic. Because they see humor as one important means for combatting the ultimate meaninglessness of life, they hardly resemble Camus's grim Sisyphus at all. Instead they act more like Mark Twain's famous bluejay, who comes across "a perfectly elegant hole" and decides to fill it with acorns. The jay is soon "of the opinion it's a totally new kind of a hole . . . a long hole, and a deep hole, and a mighty singular hole altogether—but I've started in to fill you and I'm d____d if I *don't* fill you, if it takes a hundred years!" After dropping enough acorns in the hole "to keep the family thirty years," the jay finally discovers the "whole absurdity" of his situation: He's been trying to fill up an empty house with acorns![97]

So the jay never even comes close to filling that "mighty singular hole." But in the meantime he has provided a good laugh for the entire bird population.

And this is very much like the way in which Vonnegut & Twain work. They both know they can never fill up the "mighty singular hole" of the godless life's ultimate meaninglessness. But still they do what they can, for themselves and others, to keep the despair of meaninglessness at bay. They drop whatever acorns they can find into this "totally new kind of hole"—the long and deep hole of life when there is no God and immortality to fill life with meaning.

Generally speaking, Vonnegut & Twain drop the same six acorns into the hole of nihilism. And in so doing they just about exhaust all the acorns that any atheist has been able to come up with for attempting to fill the nihilistic void.

The first three acorns belong to the realm of the "natural"—the "So-it-goes" realm. The last three belong to the sphere of human creativity—the "Cat's Cradle" category. Here is their first acorn:

30. The Gospel of Determinism

Vonnegut's & Twain's first three acorns are attempts to make the most of their view that this is finally only a natural universe in which we live. A central part of this view is their thoroughgoing *determinism*. Determinism simply says that all things are a part of a vast, interrelated network of totally natural cause-and-effect chain reactions. For the determinist nothing ever happens anywhere, including human choices and decisions, without completely natural causes that force things to happen in just the way they do.

This totally materialistic and "scientific" view is to be expected from two such offspring of the Enlightenment as Vonnegut & Twain. But the deterministic argument gets an extra boost in Twain's thinking by the emphasis on predestination in his Presbyterian upbringing. For as we have seen, determinism is the secularized form of the biblical doctrine of predestination. But Vonnegut & Twain are both enthusiastic preachers of the "gospel"—the good news—of determinism. Twain actually called it his "Gospel." [98] Why is determinism such good news for them? There are two reasons. *First—*

31. Determinism Gets Rid of Pitilessness in People

Vonnegut & Twain agree that much of man's inhumanity to man comes from the cruel attitude of self-righteousness. This is the attitude that says: I myself am free to choose to do the right thing. And since my own *self* has made the *right* choice, I am literally *self-right-eous*. Therefore, I am justified in looking down on my neighbors—or even treating them much worse!—if they freely choose to do the *wrong* thing.

But determinism nips self-righteousness in the bud. It says that people have no such freedom at all. Their so-called "free will" is an illusion since all their choices and decisions are determined by forces ultimately not their own. "Everybody has to do exactly what he does," says Vonnegut. People always "doodley do" what they "muddily must," he says.[99]

Twain made his strongest argument for determinism in his book *What Is Man?* And what is man? He is—

Man the machine—man, the impersonal engine. Whatsoever a man is, is due to his *make,* and to the *influences* brought to bear upon it by his heredities, his habitat, his associations. He is moved, directed, COMMANDED, by *exterior* influences—*solely.* He *originates* nothing, himself—not even an opinion, not even a thought.[100]

As Vonnegut points out in *Slaughterhouse-Five,* "Many Earthlings are offended by the idea of being machines."[101] But they might not be so offended by this view if they understood why Vonnegut & Twain emphasize it so strongly: They believe this view will teach people humility and to pity and understand one another, rather than teaching them self-righteous blame. Said Twain:

I wish I could learn to remember that it is unjust and dishonorable to put blame upon the human race for any of its acts. For it did not make itself, it did not make its nature, it is merely a machine, it is moved wholly by outside influences, it has no hand in creating the outside influences nor in choosing which of them it will welcome or reject . . . ; wherefore, whatever the machine does . . . is the personal act of its Maker, and He, solely, is responsible. I wish I could learn to pity the human race intead of censuring it . . . and I could, if the outside influences of old habit were not so strong upon my machine.[102]

For this same reason, Vonnegut expressly refuses to give us any "villains" in his books. How can there ever be any real villains when you see all your characters, as Vonnegut does, as "the listless playthings of enormous forces"?[103] When called upon to judge others, Vonnegut has the same attitude as Ziggy:

..i WISH THEY WOULDN'T
CALL ME FOR JURY DUTY

i ALWAYS THINK
"THERE BUT FOR THE GRACE
OF GOD GO i "...

..THEN i DECIDE
NOBODY'S GUILTY
OF ANYTHING !!

ZIGGY

When Billy Pilgrim is on his way to Tralfamadore on board a flying saucer, he says to one of the Tralfamadorians:

> "You sound to me as though you don't believe in free will," said Billy Pilgrim.
> "If I hadn't spent so much time studying Earthlings," said the Tralfamadorian, "I wouldn't have any idea what was meant by 'free will.' I've visited thirty-one inhabited planets in the universe, and I have studied reports on one hundred more. Only on Earth is there any talk of free will."[104]

If the Tralfamadorian had visited what Karl Barth calls "the strange new world in the Bible,"[105] he still wouldn't have any idea what is meant by *free will*. The Bible never mentions *free will*. Instead it is saturated with concepts totally opposed to free will—concepts such as God's *omnipotence,* his *grace,* his *predestination* and *foreknowledge* of all things. Furthermore, the Bible emphasizes people's lack of free will for the same reason that Vonnegut & Twain do. All three—the Bible, Vonnegut, & Twain—want to do away with all human self-righteousness. And from the biblical point of view self-righteousness, or free will, is also idolatry. It is finally trusting in one's self rather than in God. The following statement by St. Paul is typical of the entire Bible's attitude about human "free will":

> It was nothing you could or did achieve—it was God's gift of grace which saved you. No one can pride himself upon earning the love of God. The fact is that what we are we owe to the hand of God upon us. For we are his workmanship, created in Jesus Christ, to do those good deeds which God planned for us to do (Eph. 2:8—10, Phillips).

But if all this is true, then where on earth does the Earthling idea of free will come from? And among Earthlings, why does the "Christian West" turn out to be free will's biggest fan club? These questions lead us to the second reason why determinism is good news for Vonnegut & Twain—

32. Determinism Gets Rid of the Pitiless God

A God who creates error-prone children, and then also creates a literal hell in which to throw these error-prone children when they make their inevitable errors, is a pitiless God.

Obviously, the only way such a cruel God and his "hell" could ever be defended is by saying that people have the free will to send themselves to hell. If they are free and they end up in hell, then it is only because of their own free choice and God's "justice." But human free will can be supported neither by the Bible nor by modern science. Therefore, in order to get rid of this pitiful pitiless God, Vonnegut & Twain show us how free will is absolute nonsense in view of what nature and science tell us about human behavior. Without human free will, they reason, there certainly can be no "hell." And without hell, there certainly can be no oppressive God of hell—this being the only "Christian God" they are aware of.

But the Earthling illusion of free will is not so easily exorcised. In spite of what the Bible and modern science say, as long as the Christian West is even vaguely worried about a literal hell, it *must* hang on to the heresy of free will—the heresy of "Pelagianism."

This is the heresy that claims that people are ultimately their own saviors. When faced with the threat of a real hell, we naturally want the power to save ourselves left finally in our own hands. There we can be sure of it.

Thus "hell" forces us to be *self*-righteous. The heresy of a literal hell forces us into the heresy of *self*-salvation. And once the church has made this mistake, its ability to really understand people is completely lost. It will then only be able to look down its nose at the "sinner" with an uncompassionate arrogance.

©1967 Daily Mirror Newspapers Ltd. ANDY CAPP Dist. Field Newspaper Syndicate.

33. What Dresden Was

Dear Kurt:

I know you don't think about Dresden much, unless somebody makes you think about it. I don't blame you. I never thought about it either until you made me think about it, and for that I thank you.

You have asked: "What is there to think about it, except that man, for one reason or another, can be a very ferocious animal indeed? So what else is new?" [106]

I agree. It's an old story, the ferocity of the human being. But the thing that set my head spinning was that business about "for one reason or another." I wanted to try to see some reasons for this ferocity.

For a long time now I've believed that men and women are sinners, and all that. But I wanted to see if I could get a clearer look at some of the connections between their sin and their ferocity. I also wanted to see if I could find "one reason or another" behind Dresden. And here's what I think I've found:

It seems to me that the Holocaust, the murder of six million Jews by the Nazis, was obviously history's most glaring result—so far—of Western nihilism. But what about Dresden? Dresden would seem to be more complicated.

Dresden, it seems to me, was a confrontation between *two* enormous forces: Western nihilism, represented by the Nazis, and the self-righteousness of the "Christian West," represented by all those Allied bombers that burned to death 135,000 German civilians and children living in that nonstrategic city.

And I think you do a sensational job in *Slaughterhouse-Five,* Kurt, of showing us that it was precisely these two terrible forces that clashed at Dresden. But when I try to locate the single error in the thinking of the "Christian West" that can produce both this horrible self-righteousness and the nightmare of atheism-nihilism, I always come back to the "Christian" teaching of eternal damnation.

In other words, I think it is the teaching of a real "hell" to come later that actually produces most of the manmade hells we live through now.

Isn't that a hell of a note?

Thine,

Bob

34. God Is Responsible for All, and Yet He Commands Us to Act Responsibly—How Can We Believe the Former and Do the Latter?

A peculiar thing about Vonnegut & Twain: They are both absolutely emphatic that people have no more free will than, as Vonnegut puts it, "a piggy-wig arriving at the Chicago stockyards" or "ladybugs trapped in a blob of polished amber." [107] And yet at the same time they both practically bust a gut telling the human race to get itself together and do something about its sad condition, just as though the human race had all the freedom of God Almighty himself. And, strangely enough, this has generally been the case historically with people who have believed in determinism or in God's predestination: They are the same people who have been the most anxious that things get done and have gotten the most things done. This is especially apparent in the New Testament. For instance, no mere mortal has ever changed history more than St. Paul. He did this by acting in history and by teaching others to act. But he also changed the course of history by teaching this:

> Those whom he [God] foreknew he also predestined to be conformed to the image of his Son, in order that he might be the first-born among many brethren. And those whom he predestined he also called; and those whom he called he also justified (Rom. 8:29–30, RSV).

What is it, then, that prevents determinists, who believe that all things are exactly what they have to be, from simply resigning themselves to things as they are? Similarly, Christians will always believe that God is completely in control of all things. So what prevents Christians from making this kind of blunder?—

"If God hadn't wanted there to be poor people, He would have made us rich people more generous."

Drawing by Dana Fradon; ©1973. The New Yorker Magazine, Inc.

Why is it that the people who believe in the necessity of all things to be what they are, are usually the very people who find it most necessary to try to improve things from what they are?

The answer to this question lies in the two different ways we can understand *necessity:* objectively and emotionally. From a strictly objective or analytical standpoint, the determinist and the Christian can *observe* how all things come about by necessity, how "all things work together" (Rom. 8:28, KJV).

Also from an objectively logical standpint, Christians can see that by trusting first their own freedom to do the right thing, necessarily they are not trusting first in God. If we believe in free will, and hence basically in our *own* righteousness, logically we cannot "seek first his [God's] kingdom and *his* righteousness" (Matt. 6:33, RSV).

But this coolly objective awareness of the lack of free will doesn't keep determinists and Christians from acting, for their own *emotions* are also totally involved in this cause-and-effect scheme. For instance, determinists, like anyone else, are saddened by certain types of human behavior. Vonnegut was reduced to tears by what he saw in Biafra. Therefore, he set out to do something about that situation. But this doesn't mean his actions took place outside the realm of necessity. It simply means he can't stand being reduced to tears, or seeing anyone else so reduced. And, being a determinist, he has a healthy respect for the way particular actions will bring about particular results.

Likewise Christians, from their own emotional or personal or "existential" experiences, come to a very clear awareness that whenever they disobey God they always catch hell from God—the *real* hell, the only real hell there is, a misery that occurs right here and now. Christians learn from hard experience that they can no more be free from this "emotional" law of God than they can be free from the "objective" law of gravity. So Christians also act out of necessity—emotional necessity. "Knowing the fear of the Lord," said St. Paul, "we persuade men" (2 Cor. 5:11, RSV).

When people really are Christians, and therefore don't have an idolatrous and boastful pride in their *own* freedom to act, they will always be the first to admit that they are what they are out of God's acting on them. Again, St. Paul:

Even if I preach the Gospel, I can claim no credit for it; I cannot help myself; it would be misery to me not to preach. If I did it of my own choice, I should be earning my pay; but since I do it apart from my own choice, I am simply discharging a trust (1 Cor. 9:16, 17, NEB).

And so the world is wrong whenever it admires Christians for what seem to be totally free and unselfish acts. Christians are simply people who have learned "the fear of the Lord"—a fear that comes in trying to go it alone without the Lord. Therefore, Christians, though the *object* of their faith is God, act *from* self-interested necessity like all people do.[108]

©1971 United Feature Syndicate, Inc.

Rather than being paralyzed by their awareness that all things occur by necessity, Christians are strengthened in their actions by this knowledge. The very recognition that they do *not* have this kind of self-determination, forces Christians to take God and *his* determination more seriously. Christians then act, not with an arrogant yet basically insecure *self*-confidence, but with a genuine humility, a far greater *understanding* of themselves and others, and their obedience totally based on their confidence in God. Both determinists and Christians act out of a grateful and respectful awareness of this dependable and orderly law of nature or God's creation: that we can always depend on particular results—inward and outward—to come from particular ways of acting or failing to act. Christians are simply people who have learned through their own experience this dependable "inward" law of God: The results of a misplaced confidence—including self-confidence—is hell. Or again, as St. Paul put it: "The wages of sin is death" (Rom. 6:23, RSV).

Nevertheless, in spite of the similarities, there is still an infinite difference between the biblical belief in predestination and the determinism preached by Vonnegut & Twain. If Twain thought of the acorn of determinism as "gospel," how much more would the message of the New Testament have been "good news" to him if he had understood it and believed it. For behind determinism there are only the indifferent, impersonal forces of nature, which will finally reduce all of us to zero. But behind the Bible's predestination there is the all-powerful and all-loving God, who will finally save all men. For the determinist, everything that happens fits into a causal pattern. But this pattern is nevertheless ultimately purposeless and meaningless and without any "plan" behind it. Christians, on the other hand, "know that to those who love God, who are called according to his plan, everything that happens fits into a pattern for good" (Rom. 8:28, Phillips).

35. Better Things for Better Living Through Chemistry

Although his determinism would have made him open to the suggestion, Mark Twain never got around to speculating very seriously about the possibility of making people happier by tinkering with their biological insides. But Vonnegut does. Vonnegut is apparently deeply serious about using "chemistry" to make us happier and kinder to one another. For instance, in *Mother Night* there is the following conversation between Howard Campbell, the book's central character, and a New York City patrolman:

"I guess it's partly chemistry," he said.
"What is?" I said.
"Getting down in the dumps," he said. "Isn't that what they're finding out—that a lot of that's chemicals?"

"I don't know," I said. . . .

"Maybe it's different chemicals that different countries eat that makes people act in different ways at different times," he said.

"I'd never thought of that before," I said.

"Why else would people change so much?" he said. "My brother was over in Japan, and he said the Japanese were the nicest people he ever met, and it was the Japanese who'd killed our father! Think about that for a minute!"

"All right," I said. . . .

"Maybe, when they find out more about chemicals," he said, "there won't have to be policemen or wars or crazy houses or divorces or drunks or juvenile delinquents or women gone bad or anything any more. . . .

"Look how some women go half off their nut once a month," he said. "Certain chemicals get loose, and the women can't help but act that way. Sometimes a certain chemical will get loose after a woman's had a baby, and she'll kill her baby. That happened four doors down from here just last week."

"How awful," I said. "I hadn't heard—"

"Most unnatural thing a woman can do is kill her own baby, but she did it," he said. "Certain chemicals in the blood made her do it, even though she knew better, didn't want to do it at all."

"Um," I said.

"You wonder what's wrong with the world—" he said, "well, there's an important clue right there." [109]

Well, right there is one of Cornell-chemistry-major Vonnegut's most important theories for curing what's wrong with the world. It's a theory that constantly pops up in his writings and is sometimes even proposed as *the* answer for all that ails us. In 1971, addressing the National Institute of Arts and Letters, he said: "What other sweet mysteries of life are chemicals? All of them, I believe. Biochemistry is everything. . . . Happiness is chemical." [110]

In personality Vonnegut is just the opposite of Rakitin, Dostoevsky's portrait of the atheistic humanist as a "sniveling idiot." But it is amazing the way their *ideas* correspond point by point. For instance, here's the conversation where we learn about Rakitin's ideas on chemistry, ideas that are remarkably similar to Vonnegut's. Dmitri is saying to his brother Alyosha:

"Just imagine: there are those nerves in my head, I mean in the brain—damn them!—and those nerves have some kind of little tails which vibrate. . . . And whenever I look at something with my eyes, those little tails vibrate and the image appears. . . . That's how I perceive things and how I think. . . . So I think because of those little tails and not at all because I have a soul, or because I'm made in God's image, which is all nonsense. Rakitin explained all that to me yesterday and it really hit me hard. Science is wonderful, Alyosha—it will produce a new man. I understand all that very well. But I am unhappy about God—I miss Him!"

"That's something at least. I'm thankful for that," Alyosha said.

"You think it's good that I miss God? Why, if I feel like that, it's just chemistry. Yes, everything's chemistry! It's no use, my holy brother, you'll just have to move out of the way a bit, to make room for chemistry. Rakitin now—he doesn't like God, doesn't like him at all. To people like him, God is a sore spot. But they hide it, they lie, they pretend. . . . 'But tell me,' I asked him. 'What will happen to men? If there's no God and no life beyond the grave, doesn't that mean that men will be allowed to do whatever they want?' 'Didn't you know that already?' he said and laughed. . . . 'An intelligent man can do anything he likes as long as he's clever enough to get away with it.' "[111]

And so Dostoevsky has here again put his finger on the weakness of the Vonnegut-Rakitin argument. *Chemistry* is just another acorn. Like psychiatry, another method of rearranging people's insides, chemistry can help, but it can never provide ultimate meaning for people's lives. And as Dostoevsky made even clearer in *Notes from Underground*, the chemical theory of life will only make people's need for meaning more apparent. The more people's chemical (and psychological) problems are solved, the more they will become aware of the lack of meaning in their lives, and the more they will then violently rebel against being thought of as a complex of merely natural, or nonspiritual, responses:

"True. We do eat right; we do get plenty of exercise; we have our health,
which is the main thing. But I still say to hell with everything!"

Drawing by Weber; ©1974. The New Yorker Magazine, Inc.

The only way chemistry (and psychiatry) can solve people's need for meaning is to reduce them to something less than people—to beings who have no need for meaning. Only if we let chemistry reduce us to something approaching bugs will we not be bugged by the need for meaning. But I don't think this is an acorn Vonnegut is ready to drop.

"There was a time when everything bugged him. Now nothing bugs him."

Drawing by Mulligan; ©1976. The New Yorker Magazine, Inc.

36. Acorn Three—The Negligibility of Death and Suffering in an Indifferent Universe

Vonnegut & Twain both know that death, to use St. Paul's words, is "the last enemy" (1 Cor. 15:26, RSV). And because as atheists they also believe this enemy will finally defeat them and all other things, they both do their best to meet this defeat by trying to make death seem less tragic. Because it is death that finally makes life meaningless for them, they both try to play down death's triumph by making death seem to be either a friend in disguise or else a thing so natural and so commonplace as to be unimportant.

Twain, especially in his tragedy-filled last years, came to see death as a "most prized friend." Death is the "gift" that alone can put an end to the insane meaninglessness of life when there is no God:

> A myriad of men are born; they labor and sweat and struggle for bread; they squabble and scold and fight; they scramble for little mean advantages over each other. Age creeps upon them; infirmities follow; shames and humiliations bring down their prides and their vanities. Those they love are taken from them, and the joy of life is turned to aching grief. The burden of pain, care, misery, grows heavier year by year. At length ambition is dead; pride is dead; vanity is dead; longing for release is in their place. It comes at last—the only unpoisoned gift earth ever had for them—and they vanish from a world where they were of no consequence; where they achieved nothing; where they were a mistake and a failure and a fool-ishness; where they have left no sign that they have existed—a world which will lament them a day and forget them for-ever. Then another myriad takes their place, and copies all they did, and goes along the same profitless road, and van-ishes as they vanished—to make room for another and an-other and a million other myriads to follow the same arid path through the same desert and accomplish what the first myriad, and all the myriads that came after it, accomplished—nothing![112]

Vonnegut's defense against death is similar but not quite the same as Twain's. He wants to neutralize death's sting by "naturalizing" it. Death is simply a part of blind, impersonal nature. Therefore, we shouldn't "take it personally." It is simply the nature of all things to go into oblivion. Therefore, when anyone or anything so goes into oblivion, we shouldn't be upset. Instead, our attitude should be, "So it goes,' or, "It's all right." Here is Vonnegut's explanation for this way of dealing with death and suffering:

> I only now understand what I took from Céline and put into . . . *Slaughterhouse-5.* In that book, I felt the need to say this everytime a character died: "So it goes." This exasperated many critics, and it seemed fancy and tiresome to me, too. But it somehow had to be said.
>
> It was a clumsy way of saying what Céline managed to imply so much more naturally in everything he wrote, in effect: "Death and suffering can't matter nearly as much as I think they do. Since they are so common, my taking them so seriously must mean that I am insane. I must try to be saner." [113]

Thus it is the "mind over matter" solution that Vonnegut recommends for the problems of suffering and death: If we don't mind, they won't matter. And we won't mind if we'll just consider how common and natural they both are. Obviously, our problem is the same as Ziggy's: We all have this foolish desire to survive, when in actual fact *nothing* survives:

Here, Kurt, is a little scene from *Hamlet* that I know you're familiar with. Hamlet's father has recently died, and Hamlet is still upset.
So his mother, the queen, is trying to cheer him up.

> Good Hamlet. . . .
> Thou know'st 'tis common—all that lives must die,
> Passing through nature to eternity.
> *Hamlet:* Aye, madam, it is common.
> *Queen:*   If it be,
> Why seems it so particular with thee?
> *Hamlet:* Seems, madam! Nay, it is. I know not "seems."
>
> (I, ii, 73—76)

Two things need to be said about this "adjustment" to death that
Queen Gertrude is recommending. First, the fact that death is so
natural and common just doesn't get the job done for Hamlet—or
for any sensitive person. In effect, what Gertrude is saying to her
son is this: "So it goes, Hamlet! It's all right! Nobody survives!" And
Hamlet replies: "Gosh, mom, that's true, but that doesn't help the
way I *feel*. And the way I feel doesn't just 'seem.' It *is*."

Gertrude uses the approach of cold, unfeeling reason. She's all
head. Hamlet's approach is "existential"—the attitude of a thinking
person who is also burdened with a heart.

Second, Hamlet doesn't yet know it, but the queen is deeply
implicated in the murder of Hamlet's father. What does this mean?
Simply this: Whenever we try to overcome the tragedy of death by
making death "common" and "negligible," logically we are at the
same time making *life* common and negligible. And this attitude
toward life can easily lead to such actions as murder.

So here again is the dilemma of atheistic humanists. They are in
the situation of Dostoevsky's Shigalov in *The Possessed:* "My conclusion is a direct contradiction of the original idea with which I
start." [114] Likewise Vonnegut & Twain end with the very thing they
seek to avoid. Twain begins with a great humanitarian love for
humankind and ends by saying that humankind is "of no consequence . . . a mistake and a failure and a foolishness." Vonnegut
begins by hoping to alleviate death and suffering, and ends by saying that "death and suffering can't matter nearly as much as I think
they do" and that he must not "take them so seriously." These
ideas may not seem so dangerous coming from lovable clowns like

Vonnegut & Twain. But just let an Adolf Hitler get hold of them and then everybody had better duck for cover. The step from atheism to nihilism is easy and logical, just as the step from Nietzsche to Hitler was easy and logical. No one would think of comparing Vonnegut or Twain with Hitler. But both of them can be—and have been—compared with Nietzsche. So it is important to see where our thinking is leading us. And in the case of the acorn that Vonnegut calls "the negligibility of death," atheism leads to the meaninglessness of life because of the finality of death; this leads to an attempt to "play down" death; playing down death also means playing down life; and playing down life is nihilism. Thus the philosophy of "So it goes" quickly leads to the life of "Anything goes".

And here is the moral of this downward path of atheism into nihilism: whenever the world turns its back on Christ—and therefore has no ultimate hope or satisfying answer to the question of "Why?"—it will soon find itself living by the crazy and desperate philosophy of "Why not?"

Funky Winkerbean

FUNKY WINKERBEAN by Tom Batiuk. ©Field Enterprises, Inc., 1975. Courtesy of Field Newspaper Syndicate.

Our friend Bonhoeffer, Kurt, had a lot of experience with people for whom death was the last thing. He fought Nazis. And here is an observation he once made in the thick of that battle:

> Where death is the last thing, earthly life is all or nothing. Boastful reliance on earthly eternities goes side by side with a frivolous playing with life. A convulsive acceptance and seizing hold of life stands cheek by jowl with indifference and contempt for life. (*Ethics*, page 78)

Hi ho.

37. The Cat's Cradle of Creative Acorns

Vonnegut & Twain both know that these three "natural" acorns are sadly insufficient for filling up the huge empty house of meaninglessness. This is proven by the way they continue flitting about looking for more acorns. For now they turn to acorns of a different type: acorns of human creativity.

Back at signpost #28 we saw how John in *Cat's Cradle* was saved from becoming a nihilist by Mr. Krebbs, the nihilist who converted John's apartment into a pigsty and hanged his cat. We also said that it likewise seems to be the mission nowadays of most of our best writers and artists to save all of us from the living hell of nihilism. One principle way they try to do this is by creating what Vonnegut calls "cat's cradles."

"A cat's cradle," Vonnegut reminds us, "is nothing but a bunch of X's between somebody's hands"—X's made from a loop of string between our fingers. Also, it is "one of the oldest games there is. . . . Even the Eskimos know it." [115] But for Vonnegut, a cat's cradle represents something infinitely more important: It is the only thing that can finally prevent people from falling into nihilism's abyss. It is the "catcher" Vonnegut wants to place among his pages of nihilistic wry. It represents creativity and imagination, for it takes creativity and imagination to see a cat and its cradle where actually there's *"No damn cat, and no damn cradle."* [116] A cat's cradle represents games, play, dreams, harmless lies or *foma*—those "harmless untruths . . . that make you brave and kind and happy." [117]

In *Cat's Cradle* Dr. Felix Hoenikker is "one of the chief creators" of the atomic bomb. "Nobody could predict what he was going to be interested in next. On the day of the bomb [when the atomic bomb was dropped on Hiroshima] it was string." [118] Why string? So he could make a cat's cradle for his little son, Newt. But before the bomb was dropped, Hoenikker never played with Newt and rarely even spoke to him. In other words, when we come face-to-face with the gruesome possibilities of nihilism, as represented here by the atomic bomb, the first thing Vonnegut believes we must reach for is the "cat's cradle"—the cradling protection we can find in human creativity and imagination.

Two Vonnegut poems put these views in a nutshell. The first is a "Calypso" from the new religion of Bokononism in *Cat's Cradle:*

> I wanted all things
> To seem to make some sense,
> So we could all be happy, yes,
> Instead of tense.
> And I made up lies
> So that they all fit nice,
> And I made this sad world
> A par-a-dise.[119]

The second poem is from his 1976 novel *Slapstick:*

> "And how did we then face the odds,
> "Of man's rude slapstick, yes, and God's?
> "Quite at home and unafraid,
> "Thank you,
> "In a game our dreams remade."[120]

Our best hope is for reality "to *seem* to make some sense," says Vonnegut, for we can't escape recognizing that it actually doesn't make sense. The "reality of life," with its many deep disappointments and its ultimate futility, is the reality that "Everyman" Charlie Brown faces every day. Therefore, he has to have new "old legends" or new illusions to keep from being crushed by disillusionment. He must *lie* about reality:

SOMEBODY HAS TO MAKE UP THOSE OLD LEGENDS, DON'T THEY?

©1970 United Feature Syndicate, Inc.

According to Vonnegut, we are all like Charlie Brown; we are all caught in "the cruel paradox of Bokononist thought, the heartbreaking necessity of lying about reality, and the heartbreaking impossibility of lying about it." [121] The insane and inescapable evil and suffering and meaninglessness of life ("man's rude slapstick, yes, and God's") are odds that we can face only by remaking this cruel comedy with our "dreams."

Especially at this point, Vonnegut shows himself to be a literary and philosophical continuation of Mark Twain. At the end of *The Mysterious Stranger,* one of the last things Twain wrote, only a few sentences save the entire work from being swallowed whole by nihilistic hopelessness. And what does Twain finally propose for our hope? The same thing proposed later by Vonnegut—dreams. Said Twain—

> "*Nothing* exists; all is a dream. God—man—the world— the sun, the moon, the wilderness of stars—a dream, all a dream; they have no existence. *Nothing exists save empty space—and you! . . .*"
>
> "I am perishing already—I am failing—I am passing away. In a little while you will be alone in shoreless space, to wander its limitless solitudes without friend or comrade forever—for you will remain a *thought,* the only existent thought, and by your nature inextinguishable, indestructible. But I, your poor servant, have revealed you to yourself and set you free. Dream other dreams, and better!" [122]

Or, as Vonnegut puts it, the role of the artist "is to make mankind aware of itself . . . and to dream its dreams." [123]

Vonnegut & Twain recommend to us three forms of "dreams" or "games" or "lies" or "cat's cradles": laughter, art, and religion. These are their three "acorns of creativity."

38. Laughter

In this famous passage from *The Mysterious Stranger,* Twain said to all of us:

> You have a mongrel perception of humor, nothing more; a multitude of you possess that. This multitude see the comic side of a thousand low-grade and trivial things—broad incongruities, mainly; grotesqueries, absurdities, evokers of the horselaugh. The ten thousand high-grade comicalities which exist in the world are sealed from their dull vision. Will a day come when the race will detect the funniness of these juvenilities and laugh at them—and by laughing at them destroy them? For your race, in its poverty, has unquestionably one really effective weapon—laughter. . . . Against the assault of laughter nothing can stand.[124]

This is why the works of Vonnegut & Twain are brim full of "the high-grade comicalities" of black humor. Their humor is *black* because it looks at life realistically. It clearly exposes the evil and suffering and meaninglessness in life. And yet this humor is not sick. It is healthy. It attempts to assault the blackness with laughter. It wants human laughter and courage to have the last laugh. But of course this is not really possible when death is the end of all things.

B.C.

B.C. by permission of Johnny Hart and Field Enterprises, Inc.

For Vonnegut, the slapdash stickiness of slapstick is one of the best means we have for holding a slapped sick world together. We must challenge life's rude slapstick with our own kinder version of the same thing. "Maturity," Bokonon tells us in *Cat's Cradle,* "is a bitter disappointment for which no remedy exists, unless laughter can be said to remedy anything." [125]

But as long as we're talking about human laughter alone, when there is no God, I'm afraid no remedy exists. Certainly a literal hell is not going to remedy anything—an eternity of torture to teach us a lesson we can no longer use: "Whoops! You missed your chance to trust in God! Too bad!" The only remedy comes in understanding "bitter disappointment" as one of the tortures of the *living* hell—the hell that teaches us to trust in God *now*. If we don't believe this, then it's true that a sense of humor can become crucially important to us. It can help us keep a touch of our sanity in an otherwise totally insane world. But if there is no God, neither sanity nor a sense of humor is anything we can *finally* keep.

HAGAR THE HORRIBLE

©King Features Syndicate, Inc. 1976.

39. Art—The Helpful Fiction

"We have Art in order that we may not perish from Truth," said Nietzsche.[126] And Twain & Vonnegut agree. For "the truth is death," as Vonnegut, Twain, Nietzsche, Céline, and multitudes of others all agree. Therefore, we must use art as one of the "creative acorns," one of the lies with which we try to fill up the void of meaninglessness that comes from this truth. The purpose of the arts, says Vonnegut, is to use frauds in order to make human beings seem more wonderful than they really are. Dancers show us human beings who move much more gracefully than human beings really move. Films and books and plays show us people talking much more entertainingly than people really talk, make paltry human enterprises seem important. Singers and musicians show us human beings making sounds far more lovely than human beings really make. Architects give us temples in which something marvelous is obviously going on. Actually, practically nothing is going on inside. And on and on.

The arts put man at the center of the universe, whether he belongs there or not. Military science, on the other hand, treats man as garbage—and his children, and his cities, too. Military science is probably right about the contemptibility of man in the vastness of the universe. Still—I deny that contemptibility, and I beg you to deny it, through the creation and appreciation of art.[127]

Vonnegut should know better than this. He should know that history has taught us there is no correlation between humanistic culture and humaneness. And in his more sober moments, he probably does know this. In *Mother Night* there is a grotesque incongruity that is based on historical fact: The loudspeakers all over the Nazi's extermination camp of Auschwitz broadcast two things all day long—the world's *best music,* and frequent interruptions by a pleasantly crooned command of "Leichenträger zu Wache"[128] ("Corpse-carriers to the guardhouse").

Many modern thinkers, like critic George Steiner, even see a negative relation between culture and the way people act:

Our present knowledge of a negative transfer from civilization to behavior, in the individual and the society, runs counter to the faith, to the operative assumptions, on which . . . the dissemination of the arts were grounded. What we now know makes a mock of the vision of history penetrated, made malleable by, intelligence and educated feeling . . . of a carryover from civilization to civility, from humanism to the humane . . .[129]

"In other words," says Steiner, "the libraries, museums, theatres, universities, research centers, in and through which the transmission of the humanities and of the sciences mainly takes place, can prosper next to the concentration camps."[130]

The reason the arts cannot humanize us is that they themselves cannot give ultimate meaning to our lives. They can communicate important ideas and strong feelings to us, but whenever we expect too much from them, they will fail us like any other false god. And this failure will again cause us to *despair* and *despise,* which is exactly what happened to Eliot Rosewater in *God Bless You, Mr. Rosewater:*

> —he despises art. Can you imagine? *Despises* it—and yet he does it in such a way that I can't help loving him for it. What he's saying I think, is that art has failed him, which I must admit, is a very fair thing for a man who has bayoneted a fourteen-year-old boy in the line of duty to say.[131]

Fortunately we don't usually need a horrible shock like Eliot Rosewater's to help us realize that the arts can't supply us with ultimate meaning. This realization can occur anytime:

THE NOW SOCIETY

"What do you suppose it means when really meaningful books and plays and paintings no longer mean anything to you."

What does it mean? Simply this: Only God can give our lives ultimate meaning.

40. Religion—The Comforting Lie

Vonnegut & Twain and many like them believe that the purpose of religion, in common with the arts, is to use manmade "frauds" to help people feel better about their lives. Religion gives people meaning and hope even though there really is no meaning and nothing to hope for. Religion—all religion—is merely "superstition." But at the same time it is, like art, "a useful, comforting lie." Therefore, Vonnegut can say:

> We would be a lot safer if the Government would take its money out of science and put it into astrology and the reading of palms. I used to think that science would save us, and science certainly tried. But we can't stand any more tremendous explosions, either for or against democracy. Only in superstition is there hope. If you want to become a friend of civilization, then become an enemy of truth and a fanatic for harmless balderdash.
>
> I know that millions of dollars have been spent to produce this splendid graduating class, and that the main hope of your teachers was, once they got through with you, that you would no longer be superstitious. I'm sorry—I have to undo that now. I beg you to believe in the most ridiculous superstition of all: that humanity is at the center of the universe, the fulfiller or the frustrator of the grandest dreams of God Almighty.
>
> If you can believe that, and make others believe it, then there might be hope for us. Human beings might stop treating each other like garbage, might begin to treasure and protect each other instead.[132]

Twain was less convinced of the social usefulness of "the lie of religion," but could nevertheless make statements like this: "I am not able to believe one's religion can affect his hereafter one way or the other, no matter what that religion may be. But it may easily be a great comfort to him in this life—hence it is a valuable possession to him."[133]

But of course there is an obvious problem in trying to promote religion as something helpful and comforting and at the same time openly declaring that it is only a lie. It's a funny thing, Kurt, but people can't be very seriously or deeply comforted by "truths" that they know are really lies. It's like trying to have your cake and eat it too. Nope. "Truth" can only comfort us deeply when we deeply believe it is true.

Vonnegut's mistake here is that he makes no distinction between art and religion. Art is admittedly a "lie" that can sometimes comfort us, but it never calls itself "truth." Religion, on the other hand, by definition speaks of "the truth," and its ability to comfort depends on its truth being seriously believed as truth.

Dostoevsky's Grand Inquisitor deliberately gives people a fraudulent, manmade religious lie in order to make them "happy." And the Inquisitor knows that if they are to remain "happy," he will have to keep this secret to himself—the secret that the object of their devotion is only a lie. He does not take away with one hand what he has given with the other, as Vonnegut would have us do. He does not give people "religious truth" and then tell them that this "truth" is after all only "harmless balderdash." Vonnegut's running-mate, Twain, could see easily enough that "the one sole condition that makes spiritual happiness and preserves it is the absence of doubt."[134]

"Literature always involves an *as-if*," says literary critic Cleanth Brooks. "But religion always involves," Brooks goes on to say,

> . . . some kind of commitment, something deeper than any *as-if*. It is notorious that when religions lose their hold on their adherents, they tend to turn into a kind of poetry, no longer exerting an absolute claim or demanding certain actions by way of response, but grading off into a series of possibilities for contemplation with which we refresh our imaginations or enlarge our spirits, or in which we simply indulge . . . .
>
> For Christians, the problem is to prevent our religion from turning into mere literature, a fairy tale with ethical implications.[135]

But Vonnegut is only trying to help us while at the same time remaining true to what he really believes. He really believes that "everything is a lie," [136] that there are no absolutes, no ultimate truths or "eternal verities." But at the same time, he can see that "man cannot live by lies alone." So he gives us some lies obviously masquerading as "truths." He suggests that we consciously kid ourselves. But of course kidding oneself is comforting only if one isn't conscious of doing it.

So falls another beautifully creative little acorn into the huge house of nihilistic meaninglessness.

So they go.

41. I Love Thee, Lord Jesus, Look Down from the Sky, And Stay by My Cradle Till Morning Is Nigh.

"There is nothing on earth," said Pascal, "that does not show either the wretchedness of man without God, or the strength of man with God." [137] And the atheism of Vonnegut & Twain, unintentionally dramatizing "the wretchedness of man without God," proves once again that Pascal was right. As T. S. Eliot has said, "The World is trying the experiment of attempting to form a civilized but non-Christian mentality. The experiment will fail." [138] Vonnegut & Twain give us a startling preview of this failure and hence warn us against it. They are sensitive canaries in the deep and vast mine of modern atheism, and their attractive singing serves to warn us of this "new kind of hole's" rapidly increasing poisonousness.

And here is the important lesson that Vonnegut & Twain have unintentionally taught us: There is no way atheism can remain atheism and avoid the void of meaninglessness and nihilism. Atheism's struggle against meaninglessness and nihilism is a losing battle that threatens to drag all civilization down with it.

Thus Vonnegut & Twain only unintentionally reinforce what Dostoevsky was intentionally teaching a hundred years ago:

> Even those who have renounced Christianity, even those who rebel against it—even they, in their essence, were created in the image of Christ and have remained in His image. Their combined wisdom and their desperate efforts to create a nobler man with greater dignity, the ideal set by Christ, have come to naught. From all their attempts, only freaks have resulted.[139]

All merely human efforts to satisfy the hungry abyss of meaninglessness and nihilism, are hopelessly insufficient little acorns. All merely human attempts to insure us against a world without God, are quickly swallowed by the world itself.

Not even the "cat's cradle" of human creativity can save us from falling into this void. Which brings us back to Bonhoeffer's statement about our situation today:

> For us the world has lost its gods; we no longer worship anything. We have experienced too clearly the frailty and invalidity of all things, of all men, and of ourselves for us still to be able to deify them. We have lost too much confidence in the whole of existence for us still to be capable of having and worshiping gods. If we still have an idol, perhaps it is nothingness, obliteration, meaninglessness.

Bonhoeffer made this statement in the context of an interpretation of the Ten Commandments, an essay written while he was in prison awaiting execution. He then added these words:

> So the First Commandment calls us to the sole, true God, to the omnipotent, righteous, and merciful One, who saves us from falling into nothingness and sustains us in his congregation.[140]

People's cradle.

This is why I quoted the above verse from the famous Christmas carol. You may recognize it, Kurt. It is the quatrain that follows the one you used as the epigraph for *Slaughterhouse-Five*. It talks about a cradle—a "people's cradle"—in the night.

It also mentions the one single thing in this world that *stays*. Everything else in the world finally passes away. So it goes.

But the Lord Jesus *stays*.

As a matter of fact, these are reported to be his last words to the world: "Remember, I am with you always, even to the end of the world" (Mt. 28:20, Phillips).

So he stays.

4

The Exorcist—Nihilism's Search in the Wrong Places for God and Meaning
—or—
The Return of Religion

There is no lack of attempts to revitalize the mythical way of thinking and the pagan polytheistic reminiscences bound up with it. . . .

If we would do justice to such attempts to regain the mythical, then we must see them against the background of an atheism which governs our spiritual situation to an extent that church and theology as a rule do not even come anywhere near to adequately realizing.

—Gerhard Ebeling, *Word and Faith* [1]

It is certainly strange and unexpected that in a generation that belongs by birth to the space age, so many young people have turned away from the sciences that have made possible the world they live in and the extraordinary expansion of our knowledge about the universe. . . .

How can we explain all this? . . .

Modern science and its application—for example in medicine—has become increasingly impersonal and detached from the problems that beset individuals as they grow and mature, suffer disappointment and loss and try to find satisfaction and happiness—or simply health and quiet. So in their search for some alternative life-style a great many young people turn to those occult beliefs and disciplines in other cultures—Chinese or Indian, Japanese or Persian in origin—that promise both a greater understanding of one's own self and some sense of unity between one's private, personal self and the infinite, impersonal universe. In the predicament in which these young people find themselves, the familiar disciplines of Christianity and Judaism have become bonds to be cast off and only the unfamiliar disciplines of Zen or Yoga or one of the new cultist groups have the imaginative power to give them access to their own minds and bodies and a sense of participation in some larger, spiritual whole.

This is, I think, a use of the occult that is quite different from anything in the past, for it is a specific response to needs unmet in our very troubled present.

—Margaret Mead[2]

I am secretly convinced that it is our youth that suffers and agonizes because of the absence of sublime aims of life. In our families practically no mention is made about the sublime aims of life, while not only do they not give the slightest thought to the idea of immortality but much too frequently a satirical attitude is adopted toward it—and this in the presence of children from their early childhood, and perhaps with an express didactic purpose. . . .

With our universal indifference for the sublime aims of life, perhaps in some strata of our society our family is already in a state of decomposition. At least it is obviously clear that our young generation is destined to seek ideals for itself, and the loftiest meaning of life. But its segregation, this abandonment of youth to their own resources—this is what is dreadful. This problem is all too important at this moment of our existence. Our youth is so placed that absolutely nowhere does it find advice as to the loftiest meaning of life. From our brainy people and, generally, from its leaders, youth—I repeat—can borrow merely a rather satirical view, but nothing positive, i.e., in what to believe, what should be respected and adored, what should be sought; and yet all this is so needed, so indispensable to youth; there is, always has been, craving for all this in all ages and everywhere! And even if in the family or at school youth could still be given some sound advice, nevertheless, again, the family and the school (of course, not without exceptions) have grown too indifferent to these things because of many other more practical and contemporaneously interesting problems and aims.

—Fyodor Dostoevsky, *Diary of a Writer,* 1876[3]

The great, all-pervading theme of Dostoevsky's five major novels is man's need for God. Without God, the fragile harmony between man and the outside world collapses, and he becomes a bundle of turmoil surrounded by chaos. . . .

Without that unifying idea, there can be no harmony between man and the world around him; nor, whatever he may do, can he have any inner harmony, which Dostoevsky calls "beauty." . . . And, without it, a man is only a haphazard sequence of un-synthesized impulses and reactions, instinctively searching for a sub-stitute unifying principle. That substitute will most likely be an idol, a false god, a delusion of faith, or perhaps an obsessive passion. But, whatever it is, the result will be a whole built around a false principle, a forcibly synthesized and therefore ugly and unstable identity.

> —Andrew MacAndrew, Introduction to Dostoevsky's
> *The Adolescent*[4]

Once again we must insist on the fact that we are not dealing with illustrations, or with exaggerations of some religious enthusi-asm. If it is said: he has overcome and swallowed death, broken the chains of the devil and destroyed his power, this is so: it is done with, it is accomplished. After Christ's resurrection death is no more, nor does sin rule. Indeed death and sin continue to exist, but as vanquished things. Their situation is similar to a chess player's who has already lost but has not acknowledged it as yet. . . . That precisely is the situation of death and sin and the devil: the king is checkmated, the game is finished and the players do not acknowl-edge it as yet. They still believe the game will go on. But it is over. The old "aeon," the old time of death and sin is over, and the game only appears somehow to be going on. "Old things are passed away; behold all things are become new" (II Cor. 5:17). . . .

In this case the myth is the belief that still views death and sin as victorious powers. No, that is not true, the demon's chains have been broken. This is the truth. And if we do not admit it, at least let us acknowledge that it is the fault of our eyes which do not see, of our ears which do not hear well, and of our imagination which replaces God's reality with sad illusions. Alone with ourselves we would fancy that the [Apostle's] Creed's declarations are the prod-uct of enthusiasm, while we in our earthly wisdom are the true real-

ists who know life, evil, and death too. Well, just the opposite is true. We are the enthusiasts, we in our pessimism, our weakness, our false respect for the devil. That is the message of Easter.
—Karl Barth, *The Faith of the Church* [5]

In a meaningless world people will desperately grasp for religious straws. Some will even agree to follow the Monster God as long as he will give them an infallible outward "certainty" (the Bible, a church, a new revelation, a miraculous sign, an absolute system of laws, a rational proof, and so on), which will insure them against the final uncertainty: falling into the Monster God's "hell."

In this way a literal hell forces those who believe in it to walk by sight and not by faith; whereas Christians "walk by faith, not by sight" (2 Cor. 5:7, RSV).

Other people, rejecting the Monster God and his "hell" as ridiculously cruel and absurd, and yet unable to live the meaningless life of an atheist, are driven into a wilderness of wildcat religions.

In this way "hell" forces all those who reject it and yet who do not know the love of God make known through Christ, to walk in meaninglessness, darkness, and fear.

1. The Christian Faith vs. Religion

Back at the beginning of chapter 2, I said that the world tends to go around in a bumpy, vicious circle: Atheism→ Nihilism →Religion→Jesus. In the last chapter we saw how atheism leads to nihilism. I now want to discuss how nihilism leads to religion.

By *religion* I don't mean the Christian faith, which, as a Christian, I believe is the only "true religion." By *religion* I mean all of people's attempts to find God and meaning in the wrong places, that is, in any place other than in Christ. This is why Christians are called *Christ-ians* and why the Christian faith is called the *Christ-ian* faith. If a person doesn't really believe that Jesus Christ is himself *"the* way, and *the* truth, and *the* life" (John 14:6, RSV), then why should one practice the deception of calling himself or herself a *Christ-ian?* If we look upon Christ as merely the highest representative or the most fitting symbol or the best front man for something else, then why not call ourselves by whatever it is that Christ is understood to represent or symbolize or front for? A lot of serious confusion in life is based on lack of serious confession. In other words, much of the world's life-crippling confusion could be avoided if people would only become conscious of and say (confess) more clearly, honestly, and courageously what they really have faith in. To evade saying what we really believe is to be dishonest about who we really are.

DOONESBURY

I believe that Jesus Christ is himself "the way, and the truth, and the life." There is no other. I believe, as my friend Bonhoeffer put it, that "without Christ we would know *nothing* of God." [6] For me, this is the absolute minimum of what it means to be a Christian or to believe in Christ. "In any other you pray to the God of your imagination," said Bonhoeffer.[7] Any other is an idol of "religion." From the Christian standpoint, the cold, terrifying silence of the universe is decisively broken only by the Word of God—Jesus, who, for precisely this reason, is called "the Christ." Anytime we look for God anywhere else than in the man on the cross, we are barking up the wrong tree—the tree of "religion."

2. Atheism → Nihilism → Religion

Many biblical texts describe the pattern of atheism leading to nihilism and nihilism leading to religion. In the quotes below, I'll use *A* and *N* and *R* to show how the gears of Atheism→ Nihilism →Religion are shifted in this general direction. Jesus said:

(A) Many will fall from their faith; (N) they will betray one another and hate one another. (R) Many false prophets will arise, and will mislead many; (N) and as lawlessness spreads, men's love for one another will grow cold. (R) . . . Then, if anyone says to you, "Look, here is the Messiah," or, "There he is," do not believe it. Imposters will come claiming to be messiahs or prophets, and they will produce great signs and wonders to mislead even God's chosen, if such a thing were possible (Matt. 24:10−12, 23−24, NEB).

Then, in his letter to the Romans, St. Paul says:

(A) They have refused to honor him [God] as God, or to render him thanks. (N) Hence all their thinking has ended in futility, and their misguided minds are plunged in darkness. (R) They boast of their wisdom, but they have made fools of themselves, exchanging the splendour of immortal God for an image shaped like mortal man, even for images like birds, beasts, and creeping things (Rom. 1:21−23, NEB).

Dostoevsky also saw this pattern in history. For example, in a letter anticipating his famous "Grand Inquisitor," Dostoevsky could say:

(A) Here is the first idea which the evil spirit proposed to Christ. You must agree that it is difficult to deal with. Contemporary socialism in Europe, and with us too, everywhere puts Christ aside and concerns itself above all else with *bread,* calls upon science and declares that the cause of all man's miseries is poverty alone, struggle for existence, "the environment has gone bad."
   To this Christ answered: "Not by bread alone does man live," i.e., He propounded the axiom of the spiritual origin of

man. The devil's idea could only apply to man-brute. (N) Christ, however, knew that by bread alone one could not keep man alive. If, moreover, there were no spiritual life, no idea of beauty, then man would fall into anguish, would die, would go out of his mind, would kill himself, (R) or would enter into pagan fantasies.[8]

Said Karl Barth:

> (A) When the atheist sees (N) the danger of the sterile negation in which he finds himself, (R) at the very last moment he usually borrows from his more cautious and far-seeing partner [the mystic]. That is why the great work which F. Mauthner wrote in praise of Western atheism concludes in . . . a "concept of God purified from the nonsense of the theologians." He commends this to his readers . . . as an "ordinary deception, a healthy lie, an unavoidable lifelong illusion."[9]

And of course Barth is here giving us a beautiful description of Kurt Vonnegut—an atheist who has seen the danger of the sterile nihilism in which he finds himself, and hence at the last moment borrows a little religion as a "healthy lie." As we've seen, Vonnegut commends religion to us as a "harmless untruth" that can help make us "brave and kind and healthy and happy." Vonnegut believes in "the power of wishful thinking." His suggestion is an amusing and entertaining one, of course. But the use of a "lie" or an "illusion" for solving our real problems is no more workable in reality than this:

Copyright, 1975, Universal Press Syndicate.

3. The Dogmatic Religion of Atheism

In 1973 Vonnegut could minimize the influence of Dresden in his life and tell us of another influence:

> The amazing adventures which shaped me were over by the time I was nine years old, I'm sure. . . . I've tried to recover some of those memories recently, and I've come up with this much, anyway; the big house where I was a little kid was empty a lot of the time except for me and a black cook named Ida Young. If it weren't for her, I wouldn't know as much about the Bible and human slavery and really poor people as I do. . . . What [man] becomes depends on his early education. I am a pacifist, and I've made my children pacifists too. But that isn't because of Dresden. It's because of the humane education I received from Ida Young.[10]

Elsewhere Vonnegut tells us that "I probably spent more time with [Ida Young] than I spent with anybody. . . . She knew the *Bible* by heart, and she found plenty of comfort and wisdom in there."[11]

Well, how about Ida Young, Kurt? Do you think that for one moment she considered the Bible a pack of "harmless lies"? And if she *had* thought this, do you think she would have been so concerned to pass it along to you? Or, to put it another way, the next time you come across a Hare Krishna group on the streets, Kurt, ask them if they don't really think their religion is merely a "helpful illusion."

But be ready to run.

Everyone has a "religion" or a basic belief or faith in something that they dare not question and that they cannot prove to be true. Even the most "tolerant" and liberal-minded people have basic sets of dogmatic assumptions by which they live. Therefore, whenever these assumptions are seriously questioned, you will see even these tolerant, open-minded folks act like the narrowest bigot.

"Look, pal, I'm undecided, and that's that!"

Drawing by C. Barsotti; ©1976. The New Yorker Magazine, Inc.

Vonnegut's faith is in scientific atheistic humanism. And he is so strongly locked into this faith that even when he sees its inadequacy he can recommend other religions only as "helpful lies." Therefore, he is asking other people to do what he himself cannot do, to accept their religions as mere lies, when he can scarcely for one moment question the truth of his own religious faith—the faith of atheistic humanism. And how can he be sure that *this* faith is true?

Therefore, when the faith of atheism totally collapses into the nihilistic void of complete meaninglessness and uncertainty, all sorts of other religions—especially if the church has not done its job!—must spring up to fill this vacuum. And these new religions must be just as sincerely believed as was the religious faith of atheism. Otherwise they can be no real help in giving people something to believe in, in the midst of radical uncertainty and meaninglessness.

Vonnegut's own appreciation of people's need for religion helps us see how this is happening today, even though he can think of (other people's) religions only as "helpful lies." But no one is going to be satisfied with lies any more than Vonnegut is. For Vonnegut himself finally falls back on a "truth"—scientific "truth"—even though he knows this truth can never give life meaning. Therefore, almost everyone today—including Kurt Vonnegut!—is desperately searching for something to believe in that is strong enough to stand up against the destructive power of nihilistic uncertainty and meaninglessness.

Finding something to believe in is now definitely "where it's at." Or, as Vonnegut can say in *Player Piano,* in a statement that fits the times closer than our skin, "The big trouble, really, was finding something to believe in." [12]

4. The Exorcist and the Return of Religion

This is why *The Exorcist* (novel and film) also well represents what's going on nowadays. *The Exorcist* is a pregnant and popular symptom of the present-day search for something to believe in, especially something religious to believe in. Almost every major viewpoint on today's religious scene is in some way represented in *The Exorcist:* Protestant evangelicalism, conservative Roman Catholicism, theological rationalism, superstition, and the occult.

This is also why *The Exorcist* is unintentionally a tremendously *ironic* work. Blatty, the author of *The Exorcist,* thinks his novel is about *exorcising,* or getting rid of "the devil." But actually his book is about the return of a whole bunch of old devils. It is about the return of religion in our time.

And therefore our present situation, so well represented by Vonnegut and *The Exorcist,* is also aptly described by this saying of Jesus:

> When an unclean spirit comes out of a man it wanders over the deserts seeking a resting-place, and finds none. Then it says, "I will go back to the home I left." So it returns and finds the house unoccupied, swept clean, and tidy. Off it goes and collects seven other spirits more wicked than itself, and they all come in and settle down; and in the end the man's plight is worse than before. That is how it will be with this wicked generation (Matt. 12:43–45, NEB).

In other words, (A) modern "enlightened" atheism, represented by Vonnegut & Twain, did indeed succeed in "cleaning the shit off practically everything." The "unclean spirit" of the Monster God and his "hell" was unceremoniously swept out of people and was last seen "wandering over the deserts seeking a resting-place." (N) But in the meantime the house remained "unoccupied." It became nihilistic. The church failed to fill the house with the meaning of life given in Jesus Christ, and well-intentioned folks like Vonnegut & Twain haven't even come close to filling it with their pitiful little acorns. Mark Twain's confession about his wife is typical of what atheistic humanism has accomplished: "I took Livy's religion away from her and gave her nothing—worse than nothing—in return. I gave her alarm."[13] (R) What we are now seeing is the return of the "unclean spirit" with "other spirits more wicked than itself, and they all come in and settle down; and in the end the man's plight is worse than before. That is how it will be with this wicked generation."

And so it goes today with this generation.

"When the gods fall," said Dostoevsky, "the demons emerge."[14] "Where there are no gods," Novalis tells us, "spirits rule."[15] When the worldly false gods of atheism finally collapse into the nihilistic cave of total darkness, then the demonic false gods of religion will appear.

BROOM-HILDA

©1975 Chicago Tribune—New York News Syndicate, Inc.

5. The Exorcist—From Demonstrations to Demons

The Exorist did a wonderful job of announcing the return of religion, the return of the "unclean spirit" and others even more wicked. It appeared in the early 1970s, just when all of us were beginning to sense an ominous change taking place. The story begins by showing us how atheism is fast falling into nihilism, and then it marks nihilism's desperate turning to religion for help.

For instance, *The Exorcist* begins by dramatizing the exhaustion of mere humanism's attempts at social reconstruction and the collapse of this humanism into nihilistic anarchy. Its opening pages express boredom with a scene that had become typical by the late 1960s: a "dumb" campus demonstration against the university authorities. But this is just as it should be. For when social "activists" are not backed up by a primary confidence in God, and therefore soon become disappointed and disillusioned, they will then begin to hear "strange noises"—just as we did in the opening scenes of *The Exorcist,* and just as Megaphone Mark does in this 1970 Doonesbury cartoon:

Copyright, 1970, G. B. Trudeau/Distributed by Universal Press Syndicate.

6. The Exorcist—From Lunar Landings to Lunacy

We also learn at the beginning of *The Exorcist,* that American astronauts are on their way to the moon. Human technological achievement is literally flying at an all-time high. Technology, like the cow of old, has jumped over the moon.

And yet *The Exorcist* also shows us that, at the same time, the human *spirit* seems to be at an all-time low. Our tremendous scientific and material advances would apparently leave us with nothing to desire—except meaning in life. In the recent past it was largely because of our overwhelming material achievements that the realm of the spiritual seemed so remote and unbelievable. But now we are beginning to realize that these successes have not made us good, secure, or happy. Therefore we're now in a big hurry to grab the nearest thing handy to help fill this void inside us—whether it be with "demon rum" or "demon possession."

Drawing by Herbert Goldberg; ©1974. The New Yorker Magazine, Inc.

7. The Exorcist—From Super Meaninglessness to Superstition

But it is in the experience of Chris that *The Exorcist* most forcefully dramatizes the contemporary experience of the meaninglessness of life. For Chris is an atheist. And for the atheist, as we have seen, it is *death* that causes all life finally to be meaningless. Chris, an actress, is talking to her British director, Burke. And this is the way she describes her experience:

> She was slowly pouring vodka. "Ever think about dying?"
> "I beg your—"

"Dying," she interrupted. "Ever think about it, Burke? What it means? I mean, *really* what it means?"

Faintly edgy, he answered, "I don't know. No, I don't. I don't think about it at all. I just *do* it. What the hell'd you bring it up for?"

She shrugged. "I don't know," she answered softly. She plopped ice into her glass; eyed it thoughtfully. "Yeah . . . yeah, I do," she amended. "I sort of . . . well, I thought about it this morning . . . like a dream . . . waking up. I don't know. I mean, it just sort of hit me . . . what it means. I mean, the end—*the end!*—like I'd never even heard of it before." She shook her head. "Oh, Jesus, did that spook me! I felt like I was falling off the goddam planet at a hundred million miles an hour."

"Oh, rubbish. Death's a comfort," Dennings sniffed.

"Not for *me* it isn't, Charlie."

"Well, you live through your children."

"Oh, come off it! My children aren't me."

"Yes, thank heaven. One's entirely enough."

"I mean, think about it, Burke! Not existing—forever! It's—"

"*Oh,* for heaven sakes! Show your bum at the faculty tea next week and perhaps those priests can give you comfort!"

He banged down his glass. "Let's another."

"You know, I didn't know they drank?"

"Well, you're stupid."

His eyes had grown mean.[16]

Atheism makes life meaningless, and meaninglessness makes people mean.

The experience Chris has described here is what theologian Wolfhart Pannenberg calls being "really seized" by the "knowledge of the inescapability of death." Here is the way Pannenberg describes the depth and power of this experience:

Whether or not hope is a meaningful attitude in life at all is decided for the individual in the final analysis in the question of whether there is anything to be hoped for beyond death.

The meaning of all provisional images of hope is threatened by the inescapability of the fate of death. . . . If death is the end, then all hope for a coming fulfillment of existence seems to be foolish. For how foolish it is to long for a future that, first, always remains uncertain and, second, even at best—namely, when it is really fulfilled—only brings one nearer to the grave. In contrast, the proper art of living would indeed consist in enjoying the present day: "Let us eat and drink, for tomorrow we die" (I Cor. 15:32). But this, too, provides no exit. When the knowledge of the inescapability of death has really seized a person, then everything that fills his days becomes stale and empty. Modern medicine has recognized that radical hopelessness has death as its consequence.[17]

Thus the experience of the meaninglessness of life is brought on by fully recognizing the "hours" of death—when there is no God.

But this same experience can easily drive us into a desperate search for "intimations of immortality"—any kind of intimations of any kind of immortality. And this desperate search is what *The Exorcist* is all about.

Whenever a culture has little or no knowledge of Christ, this vacuum of spiritual bereftness will soon begin to suck into it "strange gods" from seemingly out of nowhere. As theologian Paul Tillich could say: "Abuses occur when the right use is lacking and superstitions arise when faith has become weak."[18]

"Beg pardon, sir, but I couldn't help noticing you were spiritually bereft."

Drawing by Lorenz; ©1975. The New Yorker Magazine, Inc.

8. The Return of "the Unclean Spirit"—The Monster God and His "Hell"

People will even be desperate enough to endure the abuse of the Monster God and his literal hell whenever there is enough meaninglessness and uncertainty in their lives. But in order for such a vengeful, hot-tempered god to appeal to people in their uncertainty, he must give them a guaranteed certainty that he won't throw *them* into his "hell." The god of "hell" knows he will never get to first base with people unless he agrees to furnish his followers with a visible, seeing-is-believing proof that *they* won't end up in "hell."

This is the type of phony Christianity that is making a strong comeback in our time. It is the unclean spirit of belief in a literal hell, which therefore has to cover itself with all sorts of visible proofs. For these two things will always go together: belief in "hell" and the need for a "proof." No one can seriously believe in "hell" without hanging on to some kind of infallible guarantee that he or she is not going to spend eternity there.

This is too bad. For "to demand guarantees is to mistrust" (Bonhoeffer).[19] And this is because the guarantee, or proof, is obviously what we *really* trust. And since what we really trust is also really our god, then our proof for God is actually the god we really worship and trust. Where your "proof" is, friends, there is your god also. This is why Bonhoeffer could say:

> *Where is there proof of* [God]? A God who let us prove his existence would be an idol. The Lord whom we trust binds us so firmly to himself that we are freed from superstition and a desire for miracles. The person to whom God has given faith has faith in him, whatever happens.[20]

Nevertheless, there are lots of good "proofs" available to help us live with the god of "hell." There are, for instance, Infallible Reason, Infallible Bible, Infallible Church, Infallible Laws, an Infallible New Revelation, an Infallible Miracle, and so forth and so on. But if we base our faith on any one of these proofs, logically our faith is actually in the proof. And this proof will be a *cruel* god too, for how can we be certain this proof is really true? Especially when there are so many proofs around and they all seem to contradict one another. How do we prove the proof?

A proof for God, then, is an idol that usually grows out of the fear of frying. As a rule, a proof for God is really a form of "cosmic fire insurance." So once more we see that the fear of "hell" is the false teaching that *bedevils* the church more than any other heresy. This is why it is appropriate that whenever the fires of a literal hell are seriously feared, this demonic misunderstanding will always be accompanied by a superstitious belief in a *literal* devil.

HERMAN

"What's the first thing that comes into your head when
I say, 'fire insurance'?"

But a literal devil is not the devil of the Bible.

9. I Have Met the Devil, and He Is Me

Call me Bob. That's short for Beelzebob. For I am well acquainted
with the devil—the *real* devil. I shave him every morning. I smile at
him in the mirror, and the handsome devil smiles back. Man and
boy, I've lived with the devil for over forty years now. Forty years
with him in the wilderness. And I'll tell you something: I have met
the devil, and he is *mean*. And I'll tell you something else: I have
met the devil, and he is *me*. Or, as Dostoevsky's Ivan could say,
"And *he* [the devil], Alyosha, is me, he really is myself, everything
that is base, wicked, and despicable in me." [21]

And here's one more thing, dear reader: The devil is also *you*.

To make a long story short, this is also pretty much the biblical understanding of the matter. The biblical authors were fond of personifying things they saw around them. For example, the prophet Isaiah said that even such "concrete" things as "the mountains and the hills before you shall break forth into singing, and all the trees of the field shall clap their hands (Isa. 55:12, RSV). The biblical writers also liked to personify abstract ideas and principles, such as "wisdom": "Wisdom cries aloud in the street; in the markets she raises her voice" (Prov. 2:20, RSV). But this doesn't mean that the biblical writers believed for one minute that "wisdom" actually went tramping through the street raising "her" voice, or that the trees literally clapped whenever the hills sang. Neither does the Bible seriously believe that the "devil" has any literal personal, independent existence of "his" own apart from the devil, or sin, in people. A basic, fundamental assumption of the Bible is that all people are originally sinners. And sin is never a neutral quality. It is demonically aggressive, dangerous, intelligent, and alive, just as people are. Therefore, what could make more sense than the personification of this living and basic human tendency? Sin is a problem that only persons have. This is why it is not surprising to find sin personified in the Bible in a symbolic person known as "the devil."

The devil is therefore not some monster outside ourselves that can go into a person. The devil is rather that powerful and stubborn basic thrust of the human heart that is already in people. The devil is our heart's constitutional desire to worship false gods. Notice how emphatic Jesus was on this point:

> Hear me, all of you, and understand: there is nothing outside a man which by going into him can defile him; . . . What comes out of a man is what defiles a man. For from within, out of the heart of man, come evil thoughts, fornication, theft, murder, adultery, coveting, wickedness, deceit, licentiousness, envy, slander, pride, foolishness. All these evil things come from within, and they defile a man (Mark 7:14–15, 20–23, RSV).

Therefore, dear friend, when you peer into the Bible to see what the devil looks like, keep in mind that *this* is what you're looking at:

10. The Devil and His Demons = Sin and Its Results

The cases of "possession" in the New Testament are not "devil possession" but "demon possession." [22] So how are these two related—"the devil" and "the demons"?

It works like this: *The devil is to the demons what sin is to the results of sin.* If modern medicine has taught us anything, it is simply to confirm scientifically something the New Testament already knows: The most prevalent illness among us is emotional or "mental," illness, and, furthermore, a large percentage of the problems we have with our bodies originate with our minds, or *spirits,* to use the New Testament word. Many of our bodily problems are *psychosomatic* ("spirit-body") in nature. And as this word suggests, the *psycho* (or "spirit") has priority here: The spiritual problem leads to the bodily manifestation. First the *psycho,* then the *somatic.*

This is why in the New Testament three things are always seen as closely related, when they are not actually identified with one another: *lack of faith, demons,* and *diseases.* For instance, in the following passage notice how even in a single sentence—the final sentence—these three are held tightly together:

> And when they came to the crowd, a man came up to him and kneeling before him said, "Lord, have mercy on my son, for he is an epileptic and he suffers terribly; for often he falls into the fire, and often into the water. And I brought him to

your disciples, and they could not heal him." And Jesus answered, "O faithless and perverse generation, how long am I
to be with you? How long am I to bear with you? Bring him
here to me." And Jesus rebuked him, and the demon came
out of him, and the boy was cured instantly (Matt. 17:14–18,
RSV).

Demons, then, in the way the New Testament understands
them, are simply the outward manifestations—in our bodies or our
behavior—for the inward problem of faithlessness (sin). Demons, to
adapt the language of *The Book of Common Prayer* a bit, are
"outward and visible signs of an inward and spiritual disgrace."
This is why in the Bible there is basically only one devil but many
demons. Satan, the single "prince of demons," directs the many
demons. Why? Because for the Bible there is basically only *one*
sin—lack of faith in God—but there are many demonic results of
this faithlessness. The devil and his demons are symbols for this sin
and its results. When we "have a demon," we have the demonic
consequences of placing our heart's desire anywhere but in God.

"*Here you are, Jack. Your signature on this simple document brings
you your heart's desire. Check it out.*"

Drawing by Lorenz; ©1977. The New Yorker Magazine, Inc.

Paul Tillich has done an excellent job, I believe, in helping us understand how the New Testament stories of devils and demons are not "miracle stories of the past" but "healing stories of the present."

As in ours, so in the period of Jesus much talk was going on of sickness and healing. Jews and Greeks wrote about it. People felt that they lived in a sick period; they called it *"this world-period"* and they described it in a way which is very similar to the way in which we describe it today. They saw not only the bodily infirmity of all of us, the innumerable bodily diseases in the masses of the people, they also saw the destructive powers possessing the minds of many. They called the mentally ill the possessed or the demoniacs and they tried to expel the evil spirits. They also knew that nations can be sick and that the diseases of social classes infect every individual in it. They looked even beyond the boundary lines of mankind into nature and spoke in visionary ecstasy about this earth becoming old and sick just as we did when we were under the first shock of the atomic power of self-destruction. Out of this knowledge of a sick period the question of a new period, a reality of health and wholeness was asked. Salvation and a savior were expected. But salvation is healing. And the savior is the healer. Therefore, Jesus answers the anxious question of the Baptist about whether He is the Savior, by pointing to His healing power. This is what He says: "If I am able to heal the deaf and the blind, if I am able to liberate the mentally sick, then a new reality has come upon you!" There are many healing stories in the Gospels, a stumbling block for scholars and preachers and teachers, because they take them as miracle stories of the past instead of taking them as healing stories of the present. For this they are. They show the human situation, the relation between bodily and mental disease, between sickness and guilt, between the desire of being healed and the fear of being healed. It is astonishing how many of our profoundest modern insights into human nature are anticipated in these stories: They know that becoming healthy means becoming whole, reunited, in one's bodily and psychic functions. They know that the mentally sick are afraid of the process of healing, because it throws them out of the limited but safe house of their neurotic self-seclusion, they know that the process of mental healing is a difficult and painful one, accompanied by convulsions of body and soul. They tell of the relation of guilt and disease, of the way in which unsolved conflicts of our conscience drive us to those cleavages of body and soul which we call sickness. We are told how Jesus, knowing this, pronounces to the paralytic first the forgiveness of his sins and then his regained health. The man lived in an inner struggle with himself, with his feeling of guilt. Out of this conflict his illness had grown; and now when Jesus forgives him, he feels reconciled with himself and the world; he becomes whole and healthy. There is little in our recent psychology of depth that surpasses these insights in truth and depth. These stories also describe the attitude which makes healing possible. They call it faith.[23]

11. Demon Possession=Our Demon Possessions

The best way to understand what the New Testament means by *demon possession* is to see it as the demonic results of our possessions—those things we think we can own or have control over. Sin (or lack of faith) is simply worshiping anything that *isn't* God. And this *anything* usually has the quality of being something we think can possess or control. This is why we worship it. It seemingly puts *us* in the place of God by our possession of it or control over it.

However, only God is God. Only he controls and possesses all things. Therefore, whenever we attempt to usurp God's place by possessing something we can control ourselves, this prized possession will begin to exercise a kind of demonic control over us. " 'In very truth I tell you,' said Jesus, 'that everyone who commits sin is a slave' " (John 8:34, NEB). In other words, the worship of false gods makes us the most miserable slaves of these gods. The more precious our possessions or pursuit of possessions, the more they possess us. In this sense we become "demon possessed" by our "demon possessions."

BROOM-HILDA

12. "Hell" Produces a Literal Bible, Which Produces a Literal Devil

When anyone looks into the Bible and is frightened by the horrible specter of a literal hell, the next thing he or she will have to take literally is all the rest of the Bible. For when we are seriously afraid of being eternally damned, naturally we're going to be somewhat anxious to find information that will show us clearly, plainly, and with no monkey business how we can avoid such a destiny. The Bible, which has frightened us with damnation taken literally, had also damned sure better be literal in telling us how to avoid this fate. And no nonsense! No ambiguity! Just the clear, literal meaning of the words. You don't fool around when your soul is actually in danger of hellfire.

Thus evolves a truly vicious circle: a literal hell reinforcing a literal Bible, and a literal Bible reinforcing a literal hell.

And once a literal Bible is made necessary by a literal hell, such a Bible proceeds to cause further untold trouble for the message of Christ. In addition to its supposed clarity, literalism will also have great appeal—especially to the simple—because seemingly it is the *simplest* means of interpreting a complex document. But this supposed simplicity makes biblical literalists look like simpletons to the rest of the world, since literalists so obviously miss the point of much of what the Bible is saying.

Funky Winkerbean

FUNKY WINKERBEAN by Tom Batiuk. ©Field Enterprises, Inc., 1976. Courtesy of Field Newspaper Syndicate.

Because they so desperately want everything in the Bible to be simple, biblical literalists usually only succeed in making themselves and the Christian faith look simple-minded:

> An intelligent young man named Jitterly,
> Was told the Bible was to be taken quite literally;
> So the first time he read
> *Everything* that it said,
> He rejected the whole thing bitterly.

The Bible does not point to itself as the sole norm of truth, but only to Christ and his Holy Spirit. Only Christ is "the Word of God." The Word did not become *words* or a "paper pope," but "the Word became *flesh* and dwelt among us" (John 1:14, RSV). Therefore, Christ could say:

> You study the scriptures diligently, supposing that in having them you have eternal life; yet, although their testimony points to me, you refuse to come to me for that life (John 5:39, NEB).

→

©1970 United Feature Syndicate, Inc.

It is wholly *through* the Bible that we learn of Christ, and therefore the Bible is "Holy." But Christ is the *heart* of the Bible. And if we are to understand him, we must read the Bible with *our* hearts also. A *heart-to-heart* encounter must take place if we are to really understand the Bible. We will be lost if we try to read it only with our heads, especially if we use only the shallowest level of our heads—a literal understanding. The things of the spirit "are spiritually discerned" (1 Cor. 2:14, RSV), but biblical literalists are biblical *letteralists*. They are guilty of approaching the Bible as St. Paul said many of the Jews approached the law: They knew its "letter" but not its "spirit." Real biblical understanding, as Paul said of the law, "is a matter of the heart, spiritual and not literal" (Rom. 2:29, RSV). Literalists can—and often do—know the Bible's *words* inside out, but with this one-level view of what its words can mean, it's impossible for them to go very far in their understanding.

B.C. by permission of Johnny Hart and Field Enterprises, Inc.

It is not necessary to take the Bible literally in order to take it seriously. In fact, it is the very people who take it *only* literally who are limited in their respect for the Bible. For they deny the many different ways in which it is capable of speaking to us.

Biblical literalists can never really understand this until they have been extricated from the vicious circle of a literal hell, which makes necessary a literal Bible, which in turn reinforces a literal hell. And this tightly closed circle can usually only be penetrated by a *biblical* proclamation of God's reconciliation of *all* men in Christ. Only then can the literalists' fear of "hell" be calmed enough so that they won't have to cling so desperately to the letter of the Bible.

In the meantime, belief in a literal "devil" comes with the territory of anyone trapped in this kind of thinking. But not only do they *have* to believe in the "devil," because the Bible uses this word, but they also *want* to believe in it. As Ivan tells Alyosha: "I would like it so very much if [the "devil"] really were *him* and not me." [24]

Yes, sirree! A literal devil can come in very handy!

13. How to Prove God's Existence: Take One Devil and . . .

William Peter Blatty, the author of *The Exorcist,* figures that if people—including himself—can just be convinced of the devil's existence they'll also be well on their way to believing in God. He also figures that this "Infallible Miracle," this "negative proof" for God's existence, ought to be very convincing since there's so much *evil* around to act as supporting evidence. Yes, friends, that's what the man is actually saying: "If we can just capture ourselves a real live devil, that'll mean there's got to be a good Lord around somewhere." This is why Blatty was overjoyed when he read in a newspaper article on "possession" that a man thought he had actually cornered the devil in a teenage boy:

> I was *excited*. For here at last, in this city, in my time, was tangible evidence of transcendence. If there were demons, there were angels and probably a God and a life everlasting. [25]

Lord, Lord, how Dostoevsky would have laughed at such a sophistry! He never failed to poke fun at such harebrained "proofs" for God. He would have called William Peter Blatty "batty," or at least a mere "spiritualist." In *The Brothers Karamazov,* Dostoevsky has "the devil" (Ivan's hallucination) say to Ivan:

Take the spiritualists, for example (I love them, by the way): would you believe it—they're sure they are helpful to the propagation of the faith just because the devils allow them to peek into the other world and have a glimpse at their horns, which is supposed to be material proof that the "other world" exists. The "world beyond" and material proof—a peculiar combination that only men would think up! And then, when you come to think of it, even if they have proved the existence of the devil, why should it follow that God exists too? [26]

Shucks, William Peter Blatty. If belief in real demons implies belief in a real God, I guess old Hägar here is a mighty fortress of true faith.

HAGAR THE HORRIBLE

©King Features Syndicate, Inc. 1975.

14. Don't Blame Me, Lord—"The Devil Made Me Do It!"

The devil also comes in handy in explaining the origin of evil in the world. When we don't believe that the origin of most human suffering is found in our *own* sinful hearts (see the statement of Jesus back at signpost #9), then of course we've got to look elsewhere for the origin of this evil. When we don't believe that all people originate in life as sinners (the meaning of "origin-al sin"), then we've got to locate the origin of human sinfulness elsewhere. In this case the devil becomes an extremely convenient scapegoat. No wonder the devil is often depicted as half person and half goat. He is the *goat* who helps us persons *'scape* from being the originators of our own problems.

©King Features Syndicate, Inc. 1977.

And who wants to think of themselves as sinners, especially when faced with the threat of a literal hell? For if we really may be so deeply sinful, and if there really is a "hell" in store for sinners, then we'd much rather think of ourselves as being "essentially good," just as William Peter Blatty does.[27] In this way we can keep divinity for ourselves—our own divine goodness and "freedom" always to do the right thing; and at the same time we can blame any wrong choices on the temptations of the devil. For these reasons, hardly anything could be more comforting and self-flattering to sinful humankind than belief in a literal devil.

Drawing by Alan Dunn; ©1974. The New Yorker Magazine, Inc.

This is why even a thoroughgoing atheistic humanist like Dostoevsky's Ivan Karamazov can sometimes find it convenient to believe in the devil. He desperately wants to believe that all humankind—including himself—is basically good. Therefore, when there is no God and "everything is permitted," humankind will just naturally do all the right things. Yet Ivan cannot avoid seeing that without God, humankind—including himself—acts like a maddened animal. Therefore, he begins to "hallucinate." He begins to see an actual devil in the world—a devil who can explain all of "enlightened" humankind's evil behavior and who can in this way save from collapse Ivan's idolatrous faith in humankind.

Belief in a literal devil is always a folly of immense proportions. It mislocates the basic human problem. We see the origin of sin in the devil and not in ourselves. As Dostoevsky shows us in *The Brothers Karamazov,* it is precisely for this reason that the real devil (the power of human sinfulness) wants us to believe in the phony devil (a literal devil). "My assigned position," says Dostoevsky's literal devil (Ivan's hallucination)," is to take care of the dirty work. Somebody claims all the honor for good works, leaving me nothing but the foul play." [28] Thus the real devil, our own sinfulness, in causing us to blame the decoy of a literal devil, deceives us with the greatest of all possible lies—that we ourselves are sinless. For "if we say we have no sin, we deceive ourselves, and the truth is not in us" (1 John 1:8, RSV). This is why Jesus could call the devil, the real devil, "a liar and the father of lies" (John 8:44, RSV).

Those who believe in the reality of a personal, literal devil usually do so because they don't want to believe in the reality of their own strong and deep inclination to worship false gods, or to sin. And about the worst mistake anyone can make is to think the devil is "someone else."

HAGAR THE HORRIBLE

15. And Don't Blame God, Either!—Unless You Want to Be Excommunicated from Sunday School

The devil likewise serves the convenient purpose of taking *God* off the embarrassing hook of being responsible for evil. For if "God is God He is not good," as Archibald McLeish has said.[29] In other words, if God really is the all-powerful God, completely in control of absolutely everything that happens, then he is also responsible for all the evil in the world. Timid souls usually consider this kind of thinking blasphemous. Therefore, if we don't want to be excommunicated from Sunday school, like poor Kelly, it's safer to think that there really is a devil who is responsible for evil, and that God and this devil are *not* in cahoots:

Copyright, 1974, Universal Press Syndicate.

As Karl Barth tells us, even evil only exists as "subjected to God."[30] But if God really is all-powerful and all-loving, why *doesn't* he just zap evil with a lightning bolt? On this side of heaven there is no answer to this question. In the face of evil, the only thing that finally prevents Christians from becoming atheists and seeing all of life as "much ado about nothing," is their faith that "all's well that ends well." For we know through Christ that finally all *does* end well, that ultimately "God will be all in all" (1 Cor. 15:28, NEB). Thus Christians believe with St. Paul "that the sufferings of this present time are not worth comparing with the glory that is to be revealed to us" (Rom. 8:18, RSV).

16. A Weak God and/or Christ Leads to Devil and Demon Worship

Here is the second half of MacLeish's famous formula: "If God is good He is not God." That is, if God is responsible only for good and the devil is responsible for bad, then obviously God is not all-powerful. "He is not God." His power is shared with the devil. He is not really the almighty God that the Bible—and Barth above—say he is. God and the devil are at war with each other, and the fate of us all is up for grabs.

In this way, belief in the devil, and therefore in a God who is not responsible for everything, opens the door to devil worship. As Mark Twain observed, "The wise Fiji chief said to a missionary: 'We do not pray to the Good Spirit to spare us, but to the other one; a *good* spirit is not going to hurt us.' " [31]

GRIN AND BEAR IT

"I said my prayers, Pop . . . now to be on the safe side, maybe I should work out a little detente with the devil."

GRIN AND BEAR IT by Lichty & Wagner. ©Field Enterprises, Inc., 1975. Courtesy of Field Newspaper Syndicate.

But it's not necessary to be an "uncivilized" Fiji native or a five-year-old to live in fear of devils and bad spirits. Enlightened "man come of age" is more and more open to this fear nowadays. And here's why:

As long as Christ was worshiped as the single place of God's self-revelation in the world, everything else in all history and nature was in effect exorcised, or de-divinized. Nature no longer included divine or semidivine spirits. The natural was now understood as *only* the natural and in no way included the *super*natural. And for Christians, the same was true of all *history* after the appearance of Christ. Only in the Messiah of Israel had God once and for all fully disclosed himself and his will for humankind. Any other manifestation of the supernatural was now seen as superstition, superfluous, and idolatry. And, as we have seen, it was this exorcising of nature by the Christian faith that laid the foundations for modern science and technology. What is revealed in a "biblical demonology," said Karl Barth, is

not an earth and humanity controlled, visited and plagued by demons, but liberated from them; not a world bewitched but exorcised; not a community and Christendom believing in demons but opposing to them in faith that resolute disbelief; in short the triumph of truth over falsehood.[32]

But just as soon as Jesus is no longer worshiped as the Christ, just as soon as this single anchor of God is pulled away from all of nature and history, then all humankind will immediately be once more at sea. Humankind will be adrift without compass or anchor on the vast sea of a nature and a history that is once more filled with terrifying spirits, demons, and strange gods. Just as soon as we no longer believe in Jesus as the Christ, then even the "technological society" will become riddled with superstitious beliefs in devils, demons, spooks, goblins, spirits, gremlins, and so on. All nature will once again tend to be enchanted, haunted, or possessed.

"The men feel there is an evil spirit in your clutch housing. We've called a priest."

Drawing by Booth; ©1974. The New Yorker Magazine, Inc.

17. "Hell"—The Greatest Producer of False Gods or No God

Now note this question, dear friend: What is by far the most formidable obstacle preventing Jesus from being understood as *the* Christ, as *the* single place of God's self-revelation in the world? Answer: The monstrous idea of a literal hell, the misunderstanding that pictures Christ as only saving Christians from "hell," rather than picturing him as "the Savior of the world" (John 4:42, 1 John 4:14, RSV). As long as "Christians" persist in thinking that all eternity is divided into the two spheres of heaven and "hell," the religious world will also be divided into two miserable spheres: the sphere of a weak Christ, limited in power or love or both, with his supplemental idols to assure us of our salvation; and the sphere of the constant proliferation of "wildcat" religions. Many people will always rightly reject the monstrous misunderstanding—a literal hell—as ridiculously cruel and absurd, but they will not necessarily be able to live the meaningless life of an atheist. Therefore, if these people do not know that in Christ *all* persons are reconciled to God and have their destinies in heaven, they will be driven into the wilderness of what Mark Twain called "wildcat religions." [33] A literal hell, then, is *this* door:

HAGAR THE HORRIBLE

OH! WHO LEFT THAT DOOR OPEN AGAIN ?!!

©King Features Syndicate, Inc. 1977.

Bonhoeffer could clearly see the urgent need for the church to "leave behind" the monstrous misunderstanding of thinking in "two spheres": the saved and the lost, Christ and a literal devil, heaven and a literal hell:

The world is not divided between Christ and the devil, but, whether it recognizes it or not, it is solely and entirely the world of Christ. The world is to be called to this, its reality in Christ, and in this way the false reality will be destroyed which it believes that it possesses in itself as in the devil. The dark and evil world must not be abandoned to the devil. It must be claimed for Him who has won it by His incarnation, His death and His resurrection. Christ gives up nothing of what He has won. He holds it fast in His hands. It is Christ, therefore, who renders inadmissible the dichotomy of a bedevilled and a Christian world. Any static delimitation of a region which belongs to the devil and a region which belongs to Christ is a denial of the reality of God's having reconciled the whole world with Himself in Christ.

That God loved the world and reconciled it with Himself in Christ is the central message proclaimed in the New Testament. It is assumed there that the world stands in need of reconciliation with God but that it is not capable of achieving it by itself. . . .

And yet it is the task and the essential character of the Church that she shall impart to precisely this world its reconciliation with God and that she shall open its eyes to the reality of the love of God, against which it is blindly raging. . . .

It is hard to abandon a picture which one has grown accustomed to using for the ordering of one's ideas and concepts. And yet we must leave behind us the picture of the two spheres, and the question now is whether we can replace it with another picture which is equally simple and obvious.

We shall need above all to direct our gaze to the picture of the body of Christ Himself, who became man, was crucified and rose again. In the body of Jesus Christ God is united with humanity, the whole of humanity is accepted by God, and the world is reconciled with God. In the body of Jesus Christ God took upon himself the sin of the whole world and bore it. There is no part of the world, be it never so forlorn and never so godless, which is not accepted by God and reconciled with God in Jesus Christ. Whoever sets eyes on the body of Jesus Christ in faith can never again speak of the world as though it were lost, as though it were separated from Christ; he can never again with clerical arrogance set himself apart from the world. The world belongs to Christ, and it is only in Christ that the world is what it is. It has need, therefore, of nothing less than Christ Himself. . . .

If we now follow the New Testament in applying to the Church the concept of the body of Christ, this is not by any means intended primarily as representing the separation of the Church from the world. On the contrary, it is implicit in the New Testament statement concerning the incarnation of God in Christ that all men are taken up, enclosed and borne within the body of Christ and that this is just what the congregation of the faithful are to make known to the world by their words and by their lives. What is intended here is not separation from the world but the summoning of the world into the fellowship of this body of Christ, to which in truth it already belongs. This testimony of the Church is foreign to the world; the Church herself, in bearing this testimony, finds herself to be foreign to the world. Yet . . . the Church is divided from the world solely by the fact that she affirms in faith the reality of God's acceptance of man, a reality which is the property of the whole world. By allowing this reality to take effect within herself, she testifies that it is effectual for the whole world.[34]

In "the incarnation of God in Christ . . . *all* men are taken up, enclosed and borne within the body of Christ." *All* people are reconciled with God and are destined to live eternally with him in heaven, *but not all people know this.* As St. Paul put it:

Indeed there are many "gods" and many "lords"—yet for us there is one God, the Father, from whom all being comes, towards whom we move; and there is one Lord, Jesus Christ, through whom all things came to be, and we through him. But not everyone knows this (1 Cor. 8:5–7, NEB).

And this knowledge comes to us in this lifetime only through Christ. Christ is *the only way* through which people can now safely be sure that this good news is true. And therefore Christ could say:

In truth I tell you, in very truth, the man who does not enter the sheepfold by the door, but climbs in some other way, is nothing but a thief or a robber. . . . In truth, in very truth I tell you, I am the door of the sheepfold. The sheep paid no heed to any who came before me, for these were all thieves and robbers. I am the door; anyone who comes into the fold through me shall be safe. He shall go in and out and shall find pasturage (John 10:1, 7–9, NEB).

But those who assure us of a literal hell are those who "shut the door of the kingdom of Heaven in men's faces" (Matt. 23:13, NEB). Therefore whenever this door, Christ, has been shut in people's faces so that they cannot have the knowledge that alone is adequate for their hearts' deepest needs, this door will be further hidden behind all sorts of "thieves and robbers."

Drawing by Mort Gerberg; ©1976. The New Yorker Magazine, Inc.

"The thief," said Jesus, "comes only to steal, to kill, to destroy; I have come that men may have life, and may have it in all its fullness" (John 10:10, NEB).

Sounds good! But how do we know it's true? And how do we know that all the "others" are really *false* gods? How do we really know that they are "thieves and robbers"?

18. "Life"—The Inward Proof

The "proof" that any person has for the validity of whatever he or she finally has faith in or believes or holds to be true lies finally in their heart. Even the faith that so-called rationalists have in reason is finally anchored in their hearts and not in their heads. "It is conviction that actually supports our reasons," Kierkegaard said, "not our reasons that support our conviction." [35]

The "proof" the Christian has for the truth of his or her faith is finally a subjective one also. "The heart has its reasons, which reason does not know," Pascal told us. "This, then, is faith: God felt by the heart, not by the reason." [36] And this feeling is sufficient for the Christian. It is far stronger than any intellectual objection or confirmation that the mind can possibly come up with, for this feeling is actually God himself in the person of his Holy Spirit. Real Christians are never contemptuous of reason or intellect. They know that this is one of God's greatest gifts to humankind. But neither do they worship reason, for their hearts have reason to believe that mere reason is not God.

Because the Christian faith is not ultimately proved by any visible reality, Christians often appear as fools to those who *do* place their faith in something visible—in wisdom or miracles, for instance. But the Christian faith quickly admits to being "foolishness" in this sense. St. Paul began his First Letter to the Corinthians by telling them frankly:

> He [God] chose to save those who have faith by the folly of the Gospel. Jews call for miracles, Greeks look for wisdom; but we proclaim Christ—yes, Christ nailed to the cross; and though this is a stumbling-block to Jews and folly to Greeks, yet to those who have heard his call, Jews and Greeks alike, he is the power of God and the wisdom of God (1 Cor. 1:21–24, NEB).

And so when anyone not hearing this inward call looks at a Christian, it works about like this:

"Now, there goes a happy man, the damn fool."

Drawing by Stan Hunt; ©1972. The New Yorker Magazine, Inc.

19. To *Really* Live Is to Obey, and to Obey Is to Live "That Men May Have Life"

And so the gospel is folly for not having any unquestionable visible proofs to back it up, no infallible miracles or wisdom. Yet everything the Christian does is done basically to convince the world that Jesus is the Christ. One cannot be a Christian without living for this primary purpose. "Only unbelief can wish to give the world something less than Christ" (Bonhoeffer).[37] Only lack of love can wish to give others something less than God, who is love. To be a Christian simply means to obey God. And for Christians, obedience to God ultimately means living for the single overruling purpose of also bringing—and keeping—others within this relationship to God through Christ. Indeed, it is only in being obedient in this way that Christians themselves learn what real "life" really is.

"Keeping the faith," then, always means living to give this greatest of all gifts to as many people as possible. All that the Christian does must finally be for "edification" or "to build up the Church," as St. Paul tells us over and over (1 Cor. 14:4, 5, 12, 26). Every Christian word and deed has this ultimate purpose behind it: "to win over as many as possible" (1 Cor. 9:19, NEB).

But such obedience does not mean slavish adherence to any absolute set of rules or system of laws. Christians, as St. Paul said, "Now . . . are discharged from the law, dead to that which held us captive, so that we serve not under the old written code but in the new life of the Spirit" (Rom. 7:6, RSV). This means that ultimately Christians are free to use "all means [to] save some" (1 Cor. 9:22, RSV). A good example at this point would be Bonhoeffer himself. Why did he try to kill Adolf Hitler? I have no doubt that it was in faithful obedience to Jesus Christ. Christians finally have only *one* absolute rule of conduct: " 'We are free to do anything,' you say. Yes, . . . but does everything help the building of the community?" (1 Cor. 10:23, NEB).

Christians know that no one can really be convinced that Jesus is the Christ without the inward witness of an invisible reality—the Holy Spirit, a reality that only comes into our hearts through obedience to God, and yet a reality no one can control. Therefore, Christians constantly pray to God that he will prove himself by entering people's hearts in the person of his Holy Spirit. This is why, for instance, Bonhoeffer could say that Christian love "will speak to

Christ about a brother more than to a brother about Christ." [38]

In the meantime, however, Christians must also do all they can in the realm of the visible to hasten the coming of this invisible reality. And therefore the Christian life, which is always a life of obedience, a life of evangelization, will necessarily take at least one of these four forms:

1. *Praying* for the truth to come;
2. *Preparing* the way for the truth to come;
3. *Proclaiming* what the truth is, in words, in symbolic action, or in the language of art;
4. *Proving* what the truth is.

Proving!? How can Christians "prove" what the truth is without compromising this truth? For if the truth alone is really the truth, what greater truth can act as its judge or prove it?

20. The New Testament's Two "Living Proofs"

In the New Testament there are only two "living proofs" that Christians are permitted to use to prove that Jesus is the Christ. We must remember that these two proofs are not proofs in the absolute sense. For if our confidence was finally placed in them, then the proof itself would actually be our God, rather than the God we thought we had proven. This is why Jesus consistently refused to give any "signs," or miracles, or proofs to those who demanded them.

These two proofs, then, should be understood more as evidence for or indications of the truth, rather than as once-and-for-all infallible proofs that turn faith in Christ into knowledge. But because these two proofs come so close to being Christ himself, when they are not actually identified with him, the Christian is allowed to use them as living, visible evidence for the truth of Christ.

As I've said, *everyone* has a faith in something, and this faith is always finally "proven" to its believer by reasons of the heart. But with these two types of *visible* evidence, the discussions between Christians and non-Christians move out of the stalemate of mere assertion of opposing heart-held faiths, and Christians are given "something to say to those whose pride is all in outward show and not in inward worth" (2 Cor. 5:12, NEB). The New Testament most often speaks of these two things to show for the truth of the Christian faith as its *fruits,* or *works.* And these fruits are *living* proofs because they consist, first, in the life of Jesus and, second, in the lives of his followers.

21. The Christian's "Life in All Its Fullness"

Jesus said that he came "that all men may have life, and may have it in all its fullness." By *fullness,* he meant the greatest fruition of every aspect of people's lives: their *spirits,* their *minds,* and their *bodies.* Or, to express these three another way: their *hearts,* their *heads,* and their *hands.* This is why Jesus could express the first commandment in terms of this three-part division of human life. The complete fullness of our lives is to be given to God, for only in this way will life in all its fullness then be given to us:

Hear, O Israel: the Lord your God is the only Lord; love the Lord your God . . . with all your heart, all your understanding, and all your strength (Mark 12:29, 33, NEB).

Those who try to live without giving their whole lives to Christ, said Bonhoeffer in a letter written in prison between Allied bomber attacks,

. . . miss the fullness of life and the wholeness of an independent existence; everything objective and subjective is dissolved for them into fragments. By contrast, Christianity puts us into many different dimensions of life at the same time; we make room in ourselves, to some extent, for God and the whole world. . . . We are anxious (—I was again interrupted just then by the [bomber raid] alert, and am now sitting out of doors enjoying the sun—) about our life, but at the same time we must think about things much more important to us than life itself. When the alert goes, for instance: as soon as we turn our minds from worrying about our own safety to the task of helping other people to keep calm, the situation is completely changed. . . . We have to get people out of their one-track minds; that is a kind of "preparation" for faith, or something that makes faith possible, although really its's only faith itself that can make possible a multi-dimensional life.[39]

But if faith in Christ actually gives his followers this "life in all its fullness," then this fullness should be visibly evident. The actual contents of any person's heart are of course a closed book to us. But fullness of heart should bear visible fruit through our heads and hands; through our understanding and strength; through active intelligence and intelligent action.

In this way false prophets as well as true prophets are to be recognized, according to Jesus. "I say you will recognize them by their fruits" (Matt. 7:20, NEB). And this means fullness of fruits of both hand and head—goodness and intelligence. "Christ not only makes people 'good'; he makes them strong, too," said Bonhoeffer.[40] For instance, if someone does a good job of showing love with action but not with understanding, this probably means that genuine truth and love is somewhat lacking in his or her heart. On the other hand, there are those who—to use St. Paul's words—"profess to acknowledge God, but deny him with their actions" (Titus 1:16, NEB).

©1969 United Feature Syndicate, Inc.

But Christians are called to prove the truth not only in the fullness of the types of fruit they yield—fruits of both hand and head—but also in terms of the quality of the yield. Clearly, as Jesus taught us, this yield must be extraordinary:

> What I tell you is this: Love your enemies and pray for your persecutors; only so can you be children of your heavenly Father, who makes his sun rise on good and bad alike, and sends the rain on the honest and the dishonest. If you love only those who love you, what reward can you expect? Surely the taxgatherers do as much as that. And if you greet only your brothers, what is there extraordinary about that? Even the heathen do as much. There must be no limit to your goodness, as your heavenly Father's goodness knows no bounds (Matt. 5:44−48, NEB).

The purpose of Christians' good works is certainly not to call attention to themselves or to give themselves something in which they can be proud, but solely to prove the truth of the Father. Not *pride* but *proof* motivates the Christian to do good works. For "God's wisdom is proved right by its results" (Matt. 11:19, NEB). And in this way the very house that Vonnegut & Twain can't fill with acorns, the same house that is now haunted by all sorts of "wicked spirits" represented by *The Exorcist,* this darkened house must be illuminated by the good works of Christians if it is to be illuminated at all. As Jesus said to his followers:

> You are the light of the world. A city set on a hill cannot be hid. Nor do men light a lamp and put it under a bushel, but on a stand, and it gives light to all in the house. Let your light so shine before men, that they may see your good works and give glory to your Father who is in heaven (Matt. 5:14−16, RSV).

Before a word is ever spoken, the good works or fruits of Christians' faith should point clearly to "the true vine," Christ, from whom these fruits ultimately come.

As the branch cannot bear fruit by itself, unless it abides in the vine, neither can you, unless you abide in me. I am the vine, you are the branches. He who abides in me, and I in him, he it is that bears much fruit, for apart from me you can do nothing. If a man does not abide in me, he is cast forth as a branch and withers; and the branches are gathered, thrown into the fire and burned. . . . By this my Father is glorified, that you bear much fruit, and so prove to be my disciples (John 15:4–6, 8, RSV).

This is why Christians have a right to be disturbed if what they *are* isn't clear from what they *do:*

Thus Jesus calls his followers "the salt of the earth" and "the light of the world" (Matt. 5:13, 14), not only because it is belief in him that alone can give the world meaning and preserve it from the destruction of meaninglessness and nihilism and idolatry, but also because the Christian's good works are to prove the divinity of Jesus to others. The Christians' witness through their *words* that Jesus is the Christ is to be proven by their *works*. Here's the way St. Paul could put it:

> Through our action such generosity will issue in thanksgiving to God, for as a piece of willing service this is not only a contribution towards the needs of God's people; more than that, it overflows in a flood of thanksgiving to God. For through the proof which this affords, many will give honour to God when they see how humbly you obey him and how faithfully you confess the gospel of Christ; and will thank him for your liberal contribution to their need and to the general good (2 Cor. 9:11–13, NEB).

22. "The Revision of Christian Apologetics"

To an "outsider" or to anyone with only a casual knowledge of the Bible and Christianity, faith and good works probably seem to belong together as obviously and naturally as man and woman. But in the history of Christian thinking, the correct relationship between faith and works has been just as controversial as the question about the correct relationship between man and woman. And, like man and woman, faith and good works haven't always done a good job of living together. Protestants especially have been alert to the way good works can be abused as a means of earning one's salvation, a view more traditionally championed by Roman Catholics. Indeed, this was one of the central disputes of the Protestant Reformation.

This is why it was something of a theological revolution when Protestant theologian Dietrich Bonhoeffer began to defend good works as one of the only two forms of "proof" or "defense" or "apologetic" legitimately available to the Christian faith.[41] For Bonhoeffer, good works were no longer to be played off against the adequacy of faith alone for salvation, as they had been for so long in classical Protestant thinking. Nor were they to be understood as something people could "freely" do to deserve their own salvation, as they were usually understood in Catholicism and generally in conservative Protestantism. As a means of self-salvation, good works are not only a basis for human pride, but they also become hardened into absolute systems of laws by the frantic need to save one's soul from "hell." Nor should good works, or "ethics," simply become a substitute for, rather than a living extension of, faith in Christ, as they usually do in liberal Protestantism.

Bonhoeffer, by contrast, saw Christian "righteous action among men,"[42] not as a means securing God's love and our own salvation, but as a means of proving that God's love and salvation of all people is *already* secure, as is known through belief in Jesus Christ.

It is implicit in the New Testament statement concerning the incarnation of God in Christ that all men are taken up, enclosed and borne within the body of Christ and that this is just what the congregation of the faithful are to make known to the world by their words and by their lives.

The following passage is from Bonhoeffer's "Outline for a Book." In "conclusions" that make up one of the concluding pages of Bonhoeffer's writings, here is the major portion of the final part of his outline:

Conclusions:
The church is the church only when it exists for others. To make a start, it should give away all its property to those in need. The clergy must live solely on the free-will offerings of their congregations, or possibly engage in some secular calling. The church must share in the secular problems of ordinary human life, not dominating, but helping and serving. It must tell men of every calling what it means to live in Christ,

to exist for others. In particular, our own church will have to take the field against the vices of *hubris,* power-worship, envy, and humbug, as the roots of all evil. It will have to speak of moderation, purity, trust, loyalty, constancy, patience, discipline, humility, contentment, and modesty. It must not under-estimate the importance of human example (which has its origin in the humanity of Jesus and is so important in Paul's teaching); it is not abstract argument, but example, that gives its word emphasis and power. (I hope to take up later this subject of "example" and its place in the New Testament; it is something that we have almost entirely forgotten.) Further: the . . . revision of Christian apologetics. . . .[43]

What a difference there is between the kind of "proof" or "apologetics" that Bonhoeffer here wants to offer for the truth of the Christian faith and the "proofs" that are being given us today—"proofs" that are so well represented by *The Exorcist.* The time of Dostoevsky's "Grand Inquisitor" is once more upon us.[44] For today we are again being given the "infallible" proofs that always go hand in hand with religion, or weak faith—*miracle, mystery,* and *authority:* the *authority* of a literal Bible or an infallible church or a new religious leader or an absolute set of laws; the *miracle* of new revelations and literal devils and real demons "and things that go bump in the night"; the *mystery* of superstition and magic and the occult and all their spooky manifestations.

As Bonhoeffer said, the "church will have to take the field against . . . humbug," which is what makes *The Exorcist* such a good place to start. *The Exorcist* is filled with religious humbug.[45]

In *The Exorcist* a priest who is "losing his faith" prays:

> *"Lord, give us a sign . . ." . . . Why not a sign? . . . Ah,*
> *my God, let me see You! Come in dreams!*
> *The yearning consumed him.*[46]

This yearning to prop up a weak faith with sight consumes a lot of people nowadays.

But presumably the priest is finally given his "sign": A literal devil takes up residence inside him. And so the priest then dies, fulfilled by "the devil" and happily believing in God!

As my seven-year-old daughter, Becky, would say: "Weird!"

Too bad this priest and William Peter Blatty, the wealthy author of *The Exorcist,* couldn't recall this often-repeated saying of Jesus: "An evil and adulterous generation seeks for a sign" (Matt. 12:39, 16:4; etc.). *The Exorcist* itself is a sign that ours is an evil and adulterous generation. For how did we decide that the evil in people is personified in the Bible? By "the devil." And what is the second way the devil tempted Christ in the wilderness? By asking him to perform a sign or miracle that would infallibly prove Christ's divinity. And how did Christ answer the devil's request? "Jesus answered him, 'Scripture says, . . . "You are not to put the Lord your God to the test" ' " (Matt. 4:5−7, NEB).

Sorry, old buddy. But the only way God's truth can ever be "tested" is with a higher truth. And where are you going to find that?

What a difference there is between what Bonhoeffer wanted to see the church do and what the church is actually doing. But this discrepancy goes a long way in explaining how we've come such a long way to something as obviously sick as *The Exorcist.*

*"I mean, it's hard to believe this is the same
country that produced 'Casablanca.' "*

Drawing by Wm. Hamilton; ©1974. The New Yorker Magazine, Inc.

But also in his "Conclusions," Bonhoeffer mentions the only other "living proof" for the truth of the Christian faith. This is our cue to leave the humbug of *The Exorcist* and turn to "the humanity of Jesus."

5

Jesus Christ Superstar—"I Don't Know How to Love Him," and I Don't Know if He Loves Me

The body of Jesus Christ, especially as it appears to us on the cross, shows to the eyes of faith the world in its sin, and how it is loved by God, no less than it shows the Church, as the congregation of those who acknowledge their sin and submit to the love of God.

—Dietrich Bonhoeffer, *Ethics* [1]

In relation to Jesus Christ they are all together (Romans 11:32) included in disobedience, the Gentiles in natural, the Jews in unnatural disobedience. . . . And in Christ God has also destined them all to participate in his mercy and so to be free. That is the knowledge in which those who are now obedient ought to regard those who are now disobedient: in this knowledge they ought to think of their future. That is how the Gospel answers those who despise it, for that is how Jesus Christ answers those who reject him. Any other answer could only be an unevangelical, an unchristian one.

—Karl Barth, *A Shorter Commentary on Romans* [2]

In Jesus God has said Yes and Amen to it all, and that Yes and Amen is the firm ground on which we stand.

In these turbulent times we repeatedly lose sight of what really makes life worth living. We think that, because this or that person is living, it makes sense for us to live too. But the truth is that if this earth was good enough for the man Jesus Christ, if such a man as Jesus lived, then, and only then, has life a meaning for us. If Jesus had not lived, then our life would be meaningless, in spite of all the

*other people whom we know and honour and love. Perhaps we
now sometimes forget the meaning and purpose of our profession.
But isn't this the simplest way of putting it? The unbiblical idea of
"meaning" is indeed only a translation of what the Bible calls
"promise."*

—Letter of Bonhoeffer to Fellow-Minister
Eberhard Bethge, *Letters and Papers from Prison* [3]

**Many people, in their sincere search for meaning, will
turn to Jesus to ask the meaning of life. If his gospel
is understood as being as truly and completely good
as it actually is, then there is a good chance that
these people will stay with Jesus and will believe in
him as Lord and Savior and as the Meaning-Giver of
life.**

**On the other hand, if the gospel, the good news of
Jesus, is understood to include the horrible bad news
of a literal hell, and thus in this way it is misunderstood, then once more this sad and ancient circle will
continue to move:**

**Atheism→Nihilism→Religion→Jesus→
Atheism→Nihilism→Religion→Jesus→
Atheism→ . . . . etc.**

1. The Return of "The Return of Religion"

In the last chapter we talked about the return of religion—how
"religion" in one creepy form after another will come creeping back
into our lives as soon as our lives have been made empty by godlessness and meaninglessness. And because none of these false
gods, or "pseudoabsolutes," is capable of ultimately satisfying us,
people will try on different religions as fast as Helga can try on hats.
"Whoever drinks from the springs of these pseudoabsolutes," says
German theologian Helmut Thielicke, "is forced to move on from
one fountain to the next." [4]

Therefore, there will come a point in many people's lives when "the return of religion" will itself be returned. Why? Simply because finally . . .

With Vonnegut & Twain, the Western world in general thought atheistic humanism was the answer. But atheistic humanism has degenerated into the nightmare of nihilism. Then, with William Peter Blatty, most of us were hoping that a little religion might bring some light into nihilsm's long, dark night. But religion has only turned out to be an odd can of weird worms. In this search for meaning—our search for something to believe in—we've gone about as far afield as we can go. But we've tried. Heaven knows we've tried.

©1977 United Feature Syndicate, Inc.

There is no denying us this quest for the answer or for an ultimate meaning; indeed this is the one great quest of our time. Precisely because of our lack of something to believe in, we, perhaps more than any other people in history, feel the truth behind this statement of Dostoevsky:

> The mystery of human existence lies not in just staying alive, but in finding something to live for. Without a concrete idea of what he is living for, man would refuse to live, would rather exterminate himself than remain on this earth, even if bread were scattered all around him.[5]

2. *"The* Answer"

Since almost everyone nowadays is looking for the answer, a word needs to be said about—and to—those folks who are scared out of their skins by the whole idea of *the* answer.

These folks can see that much of life's divisiveness and strife comes from people having different *"the* answers." Therefore, they want to do away with all *"the* answers" and boost something like tolerance for *all* answers. What they fail to see is that everyone, as

Dostoevsky says above, has to have a *"the* answer." No one wants to go on living without a *"the* answer." What the great liberal-minded fans of "tolerance" usually fail to see is that tolerance itself has become their *"the* answer." "No one can serve two masters" (Matt. 6:24, RSV), said Christ, the clear implication being that everyone does serve some one master. No one can live without a faith in some one thing as *"the* truth," and in this sense everyone is prejudiced about something. Even people who supposedly hate prejudice are finally prejudiced.

B.C.

B.C. by permission of Johnny Hart and Field Enterprises, Inc.

Therefore, the question is never whether or not we should have a *"the* answer," but which *"the* answer" should we have. Well, then, what about *"the* answer" of *unity* itself? If it is true that every person must serve some one god, wouldn't it be best if we all served something like the great god *unity*? At least then wouldn't we be getting rid of all the little narrow, provincial, special-interest gods, which are constantly at one another's throats?

The temptation to follow the great god of "unity at any price" has always been strong for humankind. But it is a paradox of history, as Dostoevsky makes so clear, that the idol of humankind's unity has itself been the most divisive idol of all. There is nothing humankind "is so anxious to do," said Dostoevsky,

> . . . as to find something to worship. But it must be something unquestionable, that all men can agree to worship communally. For the great concern of these miserable creatures is not that every individual should find something to worship that he personally considers worthy of worship, but that they

should find something in which they can *all* believe and which they can all worship *in common;* it is essential that it should be in common. And it is precisely that requirement of *shared* worship that has been the principal source of suffering for individual man and the human race since the beginning of history. In their efforts to impose universal worship, men have unsheathed their swords and killed one another. They have invented gods and challenged each other: "Discard your gods and worship mine or I will destroy both your gods and you!" And this is how it will be until the end of time, even after gods have vanished from the earth—for they are bound, in the end, to yield to idols.[6]

And even if it were possible for humankind to win such unity, Christ's question still remains: "What will a man gain by winning the whole world, at the cost of his true self?" (Matt. 16:26, NEB).

There is no doubt that apart from Christ even an outward or foced unity of humankind is extremely unlikely. As Dostoevsky pointed out, all such attempts at unity "are bound, in the end, to yield to idols." How does this come about? It works like this:

Today most of our desire for tolerance and unification of all humankind comes from the faith we once had in Christ. Obviously, the attitude of love and tolerance and peace and goodwill among men was an essential part of the ethical teachings of Jesus. All these teachings were given their authority, their definition, their unifying center, and their staying power by belief in the authority of the teacher, Jesus himself. But today we are trying to follow the "ideals" of the teachings without belief in the teacher. To those who now have only the ethical teaching of tolerance to believe in, the teacher himself looks like an intolerant authoritarian. Jesus, who claimed to be *"the* answer" or *"the* truth" (John 14:6), is now seen as an embarrassing stumbling block to those who tolerantly want to unify all peoples by seeing *"the* truth" in all the world's "truths." And for this reason, any *"the* truth" now tends to be relativized in favor of *"all* truths."

To what does this tolerant and magnanimous relativizing of all truths lead? It is an unintentional backward stumble into nihilism. For nihilism also says there is no *"the* truth." And placed in the situation of having no truth, all of us, as Dostoevsky says, "are bound, in the end, to yield to idols." Therefore, this is what will finally happen to people who fall prey to the great idols of tolerance and unity. They can expect first to become complete nihilists, renouncing *all* "truths," and then to end up as the very things they dreaded—the most narrowly intolerant and superstitious pagans.

3. Jesus Christ—The "Chrono-Synclastic Infundibulum"

As a Unitarian, Kurt Vonnegut has great love for the god of the unity of all "truths." But he also knows that this god leads to nihilism. In the introduction to his play *Happy Birthday, Wanda June,* Vonnegut says:

> I felt and I still feel that everybody is right, no matter what he says. I had, in fact, written a book about everybody's being right all the time, *The Sirens of Titan.* And I gave a name in that book to a mathematical point where all opinions, no matter how contradictory, harmonized. I called it a *chrono-synclastic infundibulum.*
>   I live in one.[7]

And what does Vonnegut mean by saying he lives in a "chrono-synclastic infundibulum"? Answer: As a nihilist, that's where he must live. For a nihilist, all truths are merely lies. "Everything is a lie," says Vonnegut.[8] When one is a nihilist, all truths are reduced to the mathematical point of *zero.* And at this point anyone is just as right as anyone else, "no matter what he says."

And so in this way Vonnegut finds unity in and tolerance for "all opinions, no matter how contradictory"—unity in nothingness. This is why Vonnegut can claim to be a Unitarian. "Unitarians don't believe in anything," he says.[9]

Some unity. .

As far as Jesus was concerned, true unity, real unity, lay only in him. Any other claim for unity is ultimately a force for disunity. From the point of view of the Christian faith, any unity we may try to achieve apart from Christ is only a false, weak, superficial, and illusory unity that will soon break apart into disastrous disunity. Only in Christ is there true unity of people with God and unity of people among and within themselves. "He who is not with me is against me," said Jesus, "and he who does not gather with me scatters" (Matt. 12:30, RSV).

But in this day of greater and greater emphasis on the values of tolerance and unity as ends in themselves, as "gods," Christians are under constant pressure to deny—or at least to water down—those aspects of their faith that separate them as Christians from others. In other words, they are under pressure to stop being Christ-ians. Unlike St. Paul, today's Christians are frequently "ashamed of the gospel" because it claims to be *the* saving power of God" (Rom. 1:16, NEB). A shallow humanitarianism causes any *"the* truth" (except of course *"the* truth" of a shallow humanitarianism) to appear as the most divisive intolerance and authoritarianism.

" 'Then the Lord spake unto them, saying'—
and I know this sounds a bit authoritarian . . ."

Drawing by Ed Fisher; ©1971. The New Yorker Magazine, Inc.

But Christians should remember that insofar as they really are "*Christ*-ians" (again, this is why they have *this* name and not another), there is no real unity anywhere apart from Jesus Christ. The reason so many people can today, with a straight face, call themselves "Christians" is that we feel this word can mean anything we want it to mean. But if the words *Christ* and *Christian* are not to become completely meaningless, then—by the simple logic of these two words themselves—they must mean at least this: that Jesus is the decisive, normative, authoritative, once-and-for-all revelation of God himself. This is precisely what the ancient Christian confession means: "Jesus is *the* Christ." The words *Jesus Christ* are a shorthand form of this confession. Therefore as *Christians,* if we do not at least believe that Jesus is the Christ, that he is "the way, and the truth, and the life" (John 14:6), that he is the only way to the truth in this life, then logically we're using the wrong word to describe ourselves. Said Bonhoeffer:

> Reality . . . in all its multiplicity is ultimately one; it is one in the incarnate God Jesus Christ, and precisely this is the testimony which the Church must give. . . .
> The will of God, which became manifest and was fulfilled in Jesus Christ embraces the whole of reality. One can gain access to this whole, without being torn asunder by its manifold variety, only in faith in Jesus Christ, "in whom dwelleth all the fulness of the Godhead bodily" (Col. 2:9 and 1:19), "by whom all things are reconciled, whether they be things in earth or things in heaven" (Col. 1:20), and whose body, the Church, is "the fulness of him that filleth all in all" (Eph. 1:23). Faith in this Jesus Christ is the sole fountain-head of all good.[10]

But how does it happen that faith in Jesus Christ "is the sole fountain-head of all good" in the world? This shouldn't be hard to understand, at least in principle. We all deal with single sources of power every day in our lives. Faith is simply the life that points to Christ and says, "Here is the sole power outlet for all good in the world!" Like this:

Drawing by Carl Rose; ©1969. The New Yorker Magazine, Inc.

Or, to use a similar illustration, Dostoevsky could point to this same single power source, this "essential point," in this way:

> The moral basis of society [in "the new humanity"] . . . not only gives no results, but cannot define itself, for it is lost in cloudy aspirations and ideals. Are there yet not enough facts to prove that society is not established thus, that these are not the paths leading to happiness, and that this is not, as has been believed till now, the source of happiness? But what

is its source then? So many volumes are written, and the essential point is ever missed: the Western World has lost Christ Jesus—and for this, and this alone, the Western world must perish.[11]

Kurt Vonnegut is just like the rest of us, at least in this: He yearns to know that one, single "point" at which "all things are reconciled." We all yearn to find—and to live in!—a "chrono-synclastic infundibulum." And the gospel, the good news, is precisely this: There really is a "chrono-synclastic infundibulum." But it is not Vonnegut's contradictory "chrono-synclastic infundibulum" of nihilism, in which he believingly denies all belief and hopes while denying all hope. Nor does it exist in the farthest reaches of the cosmos, as Vonnegut playfully suggests in *The Sirens of Titan*. No, this "chrono-synclastic infundibulum" exists right here on earth, right— as Bonhoeffer said—"in the midst of history":

This may sound very theoretical, and it is theoretical until it becomes clear at what point this attitude has its basis in reality so that it can itself become real. . . . there is a place at which God and the cosmic reality are reconciled, a place at which God and man have become one. That and that alone is what enables man to set his eyes upon God and upon the world at the same time. This place does not lie somewhere out beyond reality in the realm of ideas. It lies in the midst of history as a divine miracle. It lies in Jesus Christ, the Reconciler of the world. As an ideal the unity of simplicity and wisdom is doomed to failure, just as is any other attempt to hold one's own against reality. It is an impossible ideal and a very contradictory one. But if it is founded upon the reality of a world which is at one with Jesus Christ, the commandment of Jesus acquires reality and meaning. Whoever sees Jesus Christ does indeed see God and the world in one. He can henceforward no longer see God without the world or the world without God.[12]

This, then, is the real "chrono-synclastic infundibulum." I know because I live in it.
And it in me.

4. Jesus Christ Superstar—A Rock Passion Passionately Looking for "the Rock" of *The* Answer

To briefly review once more: Atheism leads to the harrowing experience of nihilism, and nihilism leads to the desperate search for meaning within a wilderness of the pagan and superstitious beliefs of "religion." But now, in this real hell of meaninglessness, many will look instinctively to Jesus to see if he can give them *"the* answer" to the meaning of life.

Jesus Christ Superstar is a beautiful contemporary representation of those who are truly "blessed" and "humble" in the biblical sense: Openly acknowledging they have no answer themselves, they seek out Jesus, in the hope's of finding *"the* answer" in him. This is why it is a complete misunderstanding to view *Jesus Christ Superstar* as an expression of anyone's answer. As an answer it is of course a distortion of the New Testament and leaves much to be desired. Therefore, most of *JCS*'s critics, who have understood it as an attempted "answer," have completely missed the point. Like these two gentlemen, for instance:

"Nothing like the book."

Drawing by Ed Arno ©1973, Saturday Review, Inc.

As a matter of fact, *JCS* is a *lot* "like the book," but this is not its primary purpose. Its purpose is, first, to put to Jesus the question we have today about the meaning of life, and, second, to put this question in our own *way* of putting it, to express it in our own idiom. This is precisely why *JCS* may turn out to be, as *Variety* called it, the "biggest all-media parlay in show-business history." [13] It is asking *our* question in *our* way of asking it. By contrast, the church generally continues to express itself in a language no one finds easy to understand. But this really doesn't matter much since it's not using this language to talk about anything people are very concerned about anyway. And therefore we could hardly expect these two, *JCS* and the church, to have the same kind of appeal to people:

"'Jesus Christ Superstar' has already grossed thirty million dollars. Just where did we go wrong?"

Drawing by Alan Dunn; ©1971. The New Yorker Magazine, Inc.

At Jesus' triumphal entry into Jerusalem, *JCS*'s lyricist Tim Rice, has the crowd sing:

Hosanna Heysanna Sanna Sanna Ho
Sanna Hey Sanna Ho Sanna
Hey JC, JC won't you smile at me?
Sanna Ho Sanna Hey Superstar

Then Rice has Caiaphas, the high priest of the Jews, say:

Tell the rabble to be quiet we anticipate a riot
This common crowd is much too loud
Tell the mob who sing your song that they are fools and they are
   wrong
They are a curse, they should disperse

According to Rice, Jesus replies to Caiaphas:

> Why waste your breath moaning at the crowd?
> Nothing can be done to stop the shouting
> If every tongue was still the noise would still continue
> The rocks and stones themselves would start to sing[14]

Here is the New Testament's description of the same event:

> And now, as he approached the descent from the Mount of
> Olives, the whole company of his disciples in their joy
> began to sing aloud the praises of God for all the things
> they had seen:

"Blessings on him who comes as king in
   the name of the Lord!
Peace in heaven, glory in the highest heaven!"

>   Some Pharisees who were in the crowd said to him,
> "Master, reprimand your disciples." He answered,
> "I tell you, if my disciples keep silence the
> stones will shout aloud" (Luke 19:37–40, NEB).

JCS is at least one instance in which this prophecy of Jesus has been fulfilled in our time. The disciples of Jesus are now largely keeping silent. The gospel of Jesus Christ is muted and rarely heard. But stones have shouted aloud—stones like Tim Rice and Andrew Lloyd Webber, the two young Englishmen who put together *JCS*. For Rice and Lloyd Webber make no claim of being disciples of Jesus. They consider themselves agnostics. They remain unconvinced of Jesus' divinity.[15] Yet what they have said about Jesus in *JCS*, even if it has been said unintentionally and indirectly, is a loud shout compared to the silence coming from Jesus' own disciples, the churches. What an amazing turn of events it is when disciples of Jesus must depend on agnostic "stones" just to . . .

"Oh, please! Two tickets for 'Jesus Christ Superstar,' just to help make Christmas Christmas."

Drawing by Alan Dunn; ©1971. The New Yorker Magazine, Inc.

Newsweek was right in saying that Rice's "choosing to pivot the 'plot' around the question of Jesus' divinity is a natural decision as a child of his time." [16] *JCS* bristles with questions directed to Jesus. The questioning begins at the Apostle's opening theme of "What's the buzz? Tell me what's happening," and never lets up until the final scene, in which all of Judas' many questions end with the refrain, "Don't you get me wrong—I only want to know," and the choir repeatedly asks:

> Jesus Christ Jesus Christ
> Who are you? What have you sacrificed?
> Jesus Christ Superstar
> Do you think you're what they say you are?

The two young creators of *JCS* are no doubt typical of multitudes of people in our time: They *sincerely* "only want to know." And in asking this question with this kind of intensity, they have come closer to the answer than those who attempt to find an answer without any insight into—or serious regard for—the question. The sincerity and genuineness of their question is reflected in the way they have unconsciously been drawn to the precise place where the answer is given. The events of *JCS* center around the last seven days of Jesus' life, culminating in the crucifixion. And it is precisely at this point—the crucifixion—that the biblical writers obviously saw God's own answer to all peoples' ultimate questions most clearly expressed. The biblical writers would not have been at all surprised with *JCS*'s fascination with the way Jesus died, for Jesus had told them, " 'And I shall draw all men to myself, when I am lifted up from the earth.' This he said to indicate the kind of death he was to die" (John 12:32–33, NEB).

Thus *JCS* is a marvelous musical passion of Christ. It is a *passion* because, like all passions of church music, it includes no resurrection but concentrates solely on Christ's crucifixion and the events leading to it. Indeed, *Time* magazine could say that *JCS* "rivals the *St. John* and *St. Matthew Passions* of Bach—in ambition and scope if not in piety or musical exultation." [17] And I call *JCS marvelous* because, as a modern expression of our own deepest needs, it fully *shares* in Christ's passion. It depicts *our* passion too. It looks to Christ just as most people honestly see him today, and it asks our own passionate and sincerely desperate question: "What's it all about?"

5. Jesus Christ Superstar & Vonnegut & Us—"I Don't Know How to Love Him"

In *Slaughterhouse-Five,* which Vonnegut considers the "bloom" of "whatever flower I was supposed to be," [18] he continually circles around the crucifixion of Jesus, trying to figure out what to make of it. The obvious crucifixion of Vonnegut's Billy Pilgrim and the crucifixion of Jesus stand like two separate crosses in *Slaughterhouse-Five,* and Vonnegut is constantly drawing parallels between them.

But as to what these connections mean, Vonnegut is never able to decide. He can finally only stand in amazed perplexity between these two crosses and say, in his own way, "I only want to know."

As a matter of fact, there is plenty of evidence that Vonnegut regards *Slaughterhouse-Five* as something of a "fifth gospel," a gospel in which he desperately tries to make sense of the other four. *Slaughterhouse-Five* is like the Kilgore Trout story it describes, *The Gospel from Outer Space,* in which a "visitor from outer space made a serious study of Christianity, to learn, if he could, why Christians found it so easy to be cruel." [19] For this investigation, like *JCS*, centers around the crucifixion.

Therefore it would seem that *JCS* and Vonnegut are both typical of today's men and women in that they "only want to know." They are irresistibly attracted to Jesus and his cross by their deep and basic need to find meaning in life; yet the response of most of these people as they look upon Jesus is, in the words of *JCS:* "I don't know how to love him." Like Jesus' disciples in *JCS*, they have been drawn close to Jesus and yet can still say, "Tell me what's happening." And as a result of the disciples' not knowing, hell—the real hell, the hell of not knowing "what's happening"—spreads to all around them.

"I'd just like to know what in hell is happening, that's all! I'd like to know what in hell is happening! Do you know what in hell is happening?"

Drawing by Booth; ©1974. The New Yorker Magazine, Inc.

For this reason, the empty cross at the conclusion of *JCS* should not be an offense to Christians because it is not quickly followed by a resurrection "in the final reel." But it should be a judgment on them because they have not made clear to others the meaning of that cross. The cross at the conclusion of *JCS* and the cross of Jesus in *Slaughterhouse-Five* stand like giant question marks, representing today's honest inquirers who have asked and "only want to know," and yet still haven't gotten the message. Thus the problem is not in the question being asked, but in the answer being given.

Today's generation continues to be crucified on a question mark.

6. Jesus—The Unique Visible Fruit of the Cross

The Christian faith says that only this man, Jesus, is the way to the truth that gives us the life—the real life that also assures Christians of the final "great joy which will come to all the people" (Luke 2:10, RSV). This is the picture of the Christian message that Bonhoeffer calls "simple and obvious." It says in effect: "All people are 'saved.' Finally there is nothing that will separate anyone from God's love." Our reply is: "Well, that's an awful nice promise for God to make, and all, and I wish I could believe it, but how do I know it's ture?"

And God's reply is: "Take my Word for it."

This—no more but also no less than this—is precisely what God has given us to "prove" that his promise is true: his own Word, Jesus Christ. In only this man, says the Christian faith, can anyone know this promise is really true—the promise God has made to everyone. "These two things must be carefully considered," said Karl Barth, "the uniqueness of Christ and his significance for the whole world, the concentration and the universality of grace. It is *here* that grace is found, in Jesus Christ: but it is grace intended for the whole world, since it is grace." [20]

Christians do not finally worship anything *about* Jesus; they worship Jesus himself as the Christ. They worship this particular, historical, flesh-and-blood Jewish man. Jesus does not finally represent anything else for Christians. He is the thing itself, the actual object of worship. This is why Jesus—and not something about Jesus—is called "the Christ," and this is why Christians are called "Christians."

But Jesus is not simply a mathematical point. He is not merely the point or place where the line of the divine vertical has crossed the line of the historical horizontal. For there are things *about* Jesus that draw people to this single place where God is to be found, the single point of Jesus himself. These "things," which are seen most clearly in the crucifixion of Jesus, make Jesus the unique visible fruit of the cross. The Christian faith says that while we live it is only in this man that God can be found and known. And it is this "only" and this "man" that constitute the uniqueness and the visible humanity of Jesus and attract us to him.

7. The Humanity of Jesus—Only This *Man*

"The humanity of Jesus" was for Bonhoeffer the second and only other legitimate "proof" that Jesus is the Christ. The fruits of Christians' lives should provide one sort of proof or evidence; Jesus' own life is the single fruit that provides the other. The church, as Bonhoeffer has told us, "must not under-estimate the importance of human example (which has its origin in the humanity of Jesus and is so important in Paul's teaching); it is not abstract argument, but example, that gives its word emphasis and power." [21] The Bible agrees: "It is by this that we know what love is: that Christ laid down his life for us. And we in our turn are bound to lay down our lives for our brothers" (1 John 3:16, NEB).

The fullness of the life of Jesus, as it is presented in the New Testament, appeals fully to our lives. Every aspect of his life—his hands, head, and heart—appeals to the same aspects of our lives. Through his words and symbolic actions he not only tells and shows us *what* is true, but he also proves *that* this truth is true by the power, beauty, love, and goodness of a life lived totally on the basis of this truth. The life of Jesus is the single visible fruit that is finally left hanging from "the tree" (see 1 Pet. 2:24) of the cross, and this fruit "draws all men to himself." Like the fruit that hung from "the tree of the knowledge of good and evil" in the Garden of Eden, a fruit we were not to eat, the life of Jesus, the fruit of the cross, appeals to us in much the same way: "The woman saw that the tree was good for food, and that it was a delight to the eyes, and that the tree was desired to make one wise" (Gen. 3:6, RSV).

This appeal of the life of Jesus has certainly not been lost on the creators of *JCS* or on Kurt Vonnegut. It is this very appeal of Jesus' humanity that draws them close to the cross of Jesus in search for life's meaning. The creators of *JCS* leave the supernatural divinity of Jesus, which contains the answer to life's meaning, an open question, but in the meantime they are attracted by Jesus' life, which for them makes Jesus a "Superstar." And they continue to ask:

> Jesus Christ Superstar
> Do you think you're what they say you are?

Likewise Vonnegut, in *Slaughterhouse-Five,* can speak of "all the lovely and puzzling things [Jesus] said in the . . . Gospels." [22]

Even on the strongest atheist, even on those who find much of what Jesus said puzzling or even offensive, the life of Jesus will always act like a strong magnet. For the visible loveliness of the fruit of the cross, the self-giving life of Jesus, has this ultimate purpose behind it: to point to, to prove, and to draw us to the way itself—the incarnate God, Jesus. This is why the New Testament at first emphasizes the life of Jesus and only later or secondarily begins to concentrate on the meaning of that life. First the emphasis on what he *did,* then the emphasis on who he *was:*

> If I am not acting as my Father would, do not believe me. But if I am, accept the evidence of my deeds, even if you do not believe me, so that you may recognize and know that the Father is in me, and I in the Father (John 10:37–38, NEB).

8. Admiration of This Man vs. Belief in Him

"Believe me when I say that I am in the Father and the Father in me; or else accept the evidence of the deeds themselves" (John 14:11, NEB). For mere admiration of Jesus' life and deeds, and belief in him as the Christ—the incarnation of God—are two infinitely different things.

In a poem composed for Christmas, 1969, Vonnegut wrote:

> I will dream of a baby,
> A boy and a man,
> Who taught simple kindness;
> I'll learn it if I can.
> I'm sorry they killed you,
> I'm glad you were born.
> I'll be a mild Christian
> On mild Christmas morn.[23]

But Vonnegut is admittedly no believer. He is only an admirer of Jesus' life and moral teachings. Similarly, the creators of *JCS* "consider Christ a fascinating man, a very remarkable man, a very good man."[24] They admire the *good* in this man but doubt that *God* was in him. Like Vonnegut, they are admirers without being followers. For Rice, Lloyd Webber, and Vonnegut, Jesus is merely a representative of "love" or "good works," which they believe are human possibilities quite apart from belief in God and/or Christ. But in the Bible, no one does good work unless this work is God's work. In the Bible there is no good apart from God. God "alone is good," said Jesus (Matt. 19:17, NEB). But then the Bible goes even further in sharpening its definition of *good work*. For no one does *God's work* unless it is work done in obedience to Jesus *as the Christ*.

> Then they said to him, "What must we do, to be doing the works of God?" Jesus answered them, "This is the work of God, that you believe in him whom he has sent" (John 6:28–29, RSV).

All this may sound heartless, abstract, and difficult to understand, but even an atheist like Dostoevsky's Stavrogin can see that, just as the fruits cannot exist without the vine, real good cannot exist without the real God:

> Many people think that it is enough to believe in Christ's moral teaching, in order to be a Christian. It isn't Christ's morality, or his teaching, that will save the world, but faith, and nothing else, faith in the fact that the word was made flesh. . . . Only if we have such faith do we attain the right worship,

that ecstasy which, more than anything else, ties us to him immediately and which has the power to keep man from going
astray. With anything short of such ecstasy, mankind would
have perhaps inevitably gone astray, falling into heresy to
begin with, and later into godlessness, then into amorality,
and finally into atheism and troglodytism; and it would have
vanished, and decayed.[25]

Troglodytism is "cave-dwelling"—the kind of brutish living we see
at the conclusion of Vonnegut's *Slapstick,* his novel of the future in
which humankind is "vanishing and decaying."

From faith in Jesus as "the real vine" (John 15:1, NEB), come the
rich, living fruits of a strong and real social ethic. But when Jesus is
no longer worshiped as the Christ and we attempt to replace faith in
him with only the fruits of faith, then faith's ethical fruits will also
disappear. "No branch can bear fruit by itself, but only if it remains
united with the vine; no more can you bear fruit, unless you remain
united with me. . . . for apart from me you can do nothing" (John
15:4–5, NEB).

In the world of morality and social ethics, losing Jesus as the
Christ is like losing the fuse box. If this goes, the whole system goes.
For Jesus Christ alone is that single, historical point through which
all the knowledge of God's love flows to all the people.

"You mean nobody knows where they put the fuse box?"

Drawing by Joseph Farris ©1971, Saturday Review, Inc.

9. The Uniqueness of Jesus—*Only* This Man

The New Testament points to Jesus and says, "There is salvation in no one else" (Acts 4:12, RSV). Such exclusivism and uniqueness offend only those self-contradictory individuals who specifically and dogmatically hold out for a nonspecific and undogmatic unity of humankind. These absent-minded folks forget that by finding "*the* answer" in something all-inclusive and universal they have nevertheless found "*the* answer," which ultimately is itself dogmatic and exclusive.

This is why narrow-minded conservatives, who think they have *the* answer, are especially annoying to "broad-minded" liberals, who, of course, really do have it.

But most people are clearer thinking than this and are quite aware of their personal necessity and desire to find the unity of *the* answer in some one unique thing. They are not offended by Jesus' claim to be unique. In fact, just because of all peoples' basic need for "*the* answer," this claim will always appeal to most people. This is also why *any* clear and simple "*the* answer" to life—regardless of what it is—will always find its followers.

Even broad-minded folks like Kurt Vonnegut, who have tried to live with *the* answer that there is no "*the* answer," can't help wishing that there was a more positive "*the* answer" to be found. The futile search of Vonnegut's alter ego, Billy Pilgrim, including his escapist flights of fantasy to the planet Tralfamadore, is summarized by the search of Dwayne Hoover in *Breakfast of Champions:*

"I've lost my way," said Dwayne. "I need somebody to take me by the hand and lead me out of the woods."

"You're tired," she said. "Why wouldn't you be tired? You work so hard. I feel sorry for men, they work so hard. You want to sleep for a while?"

"I can't sleep," said Dwayne, "until I get some answers."

"You want to go to a doctor?" said Francine.

"I don't want to hear the kinds of things doctors say," said Dwayne. "I want to talk to somebody brand new. Francine," he said, and he dug his fingers into her soft arm, "I want to hear new things from new people. I've heard everything anybody in Midland City ever said, ever *will* say. It's got to be somebody new."

"Like who?" said Francine.

"I don't know," said Dwayne. "Somebody from Mars, maybe."

"We could go to some other city," said Francine.

"They're all like here. They're all the same," said Dwayne.[26]

Vonnegut elsewhere mentions an awful automobile driver he once heard of, a woman "who never took her eyes off her radiator ornament." "And," says Vonnegut,

looking at one day's news or a few days' news or a few years' news is a lot like staring at the radiator ornament of a Stutz Bearcat, it seems to me. Which is why so many of us would love to have a visitor from another planet, who might have a larger view of our day-to-day enterprises, who might be able to give us some clue as to what is really going on.[27]

The Bible, sees Jesus as this same type of wholly unique "visitor," which is a strong reason why many of us are attracted to him.

Most of us come around to the opinion that if there is ever going to be any radical improvement in our lives it's finally going to have to come from somewhere totally outside ourselves. The Bible agrees. It says our only real improvement finally comes, not from ourselves or from one another, but only from God, who in the Old Testament is "One" and "Totally Other." And when in The New Testament this "One Totally Other God" visited the world and "became flesh" like us (John 1:14), he became *one* "totally same" but nevertheless "totally other" human being. The advice the Bible gives to all of us mere mortals, is the same advice Ira here gives to Francine. For among all of us "selves," only Jesus is in the biblical sense really "somebody else":

MISS PEACH by Mell Lazarus. Courtesy of Mell Lazarus and Field Newspaper Syndicate.

In the film of *JCS*, Mary Magdalene, the apostles, and the crowd sing: "I'd been living to see you/Dying to see you . . ." This is the way most of us feel. We are living—even dying—to see that single down-to-earth but unique you, that radically different somebody else, who can really make an improvement in our lives.

10. The Cross—The Necessary Way to *This Particular* Man

But if most people are so attracted to Jesus by his visible manhood and his claim of uniqueness, then why doesn't he have more believers, rather than multitudes of mere admirers? If most of us, like the admirers of Jesus in *JCS*, are "living to see you/Dying to see you," then what goes wrong? What causes most of his fans to turn cold at the crucial moment—the moment of the cross when only believers in him will still follow him? When Jesus nears the time of his crucifixion in *JCS,* his admirers sing:

> I'd been living to see you
> Dying to see you but it shouldn't be like this
> This was unexpected
> What do I do now?
> Could we start again please

The first and basic reason for our last-minute betrayal of Jesus is this: Belief in the crucified Jesus always requires one more cross— our own. The crucifixion of Jesus makes *our* crucifixion necessary before we can become his followers. And here's why:

Jesus assumed two things about all of us: First, we all need to worship the one true God, who is found only in and through himself, the man Jesus. Second, no mere mortal originates in life worshiping this true God; but all of us originally worship false gods. This means that both Jesus and his admirers must be stripped and crucified before genuine faith can take place. We idolators must be stripped and crucified in the utter loss of all our false, original gods. Jesus must be stipped and crucified and "made nothing" (Phil. 2:7, NEB) in order to divest himself of anything we might want to invest him with that we could then worship, rather than worshiping this particular flesh-and-blood man, Jesus himself.

For to worship something *about* Jesus is not to worship *Jesus,* who is himself the incarnation of God, the Word made flesh. When our false gods finally fail us, and in this sense leave us crucified, Jesus does not then supply us with other false gods, with something about himself that we can then follow. Instead, he is also crucified and is thereby finally stripped of everything about him that might divert us from worshipping him alone.

In the crucifixion, Jesus finally stripped himself of all worldy success and power and any proofs of a visible nature. And in doing so he also "crucified" his disciples by stripping them of their reliance on these false gods. And note that it wasn't until then that the disciples really began to understand Jesus and to rely solely on him. *JCS* is completely true to the New Testament when Jesus sings to Simon Zealotes and to the crowd:

> Neither you Simon, nor the fifty thousand
> Nor the Romans, nor the Jews, nor Judas nor the Twelve,

> Nor the Priests, nor the Scribes
> Nor doomed Jerusalem itself,
> Understand what power is . . .
> Understand at all . . . understand at all.

True power can come to us only when these two wires are brought together, wires that have been stripped (crucified) of their insulation: In the body of Christ on the cross, we are brought face-to-face with the literally naked object of the Christian's faith; but unless we are also stripped (crucified) of our insulating false gods, the power-producing contact can never occur. God's "power is made perfect in weakness" (2 Cor. 12:9, RSV). And this means Jesus' "weakness" *and* our own.

This is why "Christ nailed to the cross . . . is a stumbling-block to Jews and folly to Greeks" (1 Cor. 1:23, NEB). "To conquer death," sings Jesus in *JCS,* "you only have to die." This is true, and it is also why Kierkegaard said, "Between man and truth lies mortification—you can see why we are all more or less afraid." [28]

Jesus is *the* way to *the* truth of God while we live. To help convince us of this, his claim of uniqueness is certainly charming and his visible humanity is undeniably attractive. But the way to Jesus is the way of the cross: "Whoever does not bear his own cross and come after me, cannot be my disciple" (Luke 14:27, RSV). It is this way of his, the way of the cross, that irritates everyone and drives them from him in disgust. "When Christ calls a man," said Bonhoeffer, "he bids him come and die." [29] This is why there will always be crowds of people—and Vonnegut and the creators of *JCS* are good examples of these people—running back and forth between Jesus and an empty horizon.

MISS PEACH

MISS PEACH by Mell Lazarus. Courtesy of Mell Lazarus and Field Newspaper Syndicate.

11. Only This Man—The Single Flesh-and-Blood Man Who Must Be *Eaten*

Jesus looked at the people of his day and said, "The harvest is plentiful" (Matt. 9:37). The situation is much the same today. The land is filled with people who are emotionally and intellectually ripe for hearing and understanding the good news of the Christian message. Today most of us are sincerely and desperately looking for something to believe in. This means that the false gods, which all of us originally had confidence in, have been shaken all the way down to their clay feet. The inadequacy of these gods for fulfilling our deepest emotional needs is becoming more and more apparent to more and more people.

In this sense, then, the harvest is indeed plentiful with people who have already met the New Testament's first precondition for understanding and believing in God. They have already "died" to the world's false gods. They have already been "stripped" and "crucified" and have experienced what the New Testament means by *hell*. For hell, we remember—the *real* hell—comes when our false gods go.

So now these people are sincerely looking for the one, true God who will not fail them, and therefore the cross is no longer a "stumbling-block" for them. It is instead the pathway they are already on—this only pathway to Christ, the way of the cross, the cross of their own emotional deaths. However, second and third major stumbling blocks still lie in the modern pilgrim's pathway to belief in Jesus as the Christ.

The second of these obstacles also concerns the cross, for on "the tree" of the cross there fianally hangs a single fruit—Jesus of Nazareth. We have said that this fruit is beautiful and that it excites our admiration, but we have also said that mere admiration of this fruit is not enough. No, this fruit must be eaten!

This single fruit on the tree of the cross corresponds figuratively to the fruit on "the tree of the knowledge of good and evil" in the Garden of Eden. The Old Testament story about this tree is not meant to explain how our situation actually came to be. Rather it intends to tell us *what* our situation is—that none of us origin-ate in life worshiping God. Instead, we all origin-ate worshiping *false* gods, and in this sense all of us are "originally sinners." The Bible teaches that our problem is fundamentally at our "starting point." Therefore when the New Testament tells us we must "turn to Christ," it is really telling us that we must "start again please." As soon as we reach the end of the empty, lonely way on which we all originally embark, this message of the Bible startles us in its clarity:

RETURN TO
STARTING POINT

Drawing by Chas. Addams; ©1974. The New Yorker Magazine, Inc.

If we follow the Bible in answering the question "What is love?" says Bonhoeffer, we learn that "Love is the reconciliation of man with God in Jesus Christ. The disunion of men with God, with the world and with themselves, is at an end. *Man's origin is given back to him.*" [30]

This is why the New Testament calls Christ "the last Adam" (1 Cor. 15:45, RSV), and why the fruit eaten by the first Adam can be seen as "a type of the one who was to come" (Rom. 5:14 RSV)—namely, Jesus, the single fruit on the tree of the cross. Just as we were then commanded not to eat of that first tree, we now—if our old problem is to be remedied—must eat the fruit of this new tree, the tree of the cross.

The fruits of the lives of Christ's followers are meant to be strong outward indications of the truth of Christ. The beautiful and attractive fruit of the life of Christ himself is even stronger visible evidence. But like the proof of the well-known pudding, the final proof that Jesus is the Christ is in the eating. It is an inward or subjective proof. Jesus is the single fruit of the cross that we must *swallow*. "So Jesus said to them, 'Truly, truly, I say to you, unless you eat the flesh of the Son of man and drink his blood, you have no life in you' " (John 6:53, RSV).

What does it mean in practical terms to eat the flesh of Jesus and to drink his blood? It means to *obey* this man as *the* Christ, as *the* truth. *To swallow him means to follow him.* It is not until we actually obey Jesus as the Christ that we can be inwardly persuaded that he is indeed *the* truth and *the* Christ. Jesus must become our Lord in the sense of being our "Lord and Master" before we can also know him as "Lord and Savior." "True knowledge of God is born out of obedience," said Calvin.[31] Or, as Jesus himself put it:

> The teaching that I give is not my own; it is the teaching of him who sent me. Whoever has the will to do the will of God shall know whether my teaching comes from him or is merely my own (John, 7:16−17, NEB).

But the young creators of *JCS,* like so many people today, give no indication of understanding this. For them, Jesus must first prove himself through some kind of convincing demonstration. Only then will they believe and obey. In this way Jesus must first obey them. As King Herod sings to Jesus in *JCS:*

> Prove to me that you're divine—change my water into wine
> That's all you need to do then I'll know it's all true
> C'mon King of the Jews

In this same way, we modern skeptics make ourselves the judges of God whenever we demand that he prove himself to us:

So if you are the Christ yes the great Jesus Christ
Prove to me that you're no fool—walk across my swimming pool
If you can do that for me then I'll let you go free
C'mon King of the Jews

But the God of the Bible approaches our demands for proofs from exactly the opposite direction of what we naturally want or expect: He demands that we prove ourselves to him. *He* remains the judge. He does not let us lay down the conditions for proving him ("If you can do that for me . . ."); but he meets us with his own "If you . . ." designed to prove us. He does not allow us to promise him freedom if he will obey us (". . . . then I'll let you go free"); but instead he promises to make us free if we obey him.

The correct relationship to God does not begin with the knowledge of his truth and the experience of his freedom, followed by our obedience. No, it's the other way around: *first* our obedience, *then* knowledge and freedom.

Jesus then said . . . "If you continue in my word, you are truly my disciples, and you will know the truth, and the truth will make you free. . . . Truly, truly, I say to you, every one who commits sin is a slave to sin. . . . So if the Son makes you free, you will be free indeed" (John 8:31–32, 34, 36, RSV).

Only if we first obey, does Jesus then give us the deep and constant joy—the Holy Spirit—which alone is the inward satisfaction, proof, freedom, and rest for which our hearts hunger.

Come to me, all who labor and are heavy laden, and I will give you rest. Take my yoke upon you, and learn from me; for I am gentle and lowly in heart, and you will find rest for your souls. For my yoke is easy, and my burden is light (Matt. 11:28–30), RSV).

Exactly as "the proof of the pudding is in the eating," so the final "proof" for the Christian faith is also an inward one that involves "eating." We must eat the single fruit that hangs from the tree of the cross—Jesus. For to eat him also means taking into ourselves something we don't already have, something from outside. Something that isn't part of our horrible ordinary natures has got to "get into us"—as we see in this little Christmas story from "Hägar the Horrible":

©King Features Syndicate, Inc. 1973.

This *something* that must get into us is belief that *only this man* is the Christ. And belief in Jesus always means obedience to him as the Christ. Only then will we know "*the* life," the Holy Spirit of Christ, who alone fulfills us and frees us from the spiritual emptiness of sin.

What tremendous irony there often is between the ways we honestly express our deepest needs and how the Bible describes the ways Jesus meets these needs. For example, the mere admirers of Jesus in *JCS* want to "start again please," and it is only in following Jesus as the Christ that a radically new start can be made. In *Player Piano*, Vonnegut talks about all the new religions that people are nowadays looking to for help: "Harmless magic; good old-fashioned bunkum," he calls them. "But that sort of business wears thin pretty quick. . . . The . . . turnover is terrific." "But someday," Vonnegut goes on to say, "someone is going to give them something to sink their teeth in." [32]

How accurately you have put it, Kurt! For precisely *here* is something they can "sink their teeth in":

My flesh is real food; my blood is real drink. Whoever eats my flesh and drinks my blood dwells continually in me and I dwell in him. As the living Father sent me, and I live because of the

Father, so he who eats me shall live because of me (John 6:55–57, NEB).

12. "Hell"—The Great Deterrent (to Belief in Christ)

The third and most formidable obstacle to people's belief in Christ is the idea of a literal hell—"the monstrous misunderstanding." Just as God's "last enemy . . . is death" (1 Cor. 15:26, RSV), the last enemy of belief in God and/or Christ is an "eternal death for the wicked." For if there really is such an "eternal death," then God is finally either one of two types of "Monster Gods": He is either the weak God of unlimited love but limited power, or else he is the cruel God of unlimited power but limited love.

On the one hand, God is the poor, weak, pitiful God who, in his unlimited "love," has chosen to limit his own power in order to give people "free will." Out of his great love, God reduces himself to an innocent bystander. He must now stand by and watch helplessly as his own dear children freely damn themselves. But this picture of God (and that's all it is) makes no sense. Why, for instance, would any person who was really free, and hence really knew what he or she was doing, "freely" damn himself or herself for all eternity?

To attribute free will to people is to attribute divinity to them, and of course this explains why the idea of free will appeals to us so much. With free will we become our *own* "Lords and Saviors." We become our own Lords in that we create and control our own destinies. We become our own Saviors in that we save ourselves from sin.

But didn't Christ say on the cross, as Tim Rice translates it in *JCS:* "Father forgive them—they don't know what they're doing" (see Luke 23:34)? That hardly sounds like we're free, but it does sound like we're forgiven!

Otherwise Christ should have said: "Father, damn them to hell. For they have free will, and they know damned well what they're doing!"

Furthermore, if God really is "our Father," as Christ calls him, should we expect any less from him than we would from a human father? According to the Bible we should always expect much better treatment from our "heavenly Father" than from any earthly father (see Matt. 7:11). Then how can it make sense that our Father in heaven, out of his great love, allows us to freely damn ourselves, especially if he knows beforehand that this is what we are going to do?

This would be like a father telling his three-year-old child not to go into the street and then doing nothing more and simply allowing his child to be struck and killed by a car when the child does wander into the street. Certainly most earthly fathers will use all their available powers to prevent the destruction of their children, and certainly God has infinitely more power and foreknowledge in relation to his children than any earthly father has in relation to his. Therefore, it is only a cruel, barbaric Monster God—crueler than even the cruelest human father—who does not use his infinite power to save his children, but out of his great "love" only says: "It was the little fool's own fault. I told her to obey me. Too bad she wouldn't listen."

Mark Twain's *What Is Man?* is a wide-ranging dialogue between an "Old Man" (O.M.) and a "Young Man" (Y.M.). Part of their discussion goes like this:

O.M. Do you really believe that God is all-powerful?

Y.M. I do.

O.M. And do you believe that He would really like to see all men saved?

Y.M. I know it.

O.M. Then why doesn't He save them?

Y.M. He cannot save the disobedient.

O.M. Is His all-powerful power limited, then?

Y.M. By principle, yes. He cannot break His own decrees.

O.M. He could *annul* the decrees?

Y.M. Of course.

O.M. That would save the human race from a frightful fate. Why, do you suppose, doesn't He do it?

Y.M. It would not be right.

O.M. No, only cheaply charitable. I suppose you would do it if you could?

Y.M. But I am not God.
O.M. You paid yourself that compliment before.[33]

Our spirits are free from the spiritual death of a living hell, which results from idolatry, only when we participate consciously and willingly in the will of God. But we are never free to create these wills ourselves—either his will or our own. Our obedience to God is always brought about by the emotional necessity that God, the creator, himself imposes on us. Or, to use biblical terminology, our obedience is finally not any "doing" or "work" of our own. It is created only by God's "grace": "For by grace you have been saved through faith; and this is not your own doing, it is the gift of God— not because of works, lest any man should boast" (Eph. 2:8–9, RSV). The chimera of a literal hell is most often defended by a literal reading of the Bible, and then it is made to seem less cruel by the *unbiblical* notion of people's free will. The Bible and science and our own experience deny the fable of free will at every turn.

On the other hand, we may suppose that God is the mysterious God of unlimited power but apparently limited love. This God, for reasons known only to himself, predestines the great majority of people, through no fault of their own, to eternal damnation, while saving only a chosen few. But history has already shown us that no one can live very long with this kind of Monster God. Thus, the teaching of a literal hell makes a mockery of a God who is supposedly all-loving or all-powerful or both.

Even when the people of today have died to their false, original gods and thus are ripe for hearing the really good news of the Christian gospel, even when they are quite willing to obey, they still will not be seriously inclined to listen to the bad news of either of the above Monster Gods with their literal hell.

For who wants to jump out of the frying pan into the possibility of a much worse fire? Who wants to believe this gospel of "hell" when, even as he or she struggles to live by it, he or she will still remain ultimately uncertain about his or her final destiny? It is far easier simply to chuck the Monster God, his "hell," his Christ, and the whole miserable "gospel" of bad news. It's far easier to look upon the gospel of a literal hell as simply one of humanity's childhood diseases. And this is precisely what it is. Unfortunately, however, we still haven't outgrown it.

HAGAR THE HORRIBLE

©King Features Syndicate, Inc. 1976.

And who continues to take the bad dream of "hell" seriously? Mainly those inclined to self-righteousness, sadism, or both. Furthermore, those who are inclined to self-righteousness, sadism, or both are usually made this way by the very teaching of a literal hell itself. People always tend to resemble the gods they serve. A vindictive God always produces vindictiveness among those he influences.

Hi ho.

13. Who Really Believes in "Hell"?

There are so many perfectly valid reasons for not believing in "hell," that we might wonder who today, if anyone, still believes in such a monstrosity. According to historian D. P. Walker, in his excellent book *The Decline of Hell,* the teaching of a literal hell has been declining in popularity among Christians at least since the seventeenth century.[34] And Mark Twain tells us that most Christians who *think* they believe in "hell," can sleep at night for only one reason: "It is because the Christian does not believe it—in his heart; but only with his head. The heart could not bear that burden."[35]

But being rather thoroughly familiar with the ins and outs of hell myself, having been in and out of it so often, I have concluded that there are still two large groups of "Christians" who don't deny the existence of a literal hell: those who really do believe in it and aren't afraid to say so (this is about all they do say), and those who really don't believe in it but don't say so.

Both groups are as dangerous as hell—the *real* hell. For this is what both tend to produce.

14. Biblical Literalism = Mistaking a Literal Hell for the Living Hell, or Reading the Bible Upside Down

As we have seen, biblical literalists have to take the Bible literally because of the frightening specter of "hell" itself. Their problem originates from reading the Bible upside down: they start with their heads instead of their heart. For when they begin at the top level of their heads with a merely literal or surface-level understanding of what the Bible means by hell, the fear of this literal hell then puts a living hell in their hearts. In turn, this fear forces them to cling to a simplistic, literal understanding of everything else in the Bible. Unfortunately, the mistake is common enough.

HAGAR THE HORRIBLE

©King Features Syndicate, Inc. 1977.

As we have also seen, biblical literalists are always first-rate candidates for atheism. For their God, of course, is actually the Bible. And although the Bible is holy and good, it is not God. Therefore, when faith in their god, the Bible, is in any way shaken, then, like the "intelligent young man named Jitterly," they may "reject the whole thing bitterly." In the meantime, their narrow and shallow interpretation of the Bible may also cause a lot of other folks to reject it as well.

What biblical literalists need is not less Bible but more Bible. Their understanding of Scripture should be broader and deeper. In the words of Jesus, they "know neither the scriptures nor the power of God" (Mark 12:24, RSV).

Biblical literalists don't know the Scriptures? Why, they can quote chapter and verse without even thinking! That's true. They often can. They often do. But this is usually a dead giveaway that they don't know the Scriptures broadly enough. By memorizing a few pet verses that would seem to back up their position, they can then be conveniently less serious and less literal about everything else in the Bible.

Certainly biblical literalists have a perfect genius for overlooking all the Bible says directly and literally about the coming "time of universal restoration . . . of which God spoke by his holy prophets" (Acts 3:21, NEB). But anyone who claims to take the Bible seriously, said Karl Barth,

> should at least be stimulated by the passage, Colossians 1:19, which admittedly states that God has determined through His Son as His image and as the first-born of the whole Creation to "reconcile all things to himself," to consider whether the concept could not perhaps have a good meaning. The same can be said of parallel passages.[36]

No one denies that the Bible also speaks of hell. But if biblical literalists could only read the Bible more deeply, starting with their hearts, and in this way take more seriously the awesome here-and-now power of God, they could then better understand what is usually meant in the Bible by hell. If they had more respect for the depths of hell that people *now* experience, they wouldn't be forced to place hell somewhere out in the future. Hell's judgment is not something people will have to face after death; it is a biting misery that they now experience—to one degree or another—in the depths of their hearts. It is an existential reality. "For the wages of sin *is* [present tense] death" (Rom. 6:23, RSV), St. Paul said. As far as the Bible is concerned, sin always brings its own punishment while we live.

Mark Twain once wrote: "If I were going to construct a God I would furnish Him with some ways and qualities and characteristics which the Present (Bible) One lacks." Among the changes Twain would make was this:

There would not be any hell—except the one we live in from the cradle to the grave.[37]

Undoubtedly, it would have come to Mark Twain as good news indeed if someone had only told him that this present hell, according to the Bible, is the only hell that actually exists.

©1970 Chicago Tribune—New York News Syndicate, Inc.

The word *already* is a good key for properly understanding the Christian message. Christ's victory over the forces of sin, death, and evil in the world has already taken place. This victory has already been accomplished once and for all time and for all people. As Jesus said:

> "Now is the hour of judgement for this world; now shall the Prince of this world be driven out. And I shall draw all men to myself, when I am lifted up from the earth." This he said to indicate the kind of death he was to die (John 12:31–33, NEB).

The kind of death Jesus died will ultimately draw "all men" to him, not just a chosen few. In Jesus' death, *all* have been chosen. The forces of evil still cause plenty of trouble in the world, but their final defeat is already assured: *"Now* shall the Prince of this world be driven out." People now still suffer a temporary hell, or death, or judgment in this world, for they continue to disbelieve in the good news of their own ultimate salvation. And therefore in the same sense that the believer "has already passed from death to life" (John 5:24, NEB), "the unbeliever has already been judged" (John 3:18, NEB).

God's "Last Judgment" has *already* been passed on the entire world: "Now is the hour of judgment for this world." We now know through Christ that the verdict of God's final judgment is "acquital and life for all men" (Rom. 5:18, RSV). Notice how this gospel of *already* figures in the following statement by Karl Barth:

> Did you read in the paper recently that two Japanese soldiers were found in the Philippines, who had not yet heard, or did not believe, that the war had ended fourteen years ago? They continue to hide in some jungle and shoot at everybody who dares approach them. Strange people, aren't they? Well, we are such people when we refuse to perceive and to hold true what the Easter message declares to be the meaning of the Easter story. Sin and death are conquered; God's free gift prevails, his gift of eternal life for us all. Shall we not very humbly pay heed to this message? . . . "Wake up, sleeper, and rise from the dead, that Jesus Christ may be your light!" He, Jesus Christ, who made our history his own and, in a marvellous turn-about, made his wondrous history our own! He in whom the kingdom of the devil is *already* destroyed! In whom the kingdom of God and of his peace has *already* come, to us, to you and me, to us all, on the earth and in the whole world![38]

©1969 United Feature Syndicate, Inc.

The Bible not only affirms the future "universal restoration" directly and explicitly, but it also denies a literal hell, at least indirectly and implicitly. For it is simply impossible to square a literal hell with what the Bible also says literally about God's omnipotence and love.

Again the problem is one of reading the Bible "upside down." For if we begin by believing in a literal hell, then it is impossible to believe what the Bible says literally about God's infinite love and power. On the other hand, if we begin where we should, with the truly good news revealed in Jesus Christ—the complete control and ultimate triumph of God's love and power over *all* things, then we are enabled to appreciate the Bible's hell for what it really is: a dramatically charged metaphor for a very painful present reality.

"Outsider" Mark Twain could see as clearly as anyone that "hell" necessarily denies at least one of these two things: what the Bible says about an all-loving God's power or, as in the following piece of Twain dialogue bstween two blacks, what the Bible says about an all-powerful God's love:

> A man is a powful sight mo' juster en what de Lawd is! Kase de Lawd take en buil' up a man so he jes *boun'* to kill people, en lie en steal en embellish, en den he take en jam him into de everlast'n fire en brimstone for it! . . . I'll resk it, dat any book dat's got any sich stuff as dat in it warn't ever writ by de Lawd.[39]

Isn't it God himself, through Christ, who teaches us in the Bible to forgive "seventy times seven" anyone who wrongs us (see Matt. 18:22)? This, of course, is a biblical way of saying that we must never stop forgiving. Then could it be that God himself doesn't practice the same kind of love that he preaches? Could it be that even we people, "who are evil" (see Matt. 7:11), can occasionally feel universal love and forgiveness toward all people—and God can't? If God can't, then it is as Mark Twain says: "A man is a powful sight mo' juster en what de Lawd is!"

"I forgive all of you your trespasses."

Drawing by D. Fradon; ©1969. The New Yorker Magazine, Inc.

15. The Meaninglessness of a Literal Hell Causes the Real Hell: Meaninglessness in Life

Try to take a literal hell seriously for a moment (not an easy thing for most people to do). Judgment day has finally arrived, everyone has been called to their Maker, and now the good Lord is going to separate the sheep from the goats. The sheep will dwell in everlasting bliss with God in heaven. The goats will be confined to the torments of hell eternally. For how long? Eternally! Forever and ever and ever.

As the door of hell clangs shut for the final time, the last sinner says to himself: "Well, this is sure going to teach me a lesson!"

But what good is this lesson he may have learned? He can never use it. He will be eternally in hell. It cannot serve to instruct anyone else. Everyone has already been "called to their reward." A literal hell then is ultimately meaningless. It serves no ultimate purpose. It does not cure anyone of evil or deter anyone else from committing further evil. Nope. Hell is, to say the least, the worst imaginable case of . . .

B.C.

B.C. by permission of Johnny Hart and Field Enterprises, Inc.

In the past, believers of an everlasting "hell" have only rarely understood the ultimate uselessness or purposelessness or "overkill" behind such a concept. But whenever they did catch a glimpse of this completely meaningless aspect of hell, they usually tried to overcome the problem by what has been called "the abominable fancy." [40] They tried to say that, yes, hell does serve some purpose after all. And what is this purpose? It increases the bliss of those who are in heaven! Here, for example, is the abominable way Saint Thomas Aquinas could fancy it:

> That the saints may enjoy their beatitude and the grace of God more abundantly, they are permitted to see the punishment of the damned in Hell. [41]

Nowadays, however, even "hell's" most loyal defenders wouldn't be caught using this kind of argument. "Nowadays," says D. P. Walker, "vindictive justice has had to take refuge among the advocates of hanging; and it is no longer considered respectable to enjoy the infliction of even the justest punishment." [42] Only the most cruelly self-righteous could enjoy seeing anyone writhe in hell even for an instant. Real Christians, on the other hand, have always known that any righteousness they possess comes, not from themselves, but only from God. Christians know, as Shakespeare could say in *The Merchant of Venice,* "That in the course of justice none of us/Should see salvation." If it were up to our own goodness or righteousness, none of us would see God's heaven—any more than any of us would see the sun shine in a case like this:

©1971 United Feature Syndicate, Inc.

This is why it is safe to assume that if Christians got to heaven and there did turn out to be a literal hell, then they—along with Jesus Christ as their leader—would be the first to organize an assault party to liberate the place. But such an eventuality will never need to occur, for every Christian can say, to use Mark Twain's words about heaven and hell, "I have friends in both places."[43] Christians know they have friends who live in the real hell—the living hell. They live there themselves a lot of the time. But what is more important is that they also know they have a friend in heaven—Jesus Christ—who, whether people now realize it or not, is the friend and brother and savior of all people:

Should anyone commit a sin, we have one to plead our cause with the Father, Jesus Christ, and he is just. He is himself the remedy for the defilement of our sins, not our sins only but the sins of all the world (1 John 2:1–2, NEB).

©1969 Daily Mirror Newspapers Ltd. ANDY CAPP Dist. Field Newspaper Syndicate.

Every man is a *virtual* brother of Christ, because the whole world is healed in and through Christ. Everyman has his destination in Christ. . . . Even before he becomes a Christian he is in continuity with God in Christ, but he has not yet discovered it. He realises it only when he begins to believe. (Karl Barth) [44]

In the meantime, belief in a literal hell is the source of almost every idea that ails us. For hell's ultimate pointlessness, absurdity, and meaninglessness is the greatest single factor in causing people to reject belief in God as absurd and meaningless. And then, as we have seen, life itself—without God and immortality—soon becomes meaningless. And a meaningless life is the *real* hell. Mark Twain's throwing Christ out along with the dirty bath water of a literal hell is a reaction typical of millions of people:

> I believe that the Old and New Testaments were imagined and written by man, and that no line in them was authorized by God, much less inspired by Him. . . .
>
> I cannot see how eternal punishment hereafter could accomplish any good end, therefore I am not able to believe in it. To chasten a man in order to perfect him might be reasonable enough . . . but to roast him forever for the mere satisfaction of seeing him roast would not be reasonable—even the atrocious God imagined by the Jews would tire of the spectacle eventually.
>
> There may be a hereafter, and there may *not* be. I am wholly indifferent about it. If I am appointed to live again, I

feel sure it will be for some more sane and useful purpose than to flounder about for ages in a lake of fire and brimstone for having violated a confusion of ill-defined and contradictory rules said (but not evidenced,) to be of divine institution. If annihilation is to follow death, I shall not be *aware* of the annihilation, and therefore shall not care a straw about it.[45]

More than anything else, it was the teaching of a future, meaningless, literal hell that turned Mark Twain away from God. And, having no God, life itself finally became a hell of meaninglessness for Twain. This fact is significant because it is an extremely clear and typical example of the way a literal hell in eternity continues to cause a living hell here and now.

So it goes.

16. Jesus Christ Superstar—I Don't Know If He Loves Me

I have used a lot of Mark Twain in the preceding four sections because he is so obviously a victim of the literal understanding of hell. He typifies the countless number of intelligent and decent folks who would like to believe in God, but simply can't remain honest and swallow an all-loving and all-powerful God who at the same time "designed the trap, then designed the victim with a disposition to *go into* it." [46]

Here again, Kurt Vonnegut has followed in Mark Twain's footsteps. In talking with Vonnegut I attempted to express my belief that all people are finally destined for heaven, regardless of what they've done in life. Vonnegut seemed to like this idea, but at the same time it apparently remained inconceivable to him. As our discussion progressed to the idea of hope, he referred to heaven as "this wonderful thing that's going to happen to you . . . if you live systematically." [47] And so for Vonnegut also, like for so many other people, the idea of God's love with absolutely no strings attached is an idea that finally remains strange and unimaginable. Nevertheless, this is the way God loves. As Karl Barth put it:

Contrary to human mercy even in its kindest expression, God's mercy is almighty. It is almightily saving and helpful. It brings light, peace and joy. We need not be afraid that it might be limited or have strings attached. His "yes" is unequivocal, never to be reversed into "no."

Since God's mercy is divine and not human, it is poured out on all men, as emphasized in our text. ["For God has made all men prisoners, that he may have mercy upon all."—Rom. 11:32][48]

In other words, God's love and mercy do *not* work like this:

I WAS AFRAID THAT'S WHAT THAT STRING WAS FOR

The question of what strings are attached to God's love—if any—is also the fundamental question behind *Jesus Christ Superstar*. This is why *JCS* concentrates so heavily on Judas' role in the Gospel story. Judas, the disciple who betrayed Jesus, is obviously the number one sinner in the New Testament. Therefore, whenever we are primarily concerned about the quality of God's mercy, then the question about God's attitude toward Judas will inevitably take center stage. The creators of *JCS* intuitively zero in on precisely the correct point in asking about the extent of God's love. Judas Iscariot, says Barth, is *the* character in which the question about those "rejected" by God "is concentrated and developed in the New Testament."[49]

"Will he love—does he love me too? Does he care for me?" asks Judas in *JCS*. "Just don't say I'm/Damned for all time" he sings over and over.

Well, how about it? Does God and/or Christ love Judas too? Or is Judas sure 'nuf totally unforgiveable and "damned for all time"?

It is obvious that the creators of *JCS* felt that "poor old Judas" should not be damned for all time and should be loved by Jesus. Why? Because Rice and Lloyd Webber have been completely true to the New Testament's own express witness that God is always completely in control of *all* things—including the evil done by Judas! In *JCS*, Pilate warns Jesus:

You've got to be careful—you could be dead soon—could well be
Why do you not speak when I have your life in my hands?

And Jesus replies:

> You have nothing in your hands
> Any power you have comes to you from far beyond
> Everything is fixed and you can't change it

But is this really the Bible's view of things? It darn sure is! The two speeches above, for example, are only a paraphrase of the conversation that takes place in the original "script":

> When Pilate heard these words, he was the more afraid; . . . and said to Jesus, "Where are you from?" But Jesus gave no answer. Pilate therefore said to him, "You will not speak to me? Do you not know that I have power to release you and power to crucify you?" Jesus answered him, "You would have no power over me unless it had been given you from above" (John 19:8–11, RSV).

Also in *JCS*, "poor old Judas" can sing:

> —My God I am sick I've been used
> And you knew all the time
> God! I'll never ever know why you chose me
>   for your crime
> For your foul bloody crime
> You have murdered me! You have murdered me!

Neither does the New Testament tell us why God chose Judas for his particular role. But it certainly agrees with *JCS* that Judas was indeed "chosen" to play a part in a drama in which everything is fixed:

> For Jesus knew from the first . . . who it was that should betray him. And he said, "This is why I told you that no one can come to me unless it is granted him by the Father. . . . Did I not choose you, the twelve, and one of you is a devil?" He spoke of Judas the son of Simon Iscariot (John 6:64–65, 70–71, RSV).

Jesus, the New Testament further tells us, was "delivered up" to crucifixion and death "according to the definite plan and foreknowledge of God" (see Acts 2:23, RSV).

Here again *JCS* is typical of the outlook of the modern "outsider." Most modern non-Christian men and women also believe they live in a universe in which "everything is fixed." They therefore attempt to predict the course of this fixity either through scientific analysis on the one hand, or with the use of occult sciences (like astrology) on the other. Without generally recognizing it, the modern outsider is here in remarkable agreement with the Bible. For the Bible also teaches that "everthing is fixed." As Jesus said, "Not one of them [a sparrow] will fall to the ground without your Father's will" (Matt. 10:29, RSV). Paul said that God "accomplishes all things according to the counsel of his will" (Eph. 1:11, RSV).

In *The Sirens of Titan* Vonnegut tells us repeatedly: "Everything that ever has been always will be, and everything that ever will be always has been." [50] When he wrote these words, Vonnegut was evidently unaware that they are an excellent paraphrase of the Book of Ecclesiastes: "That which hath been is now; and that which is to be hath already been" (Eccles. 3:15, KJV).

Therefore at this point, at least, the modern atheist or "outsider," represented by the likes of Vonnegut & Twain & *JCS,* is much closer to the biblical way of looking at things than are most so-called Christians, who arrogantly and self-righteously believe in their own free wills, in their own power to control things. Of course, there is this difference: The modern "outsider" believes everything is fixed by an impersonal and meaningless accident. The Bible teaches that all is fixed by an all-loving and all-powerful God.

Vonnegut begins *Slaughterhouse-Five* by telling about a post card he received from a man he met in Germany, a German taxi driver whose English wasn't the best. "I hope that we'll meet again in a world of peace and freedom in the taxi cab if the accident will," wrote the German. Remarks Vonnegut: "I like that very much: 'If the accident will.' " [51]

Vonnegut likes this very much because it very much expresses his view of things: Everything happens by accident. The Bible agrees with Vonnegut that everything is caused by a power that "comes from far beyond" us. But the Bible also teaches that this power possesses a personal will. In the Bible it is not "if the accident will," but "if the Lord wills." This means that "outsiders" who only believe in "if the accident will" are actually much closer to real Christian humility than so-called Christians who boast in their own free wills.

Come now, you who say, "Today or tomorrow we will go into such and such a town and spend a year there and trade and get gain"; whereas you do not know about tomorrow. What is your life? For you are a mist that appears for a little time and then vanishes. Instead you ought to say, "If the Lord wills, we shall live and we shall do this or that." As it is, you boast in your arrogance. All such boasting is evil (James 4:13–16, RSV).

How does all this relate to Judas and whether or not he's "damned for all time"? First, it reminds us, as Karl Barth put it, that "the situation between Jesus and Judas . . . is only a heightened form of the situation between Jesus and all other men." [52] In other words, whenever we look at "poor old Judas," we should remember this:

ZIGGY

And this thought has a brother, which also I'll ask the great Barth to express:

The Church will not then preach . . . a powerless grace of Jesus Christ or a wickedness of men which is too powerful for it. But . . . it will preach the overwhelming power of grace and the weakness of human wickedness in the face of it. For this is how the "for" of Jesus and the "against" of Judas undoubtedly confront one another. . . .

As the forgiveness of sins is established in Jesus Christ alone, and as He alone has risen from the dead, so we have Him alone, both for ourselves and others, as a pledge of hope. There is all the less reason for us to deny that the rejected also stand in this light. For if in faith we can confess this for ourselves, we can do so seriously only as we recognise that we no less than they have deserved to be handed over to bondage by the wrath of God. We can confess it seriously only when we are in solidarity with them. If we are to make Paul's defiant question our own: "If God be for us, who can be against us?", the genuineness of our use of Paul's words can be tested by whether, thinking and speaking in faith, we can go on to say even in respect of apparent or obviously real Judases: "If God be for them, who can be against them?" The fact [is] that God is for them, too.[53]

"Does he love me too?" asks Judas in *JCS*. Yep, Judas. He even loves you too, which is sure good news for me. For to tell you the truth, Judas, I often feel a very close kinship with you.

Happily for you and me, Judas, God is a lot like Will Rogers: He never made a man he didn't like.

17. Those Who Tell Us *No* News—The Silent Ones

Regardless of the criticisms I've made of the biblical literalists, the so-called evangelical Christians, they usually have at least openness and honesty going for them. Albert Camus once said that "the world needs real dialogue, . . . falsehood is just as much the opposite of dialogue as is silence, and . . . the only possible dialogue is the kind between people who remain what they are and speak their minds."[54] No doubt there are believers in a literal hell who don't want to make themselves unpopular by saying so. But I think most people who really believe in "hell" remain what they are and speak their minds. Good for them.

Because on the other hand, there is also that large group of people who really don't believe in hell, but, for one bad reason or another, they keep this disbelief hushed up.

To begin with there are the *Outright Charlatans*. They no more believe in "hell" or God than they believe in the tooth fairy, but they want *other* people to believe in "hell" so they can take immoral advantage of the behavior this belief can sometimes generate. For instance, this type person sometimes learns that there is big money in marketing Jesus as the one who can save us from "hell." These are also the people who, as Vonnegut puts it, don't really "believe in a punitive afterlife," but "put such emphasis on truthfulness in order to be believed when they lie." [55] It works about like this:

Then, of course, there are the *High-Minded Impostors* who secretly disbelieve in "hell" and God. But, like Dostoevsky's "Grand Inquisitor," they boost "hell" and God because they feel that all such beliefs are merely "harmless untruths" that tend to make people brave, kind, healthy, and happy. "Hell" and God are good things for *other* people to believe. The woods are full of Outright Charlatans and High-Minded Impostors.

But the most harmful group are the *Silent Ones*. These are the timid souls who really do try to believe in God and/or Christ, and they say so; and they don't really believe in a literal hell, but they *won't* say this. Indeed, they often avoid any talk of a future life altogether.

Why don't the Silent Ones speak their minds? There are several reasons. First, many Silent Ones evidently assume that everybody already knows there is no "hell." I was recently in on a panel discussion with one of America's most famous theologians, a former president of one of our great theological seminaries. We spoke before a large group of ministers, their spouses, and many lay people. During our discussion this good man said what a happy circumstance we now live in when we no longer have to worry about "the horrible idea of hell." Twenty minutes later, when it was the great theologian's task to lead a group discussion among these people, he suffered what must have been a severe shock. These folks quickly let him know that they shared no such happy circumstance at all.

It may be true that behind his desk at the seminary there was no such worry; so it's probably a good thing that he came out from behind his desk.

This brings us back once more to Ebeling's wise words:

> It would be senseless to speak of faith on the assumption that no unbeliever is present. Christian talk of faith does indeed mostly take place on this tacit assumption. Faith is spoken of in more or less dark hints which are meant only for the initiated. . . . But . . . when faith is spoken of, the non-believer is the most appropriate listener. He is at all events a salutary criterion, which compels us not to speak too glibly of faith.[56]

Second, many Silent Ones feel that eschatology is really rather unimportant. They don't see how what happens to us after death is all that relevant to life. And life, of course, is "where it's at." This attitude is now rapidly changing, but in the meantime it would be good if all such Silent Ones could chew on this statement of Dilthey:

> The thing that more than anything else profoundly determines the way we feel about life is the way life is related to death.

Certainly Dostoevsky was an absolute master in actually showing us, through his novels, how the way we look at death "profoundly determines" the way our lives are lived, both individually and politically. "Eschatology, rightly understood," said Barth, "is the most practical thing that can be thought." (*Dogmatics in Outline,* page 154)

Also, no one could be more emphatic than Karl Barth in telling Christians that if the gospel is really to be the gospel then the totally good news of "the last things" should always be, along with Christ, at the very head of all Christian thinking, speaking and doing:

> The task which confronts us is rather a critical one, even in the face of the very best tradition. . . . The shadow must be dispersed. . . . We cannot be too soon, or too radical, in the opposition which we must offer to the classical tradition. . . . And we introduce the first and most radical point with our thesis that the doctrine of [God's election of man] must be understood quite definitely and unequivocally as Gospel; that it is not something neutral on the yonder side of Yes and No; that it is not No but Yes; that it is not Yes and No, but in its substance, in the origin and scope of its utterance, it is altogether Yes.
>
> The election of grace is the sum of the Gospel—we must put it as pointedly as that. But more, the election of grace is the whole of the Gospel, the Gospel *in nuce*. It is the very essence of all good news. . . .
>
> On the other hand, if it is the shadow which really predominates, if we must still fear, or if we can only half rejoice and half fear, if we have no truth at all to receive or proclaim but only the neutral elucidation of a neutral subject, then it is quite certain that we can never again receive or proclaim as such the Gospel. . . . In this sphere, too, the shadow will necessarily predominate.[57]

Third reason for the silence of the Silent Ones: They are often afraid. What are they afraid of? Well, probably a few of them are still afraid that the good news of God's election of all people to salvation will lead to indifference or lawlessness, but real faith knows better than this. Faith knows that real belief in Jesus Christ as the reconciler of all people can never exist apart from obedience to Christ. There can be no real certainty of the truth without *"doing the truth"* (see John 3:21).

In earlier ages, when many Christians assumed the existence of a literal hell, their most anxious question was whether or not they'd escape "hell" and make it to heaven. Nowadays, when much fewer people believe in heaven *or* hell, almost everyone assumes that:

"If it's up there, I'll be there."

Drawing by Modell; ©1973. The New Yorker Magazine, Inc.

Therefore, the big question today is, Is it up there? faith says, yes, it's up there, and eventually, "when the roll is called up yonder," we'll *all* be up there in it. But this knowledge cannot lead to indifference or lawlessness, for no one can really have this knowledge without obeying Christ. The assurance Christians have that there is indeed an eternal life for all people after this life is based on their experience of "the life," the Holy Spirit, in this life. Only from the confirmation of "the life" now, from *present* joy, do Christians now know that the Bible's witness is true about the "great joy which will come to all the people" *later* (Luke 2:10, RSV). But this experience and assurance come only through obedience. If we don't obey, we don't believe. And if we don't believe, there is absolutely no way we can finally be sure that "there's life after this one."

BROOM-HILDA   ©1975 Chicago Tribune—New York News Syndicate, Inc.

But there is another side to the danger to society that the Silent Ones sometimes see in Christian universalism. They are not only afraid that this good news might justify lawlessness (something it can never do), but they are also afraid to give up any force a literal hell may have as a *deterrent* to immorality and lawlessness.

Is "hell" such a deterrent? No sirree, and it never has been! As a matter of fact, in the long run it is just the opposite: The teaching of a literal hell *leads to* immorality and lawlessness. Why? Because bad laws breed disrespect for the law. And "hell" is the original bad law created, not by God, but by people. On the broad social level, as we have seen, "hell" leads to atheism, and atheism leads to the lawless nightmare of nihilism. In the case of the individual, "hell" has the effect that D. P. Walker describes: "Few if any men do in fact feel the degree of guilt that would merit an infinite punishment; therefore they ignore the threat altogether." [58] And because they have been told that this horrible threat comes directly from a good God, many people ignore and do not believe in him either.

This is why Karl Barth had this important comment to make to all Silent Ones who fear that talk of "universalism" might lead to indifference and lawlessness:

> One question should for a moment be asked, in view of the "danger" with which one may see this concept gradually surrounded. What of the "danger" of the eternally skeptical-critical theologian who is ever and again suspiciously questioning, because fundamentally always legalistic and therefore in the main morosely gloomy? Is not his presence among us currently more threatening than that of the unbecomingly cheerful indifferentism or even antinomianism, to which one with a

certain understanding of universalism could in fact deliver himself? This much is certain, that we have no theological right to set any sort of limits to the loving-kindness of God which has appeared in Jesus Christ. Our theological duty is to see and understand it as being still greater than we had seen before.[59]

We have been far too slow in seeing. But even as far back as 1700, there were Christians who could see the deadly relationship between "hell" and Christendom's rapidly increasing atheism. As one German theologian wrote:

What fruit has the doctrine of eternal damnation born up till now? Has it made men more pious? On the contrary, when they have properly considered the cruel, frightful disproportion between the punishments and their own finite sins, they have begun to believe nothing at all, and have thought that these books of Holy Scripture have just been compiled by the priests, who made up such threats for the common people as they thought fit, in order to keep them in check.[60]

18. The Need for an Unambiguous *Christian* Universalism

Because of "a certain understanding of universalism," Barth shied away from calling himself a universalist. Here is the understanding of *universalism* that Barth rejected: that God has to save all people because of some kind of necessity laid on him; and that this salvation of all people can be known in ways other than through Jesus Christ. Barth, on the other hand, said that God in his *freedom* has chosen to save all people. He will save all of us, "not with a natural Therefore, but with a miraculous Nevertheless."[61] Furthermore, this free and gracious decision of God is made known to us only through Christ, who is the very revelation of God himself.

A grace which automatically would ultimately have to embrace each and every one would certainly not be free grace. It surely would not be God's grace.

But would it be God's free grace if we could absolutely deny that it could do that? Has Christ been sacrificed only for our sins? Has He not, according to 1 John 2:2, been sacrificed for the whole world? Strange Christianity, whose most pressing anxiety seems to be that God's grace might prove to be all too free on this side, that hell, instead of being populated with so many people, might someday prove to be empty![62]

"God does not *have* to do anything at all," Barth reminded us,[63] least of all save people. So when Voltaire said, "God will forgive, because it is his job,"[63] he was perhaps speaking as a universalist, but not as a Christian universalist. And Lucy and Voltaire are in the same boat:

©1969 United Feature Syndicate, Inc.

For these reasons, then, Barth could say, "I don't believe in universalism, but I do believe in Jesus Christ, the reconciler of *all*."[65] Therefore, with these important qualifications of the word *universalism* in mind, it is correct to call Barth a *Christian* universalist. All Christian obedience—for Barth, Bonhoeffer, Dostoevsky, and the New Testament—means ultimately only one thing: It is to proclaim,

to the world, in word and deed, "Jesus Christ, the reconciler of all."
Barth put it this way:

> The task of the Church is to announce the good news of
> the perfect work of Christ done for all. Salvation is complete.
> There is no need for supplementation. . . . The distinction is
> not between redeemed and unredeemed, but between those
> who realise it and those who do not. The emphasis in much
> of today's preaching has to do with salvation in the future,
> something the preacher can help give, instead of speaking of
> the perfect salvation already accomplished. We only await its
> final revelation. The emphasis should be on the deed of God
> *done*. . . . Faith is a form of knowledge.[66]

But if announcing this good news is really the central task of the
church, then there must be many more people who understand this
announcement than actually say so, for this is an announcement we
rarely hear. And when we do hear it, it is spoken only timidly and
ambiguously, as though there were something here to be ashamed
or afraid of.

This brings us back to our previous question: Why is there such a
conspicuous silence from the church at just this crucial point, the
point of the gospel itself? By now the answer should be obvious:
The church's announcement of the gospel is closely tied to the people whose professions it is to make this announcement, and these
people are often afraid that they might jeopardize their jobs with
such an announcement. Sometimes an "outsider" like Kurt Vonnegut can see the main problem clearly. On "60 Minutes," when
Harry Reasoner asked Vonnegut how he explained the fact that he
is "idolized" by young people nowadays, Vonnegut said:

> Well, I'm screamingly funny, you know. . . . And I talk
> about stuff Billy Graham won't talk about for instance, you
> know, is it wrong to kill? And what's God like? And stuff like
> that because they can't get it from the minister, and I show
> what heaven is like, you know, which you can't get a minister
> to talk about. . . . And so they want to know. They want to
> know what happens after you die. And I talk about it. That's a
> very popular subject.[67]

Later, when I asked Vonnegut "about ministers not being more open in how they talk about the future," he had this to say:

> Their problem must be political . . . that they dare not be very interesting up there. It's that they're so easily fired. And their congregations just scold them. I mean, on Cape Cod I know ministers'd be in trouble and they'd be quite frightened by their congregations. They made a mistake last Sunday and next Sunday they'll try to patch it up.[68]

In other words, whenever the clergy are insecure in their jobs, it is politic that they be ambiguous, wishy-washy, and "flexible about God":

"I do like the new rector, don't you? He's very flexible about God."

Drawing by Alan Dunn; ©1970. The New Yorker Magazine, Inc.

God, on the other hand, never seems to be so flexibly ambiguous about himself. St. Paul said:

> Do I, when I frame my plans, frame them as a worldly man
> might, so that it should rest with me to say "yes" and "yes,"
> or "no" and "no"? As God is true, the language in which we
> address you is not an ambiguous blend of Yes and No. The
> Son of God, Christ Jesus, proclaimed among you by us
> . . . , was never a blend of Yes and No. With him it was,
> and is, Yes. He is the Yes pronounced upon God's promises,
> every one of them (2 Cor. 1:17–20, NEB).

Karl Barth was only echoing Paul's words when he assured us that the Christian message,

> no matter how it may be understood in detail . . . is itself
> evangel: glad tidings; news which uplifts and comforts and sus-
> tains. Once and for all, then, it is . . . a proclamation of joy. It
> is not a mixed message of joy and terror, salvation and dam-
> nation. . . . It does not proclaim in the same breath both
> good and evil, both help and destruction, both life and death.
> It does, of course, throw a shadow. We cannot overlook this
> aspect of the matter. In itself, however, it is light and not dark-
> ness. . . . The Yes cannot be heard unless the No is also
> heard. But the No is said for the sake of the Yes and not for
> its own sake. In substance, therefore, the first and last word is
> Yes and not No.[69]

When a person, any person, stands before the Christian church and bluntly asks the question of his or her own personal eternal destiny, "Fundamentally," says Barth, "this question is not unanswerable. It is not one of the questions which are destined always to remain questions. In face of it there is no place for that mysterious shaking of the head or shrugging of the shoulders or wringing of the hands which some perhaps regard as particularly pious in this connexion."[70]

And yet, in just this connection, it is obvious that our churches remain full of ministers who, behind the mask of a pious humility, find it expedient only to shake their heads or shrug their shoulders or wring their hands or to fill us with pious-sounding doubletalk.

19. "The Shadow Must Be Dispersed"

What can help this situation?

First, lay people need to revolt against it and force their ministers into clarity and openness. If it is really true that lay people have discouraged their ministers into a frightened silence (which I doubt), then the same lay people can also encourage their ministers to speak up clearly and openly.

Second, closet universalists among the clergy—who must surely realize that they have the power of the Bible and the truth in their corner, and further that they are being false to themselves, to their flocks, and to their God when they don't speak up—should also understand that they probably have less to fear than they think. I can sympathize with their fear, but I am also more and more convinced that this fear is unfounded. I'll never forget the fear I felt on the first occasion before a large group of people where I was to declare myself unambiguously for Christian universalism. I had visions of being stoned, or at least tarred and feathered, but the response was just the opposite of what I feared. I couldn't have been more happily surprised.

There is too much at stake for Christians to allow themselves to be intimidated by the wrathful self-righteousness of the "hell"-raising gloomy doomies. Hell—the real and only hell—is the hell that these people themselves already live in, and Christians of the truly good news are certainly not called to leave anyone in this hell. Therefore, our witness to them should be just as aggressive and unambiguous as theirs has been to us.

For if we don't speak up on these issues, the so-called "evangelical Christians" will only continue to give the world the untrue and ultimately unbelievable bad news of a literal hell, and the silent Christians will give it no news at all. This, of course, goes a long way in explaining "why conservative churches are growing." [71] The conservatives at least have something to say; and the fact that even this bad news can be taken so seriously shows just how desperate the world is for any news at all.

If the mainline churches are really concerned about their current lack of growth and effectiveness, they should be less concerned about obsequiously accommodating themselves to what they think their congregations are thinking, and more concerned about accommodating themselves to the truth. As an example to everyone else, the churches—before anyone else—should "seek first [God's] kingdom and his righteousness, and all these things shall be yours as well" (Matt. 6:33, RSV). The New Testament also contains this excellent bit of advice for the life of the churches today: "Whoever would save his life will lose it; and whoever loses his life for my sake and the gospel's will save it" (Mark 8:35, RSV). And just at this point, the point of "the gospel," we are again brought around to Barth's words: "I fear that much of the weakness of our Christian witness comes from this fact that we dare not frankly confess the grandeur of God, the victory of Christ, the superiority of the Spirit." But whether or not we dare make this witness, this is obviously what we have been entrusted to do:

> From first to last this has been the work of God. He has reconciled us men to himself through Christ, and he has enlisted us in this service of reconciliation. What I mean is, that God was in Christ reconciling the world to himself, no longer holding men's misdeeds against them, and that he has entrusted us with the message of reconciliation (2 Cor. 5:18–19, NEB).

How do we finally know this reconciliation of all the world is true? Certainly when we look at the gentle shepherd of Nazareth we have good reason to believe it's true. When we look at him, we have good reasons to believe with Paul that finally nothing can come between anyone "and the love of God made visible in Christ Jesus our Lord" (Rom. 8:39, JB). But if we are to be certain of this, as Paul said he was, then we must go beyond merely having reasons for believing, and we must believe in this man.

Apart from believing that Jesus is the Christ, "the Lamb of God, who takes away the sin of the world." (John 1:29, RSV), there is nothing nearly as true or nearly as good to believe in.

Robert Short Interviews Kurt Vonnegut, Chicago— June 8, 1976

SHORT: Well, I have a few questions here, and some of them may sort of put you on the spot, but I don't want to put you on the spot in any way you don't want to be put.

VONNEGUT: Well, let's see what happens.

SHORT: If you don't want to answer them, just cross your fingers, or don't answer, or I can shut this thing [tape recorder] off, or whatever. We were talking about Bonhoeffer last night. You said you hadn't read very much Bonhoeffer?

VONNEGUT: No, I don't tend to read that sort of thing. I will. I feel no urgency about reading. I'm aware of who he was. I know what the shape of his life was. I'm aware of his problems, his death. Sometime I'll find a Bonhoeffer book and start reading.

SHORT: Yeah. Well, let me send you one. I think *Letters and Papers from Prison* is probably his best known. Bonhoeffer was in prison in Berlin during the last three years of the war. Because he had all this time on his hands, he was able to do a lot of thinking—the same kind of thinking that apparently you've done since Dresden. That is, how is it that this kind of thing happened and what can we do to prevent if from happening in the future, and so on. And what part has the Christian church played in this?

VONNEGUT: Well, I think that Bonhoeffer, from what I understand of his life, worked with crippled people, defective people, and one thing that really troubled him about Nazis was that they thought these people should be killed. He knew these defective people. Bonhoeffer accepted and treasured these people, and . . . I don't know. I'm completely fatalistic about Dresden. Since it did happen, it must have had to happen. I can't reason my way through it any other way. I have the same fatalism about Dresden I have about the Battle of Fredericksburg. It seems to me that the Battle of Fredericksburg couldn't have been avoided either.

SHORT: Do you need to know anything about this book that I'm in the process of doing?

VONNEGUT: I'm certainly interested. Is that a . . .

SHORT: Yeah, I mentioned to you last night that my four favorite theologians will be quoted extensively throughout the book. That includes Bonhoeffer and Karl Barth and Dostoevsky and you.

VONNEGUT: Well, of the people you've mentioned, the one who had tremendous influence on me was Dostoevsky. When I came home from the war, the first book I read was *The Brothers* [*The Brothers Karamazov*], which really impressed me as an extraordinary book to read.

SHORT: Let me ask you about *The Brothers,* since you mentioned it. Eliot Rosewater tells Billy Pilgrim, in *Slaughterhouse-Five,* that "everything there was to know about life was in *The Brothers Karamazov* by Dostoevsky. But," Rosewater continues, "that isn't enough anymore." Now, does this correspond to your own views about *The Brothers* pretty closely?

VONNEGUT: I think Dostoevsky described the three basic attitudes that males, anyway, can have toward life with the three brothers. I'm able to classify almost everyone I know according to . . .

SHORT: Yeah, Ivan, Dmitri, or Alyosha.

VONNEGUT: Yeah, and strangely enough one doesn't shade into the other very much. But that seemed like a very complete depiction of human beings when I read it after the Second World War, and I simply realized that information wasn't much help. All this descriptive psychiatry. . . . He describes three different sorts of patients, really. And . . . I've just been reading Gail Sheehy's book [*Passages,* 1976]. It's a popularization of Erik Erikson's ideas about the stages of life, and none of this hard information helps. What's lacking from *The Brothers Karamazov*—probably what was lacking in my reading of it—was the understanding of reasons for life being shaped as it is. And Father Zossima—the explaining figure and the saint in the book—talks in the way which I immediately cut out. My family has been religiously skeptical as far back as I can trace it. My people have always been agnostics, and wilder of the elements have been atheists. H. L. Mencken said he'd been misunderstood about religion, his attitude toward religious people: He wasn't against them; he just found them comical. I find them comical too. It's been the set of mind my people haven't grown up with.

SHORT: I had always thought that perhaps one of the possible reasons why you—that *Eliot*—didn't find *The Brothers Karamazov* "enough anymore" was that Dostoevsky was writing from the other side of the "second industrial revolution" [the revolution bringing about the technologically dominated society of Vonnegut's *Player Piano*]. And he really, for that reason, wasn't able to express what he had to express in terms of the technological society that we live in nowadays, that this was one of the problems. But this isn't one of the things you think Eliot was getting at?

VONNEGUT: I operate intuitively, and I spend all day writing things down just to see what the hell they are; and if they seem right, I keep 'em. When he said that, I thought some level of my intelligence had said something smart without my really being able to say what was smart about it.

SHORT: I see.

VONNEGUT: The brothers certainly didn't have many opportunities, as they were in a medieval society, really. They didn't have that many places to go, that many different sorts of jobs to take.

SHORT: Or perhaps weren't forced to ask as many questions, or the same *kinds* of questions that we're thrown up against today.

VONNEGUT: A perfectly reasonable solution to my problems might be to go and live in France or Mexico. I can do that if I want to. There are extraordinary opportunities, and even a *poor* man or woman in this country can scrape up enough money to get the hell out and live for a year somewhere else.

SHORT: Have you read very much Kierkegaard?

VONNEGUT: No.

SHORT: Nothing?

VONNEGUT: No. See my education was as a chemist and then an anthropologist. And so I've never taken literary courses; I've never read a book for credit—except in high school. And where I got into reading important books was in the anthropology department of the University of Chicago. I read A. L. Kroeber, Ralph Linton, and Ruth Benedict and . . .

SHORT: Margaret Mead?

VONNEGUT: Margaret Mead and Clyde Kluckhohn and so forth. And all these were presented as extremely important books to me. I mean, they were my great books, because . . . I didn't get into a bookish department until I got into the department of anthropology.

SHORT: I see a lot of references to Job and Jonah in the things you've written. But when I first got on to your work, I was introduced to it through *Slaughterhouse*. But my immediate response to *Slaughterhouse* was that there is a lot of Ecclesiastes in this book.

VONNEGUT: Uh-huh.

SHORT: Since then, I've felt that hunch was correct because I see a lot of what you've written as being a sort of modern-day reworking of Ecclesiastes—as much as any Old Testament personality. The business about the "clockwork monotony of the Universe" [a phrase from Vonnegut's *Sirens of Titan*], the meaninglessness that Koheleth found in the universe, and so on. The feeling that "all is vanity" and here today and gone tomorrow and so on. Have you read Ecclesiastes closely?

VONNEGUT: No. You don't have to do that. When I teach, one of my assumptions is that a person, almost at birth, has wonderful ideas coded in his head. The most important ones, it seems to me, education often destroys. The first thing I tell a student is to trust his mind, and it can do remarkable things for him. But what people feel when they read Ecclesiastes is the shock of recognition and not of discovery. "Christ, this guy is thinking what I've always thought!" And the nature of my mail is mostly that. People don't write and say, you know, "You really gave me a whole bunch of new ideas—

my head's all awhirl." They seem to see the same things I'm thinking.

SHORT: I recently read the jacket copy on one of your records. I think it was written by Philboyd Studge? . . . Sludge? . . . one of the two! [Vonnegut has used both pseudonyms] You're talking about the very early influence that Ida Young—was that her name?—had on you, and the way she came at you with the Bible, or she *gave* you a lot of the Bible. [Ida Young was a black cook in the Vonnegut household when Kurt was a child.]

VONNEGUT: Yeah. That was Ida Young!

SHORT: Billy Pilgrim went into the war with "a meek faith in a loving Jesus," but that faith never did seem to get him through the war; it wasn't *helpful* to him. What was the problem, do you think? Was there some problem with Billy's faith, or do you think there was some problem with Jesus, or why didn't they connect, I wonder.

VONNEGUT: We Americans thank God for . . . around Thanksgiving or whenever, on the Fourth of July . . . that they're still alive, and that's supposed to be miracle enough, you know, that they're still eating. And a soldier's miracle is that he's still alive, after shellings and after incredibly long marches, and no food, no water, and all that, he's still alive. And so he thanks God for keeping him alive. I think that's all Billy Pilgrm could thank anybody for. Billy Pilgrim really was a guy named Joe Crone.

SHORT: I didn't know that.

VONNEGUT: Well, his father was a Unitarian minister in Rochester, New York. The physical condition of the American people was so bad after the Depression, it was all we could do to field an infantry. I mean, misshapened, bow-legged, badly scarred, dim-visioned people, with rotten teeth. I mean the health of the country was terrible. And Joe Crone never should have been in the army. When we made that last great push—you know, finally break into Germany—sent just hundreds of thousands of misshapened replacements over 'em over in Europe just to fill out the ranks and form a human tidal wave. And an awful lot of these people were really very sick and not very strong. And Joe Crone was such a person. He was shaped like a Coca-Cola bottle, and he was very sweet and weak, and he died in Dresden of a disease which is very characteristic of American soldiers in the army, which is "the five-thousand-mile stare." A person sits down, and stares off, stops talking to people, stops eating, and dies. It's a vitamin deficiency disease too. We had hundreds of guys in Korea die of "the five thousand mile stare." They were in prison with Turks and I guess Australians, Frenchmen—I forget who all fought in Korea . . . it was a polyglot army over there—and only our guys died of "the five-thousand-mile stare." I saw Joe Crone do it, and I saw a couple of other guys do it in Germany. Simply being alive wasn't enough. These guys tried to be grateful for the gift of life, and all of that; finally couldn't be grateful for it, that it was a great gift and—it wasn't enough.

SHORT: I have read about the experience that you're describing. I can't remember where I ran across it though. As you know, Kilgore Trout's "favorite formula" in his books is "to describe a perfectly hideous society, not unlike our own, and then toward the end to suggest ways in which it could be improved." Now, it seems to me this is pretty much the pattern that you have followed in doing your books as well. [Kilgore Trout is a character frequently appearing in Vonnegut's fiction. The quote above is from *God Bless You, Mr. Rosewater.*]

VONNEGUT: Uh-huh.

SHORT: But what about the *overall* pattern? Will you become more and more positive in suggesting ways that things can be improved, you think, as you continue to write?

VONNEGUT: Yeah, I think so. I was interviewed one time by a guy from WBAI—the liberal radio station in New York—and the interviewer told me if I ever got didactic I'd lose my audience. He thought what was tantalizing about what I wrote was the incompleteness, the failure to come up with much in the way of suggestions. I've really got a lot of suggestions now. And I'm on easy street, and my children are all grown and educated, and so I've got some ideas. I really do.

SHORT: But haven't you always had some ideas? I mean, you've always been working with "suggestions" in your mind, haven't you?

VONNEGUT: Yeah. One thing I know is that it's not going to cost any money to do with this society what I want it to do, save for dissemination of information that doesn't call for large expenditures of cash. It calls for change in attitudes, how we treat each other, forms of politeness.

SHORT: Well, most of the critics tend to interpret your work, though, in terms of nihilism and this kind of thing. "God is dead" a lot of them read in your work, that our job is simply to accept the "meaninglessness of it all" and to get on with it. Does it bother you that they tend to look upon what they see in your work in such bleak terms, that they don't find more affirmation there?

VONNEGUT: Well, what they ought to understand is that it's been an affirmative act, an affirmative attitude in my family for at least two hundred years . . . to declare, you know, that there *is* no God, that God has *always* been dead. And so if I declare that God is dead, it's no turning point in my personal history or in the history of my family. We've always found this meant an agreeable situation, to be on our own and to behave virtuously within the biological limits of being human beings. They say there are no atheists in foxholes. I was certainly one, and it was a comfort to me.

SHORT: And yet at the same time you seem to be opening the door—I don't know if this is a new development in your thinking—but you seem to be opening the door to a more positive appreciation of religion. Like in the essay "Up Is Better than Down" in *Wampeters* [*Wampeters, Foma, and Granfalloons*] you say that—and I think this is a direct quote—you say that "Only in superstition is there hope" [p. 163]. And you go on to say, in so many words, that it's only in hope that we'll stop "treating each other like garbage." So that would mean that only in *religion,* which is "superstition," can we hope to stop treating each other like garbage. And yet that positive appraisal of religion seems to be undercut at the same time by calling it "superstition," by calling it an "untruth," does it not? That is, isn't it necessary for people to believe *genuinely* in a religion in order for it to be "hopeful" for them, to furnish hope for them?

VONNEGUT: *No, it is not* . . .

SHORT: You don't think so?

VONNEGUT: . . . any more than it is necessary for an audience in a theater to believe that the people up on the stage are absolutely real people who are saying what they're saying. Everyone knows that they're actors. Everyone knows that if you go to see a symphony orchestra it's a sensationally artificial situation, which is known to be pleasurable and instructive and marvelous. When I tell stories, they have nice shapes—the "sign curves." There's: "boy meets girl . . . boy loses girl . . . boy gets girl back and is happier than he's ever been before." And so when I plot stories, I do it that way. If somebody wants something, gets it, loses it, gets it back . . . I tell stories because they're known to be very entertaining to human beings . . . on the human scale.

SHORT: Like the Cinderella story.

VONNEGUT: Yeah. I don't give a damn about baseball, and I thought the last World Series was really one of the major spiritual events in my century. Everyone was *so enchanted* by the Red Sox vs. Cincinnati. It sunk deeply into their personalities and was terribly artificial. I suppose some of the guys crossed themselves before they went to bat . . . they may have done it on camera. That was charming. It wasn't really an appeal to God at all.

SHORT: It was a sort of play, I guess.

VONNEGUT: Of course! That's all *we can* do. The line that really hits me was in George Orwell's *Burmese Days*. A native is going to his hanging under guard there and is wearing a loincloth, which he'd be wearing anyway, I guess. His musculature is exposed, and you can see his body. They're taking him to the gallows, and Orwell is walking behind him. He's watching all his musculature, his veins and arteries and everything. He's talking about the body going about—he calls it "the solemn tomfoolery of life," still pumping blood and still keeping all the tissues alive while it's on its way to death. I really think that's what life *is*. That's a very fine description of it. We *can* go about "solemn tomfoolery" when we allow each other to pretend this.

SHORT: Do you think that's going to be enough for most people? Dostoevsky, as you know, has Dmitri say in *The Brothers Karamazov*: "Rakitin says that it's possible to love other people without loving God. Well, only an idiot can believe that." This is a quote. [The actual quote is: "Rakitin says that one can love humanity without God. Well, only a sniveling idiot can maintain that."] Then in his *Diary of a Writer* he talks about how when people stop believing in God and/or immortality—and the two are almost synonymous for Dostoevsky—if they really stop believing in the possibility of immortality for *all* men (I'm not talking about somebody being condemned to hell, but *everybody* making it in the "final harmony" of things), then people have a tendency to lose hope. And as a result, not only is everything then "permitted," if there is no God, but everything, *the worst,* is positively *encouraged.* Because they lose hope, they hate life; and they're disappointed with the actions of their fellow men and so they hate them; and they become—because of their lack of hope—hysterically greedy. If this is all that is given to us— namely, "life"—then doesn't the meaning of life, insofar as it has any meaning at all, mean simply to get what you can while the getting's good?

VONNEGUT: Well, all this is logical, and sermons are *all* credible, but there's very little evidence. . . .

SHORT: That such a thing exists?

VONNEGUT: Yeah. We can sit there and argue that this must be so and if a man loses belief in an afterlife he's not going to work as hard as he would otherwise, but is this really the case? All right. Well, we have huge universities now, engines for gathering information on how millions of people behave in fact, have behaved in fact, under various stresses and deprivations and all that. And, you know, I welcomed the drug era in one way: As long as we're going to do it, let's *do* it. Let's find out what happens if you swallow this, if you swallow that. People have tried to get high on rat poison, you know, they tried to get high on everything that they've got in the back room of a drugstore; and are able to perform elaborate experiments just out of craziness . . . like "What would Europe be like if there were no Jews any more?" Heavens! It's been performed! We might as well see what the hell the answer is as long as it's been performed. I mean, do people lose faith on the way to the gas chamber? How do they act, and all that. Well, we have these enormous, these huge sociological experiments. I mean, one thing about catastrophes anyway is that they are now studied; and that we have computers that begin to generalize about what sort of animals human beings are. And, Christ, they . . . they don't lose faith the way my son . . .

SHORT: Mark.

VONNEGUT: . . . lost faith twice. I mean, he was hoping to kill. He was a dangerous maniac! He was also trying to kill *himself*. And the only reason he didn't succeed at one or the other is that schizophrenics are so screwed up they *can't* kill themselves. Neither can they murder. But anyway, he went through this *huge* spiritual crisis, and so I put him in a padded cell . . . really put him in a padded cell—once. Then several months later the Canadian Mounted Police, by Christ, slammed him back in again! And *his problem was chemical.*

SHORT: Yeah.

VONNEGUT: Of all the people who were in Germany during the Second World War, the bizarre lives being led by people, most of them far from home in terrible danger. There were South Africans and Yugoslav partisans and all that. And what these people felt from day to day was a function of their health as much as anything else.

SHORT: How's Mark doing now, by the way?

VONNEGUT: Pretty good remission. He's through his first year of med school at Harvard, and he's O.K. When he comes to stay with me, he brings embarrassing numbers of bottles and all this. He's a pill freak, and he's going to have to be for the rest of his life. He can see these great biblical visions coming with blood tests. They can see these identifiable chemicals showing up in his blood stream and adjust his diet accordingly and his blood stream straightens out. Otherwise he'd see the Apocalypse, he'd see Revelations, and he doesn't want to. So he's going to be a good solid citizen.

SHORT: Was his diet so screwed up when he was in this commune that it just cracked his confidence?

VONNEGUT: That does happen sometimes. Schizophrenia is largely inherited; and it's inherited by the Negritos, it's inherited by the Eskimos, it's inherited by the Laplanders, by everybody. It's not a disease of civilization at all: and somewhere between 2 and 5 percent of any society is schizophrenic. It has this chemical imbalance, which accounts for visionaries everywhere. I've never hallucinated, but he has. I've talked to him about it, and as a child he'd have things go out of focus and hear things no one else was hearing.

SHORT: I see. Yeah, I read the excerpts in *Playboy* from his book. I also read the interview with you in *Playboy*. Would you call yourself more of an atheist than an agnostic?

VONNEGUT: It doesn't matter. I call myself a scientist because I hang around with scientists more than other people. I welcome evidence of that sort and tend to believe it more than . . .

SHORT: Uh-huh. The position that you seem to hold I guess could be classified as "religious humanism" or "scientific humanism." And this would be very close to someone like Julian Huxley, I think.

VONNEGUT: Yeah! And I haven't come from a family that distinguished, but I've come from one that old and that aggressively rational. For instance, going into the arts in this society is taken as a startling thing to do; and I've said in lectures, you know, if you want to really hurt your parents and you didn't have courage enough to become a homosexual, the least you can do is go into the arts. But in my case my father was an artist, and my grandfather was an artist, and so I've just simply taken over the family steam laundry. There's perfect continuity here, and there are lots of people like me. I represent a wave of German immigration—the prosperous, well-educated younger sons who came over here as *speculators,* not as idealists, and history had somehow made them atheistic and agnostic. I don't even know what reasoning they might have gone through. But they were also . . . uh . . .

SHORT: Tired of religious wars, probably as much as anything.

VONNEGUT: Yeah. And there was so much they could not believe . . . what the preachers were saying, the government was saying, and they were enterprising and educated and had some doubts, so they came over here.

SHORT: I read the treatment of your family by—was it your Uncle Alex that wrote the thing . . . ["An Account of the Ancestry of Kurt

Vonnegut, Jr., by an Ancient Friend of His Family" in *Summary,* 1, No. 2, 1971.]

VONNEGUT: No. It was uncle John, and he recently died, but for some reason he did not wish it known he was a writer too. He was a lawyer, and he died at the age of about eighty-seven. He was so impressed that Edgar Lee Masters lost his law practice after he became a poet, that Masters was ruined as a lawyer . . .

SHORT: I didn't know that.

VONNEGUT: . . . because people didn't think he could be a good poet and a good lawyer too. This frightened uncle John, who really had nothing to fear, and so he wrote an awful lot anonymously.

SHORT: I'll be! I couldn't tell from reading that article if most of your family background had been northern or southern Germany, or Protestant or Catholic, and if there had been any clergymen anywhere down the line.

VONNEGUT: Well, I think there must have been in a Dostoevskian society where you could be a priest, a soldier—there were just a few jobs open. And what I've seen of the family tree, a reasonable number of people had been Protestant clergymen. They were very excited by the American experiment, and whatever the roots are of Thomas Jefferson's attitudes toward life were theirs too. It must have been the same philosophical river they all sprang from. But the first Vonnegut to come here married a Catholic girl in Germany and brought her over here. And the priest would come over frequently and upset the whole damned family, also name the children—all the sons, as he had nothing but sons, who became partners of his in the hardware business. My grandfather was one of those sons. He was Bernard after St. Bernard. All the sons were named saints until the very last child of the first generation of Vonneguts born in this country. Clemens Vonnegut, the emigrant, told the priest, "Look, I'm going to name this boy after an American, see!" And that was Franklin Vonnegut.

SHORT: When I saw that name *Clemens* I immediately was scurrying around among those pages to find out if Mark Twain was involved anywhere in your family tree. But apparently not.

VONNEGUT: No, no. This was the saint.

SHORT: I don't think the name Julian Huxley pops up anywhere in your writings, and yet you've read a lot of his things probably?

VONNEGUT: Well, somebody like myself would—you know, self-educated essentially since I was a chemist—would come to Huxley through all this . . . would read *Brave New World* and then keep coming across these other Huxley names, and finally realize . . .

SHORT: Huxley has an essay called "What Are People For?" I don't know where he got that. [This rather famous question is found in Vonnegut's *God Bless You, Mr. Rosewater.*]

VONNEGUT: That's spooky! I didn't know that!

SHORT: You haven't seen it?

VONNEGUT: Oh, sure I've seen it. I just didn't . . . I've never had to write a paper on anything I've read which would really fix it in my memory.

SHORT: I thought perhaps he got it from you. It was written after—what?—*Rosewater.*

VONNEGUT: Oh, it was? I didn't know that.

SHORT: Yeah, I believe so. [I was wrong. The question "What are People For?" appears in 1961 in Huxley's book *The Humanist Frame.* Vonnegut's *God Bless You, Mr. Rosewater* was published in 1965.]

VONNEGUT: NET had a series of programs where they started out with that question, where they attributed the quote to me. It's interesting, anyway.

SHORT: Here's another quote. As you know, "Calvary cemetery was named in honor of a hill in Jerusalem, thousands of miles away. Many people believed that the son of the Creator of the Universe had been killed on that hill thousands of years ago. Dwayne Hoover didn't know whether to believe that or not. Neither did Patty Keene." [From *Breakfast of Champions*]. What do you think?

VONNEGUT: He was another human being, and his sort of divinity is attainable by us. He had no superior connections or equipment.

SHORT: You seem to enjoy using a lot of traditional Christian symbolism. I don't know, again, whether this is conscious or unconscious. But this business about the *fish* in one way or another popping up in your things—like "Kilgore Trout"—and the fact that Harry Pena, one of the more sympathetic characters in *Rosewater*, was a fisherman; and that you liken yourself to the White Rock girl on the rock "looking for minnows" [in the preface to *Welcome to the Monkey House*]. Putting all these things together, I wondered if this symbol is being consciously used this way.

VONNEGUT: Well, you can't avoid it. I *love* to go into churches. Baptismal fonts particularly are *terribly* interesting to me. You know, I'd like to loot churches and take some of the stuff home and put it in my garden around the house and all. It's all so beautiful. Sure, you can't avoid fish symbols and all that. Same problem with Freudianism. No, everything is either a male or female symbol just because that's the way the universe is shaped, you know. It's cups and things to put into cups, and all that. And fish are marvelous without plunging in the Sea of Galilee. Fish would be marvelous anyway.

SHORT: Do you know if anyone has ever attempted to interpret you as sort of a "secret Christian," a "closet Christian," a kind of Kierkegaardian Christian who claims not to be a Christian only so he can communicate indirectly, holding his own answer back?

VONNEGUT: Well, they've said it in a way. One British critic, a guy named Tony Tanner, said that I "put bitter coatings on sugar pills," which is essentially the same thing. [In *Wampeters, Foma, and Granfalloons* this statement is attributed to American critic Robert Scholes.] It didn't offend me at all that he said that. Yeah, but again I actually belong to a minor Christian sect which not many people know much about—the Unitarians. I hang around with Unitarians and all that. Sure, I think my only disappointment with Christianity is with the cruelty of Christians.

SHORT: And the question becomes paramount: How is it that these people can become this way when it's so obviously against what they're supposed to believe? This is a question you asked explicitly in *Slaughterhouse*.

VONNEGUT: Yeah!

SHORT: Kilgore, in one of his books, is attempting to find out how it is that Christians can become so cruel.

VONNEGUT: I think the answer is *simple,* and it'd cost no money and it'd cost apparently little effort. The trouble is bad preaching.

SHORT: Bad preaching and also, in the story Kilgore wrote, it was—I think you called it . . . what is the word you used? . . . "disjointed story telling," or something like that, in the New Testament.

VONNEGUT: "Bad story telling" [Actually, Kilgore "concluded that at least part of the trouble was *slipshod* storytelling in the New Testament."] That whoever made up the Christ story didn't tell it right. An editor might have helped if he'd spent a couple of weeks figuring out how to tell the story so it wouldn't misfire, so it wouldn't be misunderstood. Because the way the story's told now, watch out for walking under people.

SHORT: Uh-huh. But bad preaching *from* the New Testament or a distortion *of* the New Testament is also a problem then, would you say?

VONNEGUT: Yeah. It's something that could be solved next Sunday. If ministers would simply talk about, you know, theft and . . . I haven't heard any minister talk about all the varieties of *stealing* that go on in this society now. We're robbing ourselves blind. New York is bankrupt because people *stole* so damned much, and we finally couldn't afford it. I've never heard a minister preach about theft. I've never heard a minister preach about murder. I don't know what the hell they *do* talk about in there. I go there from time to time. I never saw "Beyond the Fringe," but I heard that record there. But there's this discussion of the meaning of a passage in the Bible and *it is tedious* and very typical. I mean, these Englishmen broke up a theater by delivering a routine sermon. Under the circumstance it was all right to laugh—people were rolling in the aisles. But I wish there were preaching about crimes.

SHORT: You mention also, along this line, in the interview you did with Harry Reasoner [on "Sixty Minutes"], that ministers don't seem to want to talk about heaven, but this is something you did in *Wanda June* [Vonnegut's play *Happy Birthday, Wanda June.*]. Everybody wants to know what heaven is like. This is a question a lot of people have, especially young people. Do you think this is still the case? Do you still feel this way about ministers not being more open in how they talk about the future?

VONNEGUT: Their problem must be political . . . that they dare not be very interesting up there. It's that they're so easily fired, and their congregations just scold them. I mean, on Cape Cod I know ministers'd be in trouble and they'd be quite frightened by their congregations. They made a mistake last Sunday and next Sunday they'll try to patch it up.

SHORT: The Unitarians call themselves, do they not, "Unitarian Universalists." And by *Universalist* I've always understood that to mean that, as far as any kind of view of the future which their ministers or laypeople can have, this means that if there is a "sweet by n' by" or "immortality," *everybody* gets in—nobody is rejected. That means that Hitler or Eichmann and all the rest will be there?

VONNEGUT: That's right. I'm working on this now as a model for heaven—another one. It'll be my fifth or sixth.

SHORT: You mean in a literary work, you're using it this way?

VONNEGUT: Yeah. I've started a *new* book. The book that's going to be published this October [*Slapstick*] has a description of heaven in it. It's a great scientific breakthrough. They actually get in touch with people in heaven, and everybody finds out it's even worse run than what we have now, which changes people's attitude toward *this* life—that this is better than what we're headed for next. They get signals accidentally from the big particle accelerator out in Urbana, Illinois. They start hearing voices out of the damned thing, and by God they are in touch with people in the afterlife somehow. And everybody's very disconsolate. I mean, nobody's being tormented or anything.

SHORT: Everybody's there—nobody's excluded?

VONNEGUT: Yeah. A guy gets in touch with his sister, who's dead, and she says, you know, "Whoever designed *this* knew even less about human beings than whoever designed where you are."

SHORT: Is it the great desire, then, of the folks on the other side to somehow get back to where they were?

VONNEGUT: No. They'd like to fix *that* up. She wants her brother to die as soon as he can and come there and see if they can't put their heads together and see if they can't figure out how to make *that* better. But all right, that's behind me now. And I'm working on another thing about heaven which is based on Dante's model.

SHORT: Oh, oh!

VONNEGUT: At the very center of heaven, or of the inferno, is this three-headed monster that's gnawing forever on Judas and on Brutus—and I forget who the third person was . . .

SHORT: I don't know, either.

VONNEGUT: But anyway, this three-headed monster there is just gnawing on Hitler all the time. Judas has finally been retired to an outer circle, and so has Brutus, and I forget who this third guy is who was a totally unforgivable person. But Hitler is . . . just all alone, gnawed on in perpetuity!

SHORT: Is this another novel or a play?

VONNEGUT: It's a novel.

SHORT: I see. Well, so many people were willing to say that you'd stopped writing after *Breakfast of Champions.*

VONNEGUT: I thought I had. And didn't know. It'd been all right if I had. I think it's just Puritanism now that keeps me writing, as I simply . . . I don't know, whatever I was *born* to do I completed after I completed *Slaughterhouse-Five.* After that, I just had to start a new career somehow, you know. All I say is that I have a feeling of *completion* after that. I'm not counting on the quality of the work or anything else. It's just something was finished when I finished that.

SHORT: But your definition of a writer seems to be a person who *has* to write, is driven to write, he's *got.* to. Whether he happens to be good technically or not, he has to write. And I've always thought that this is probably *you!* I couldn't understand how you could deliberately turn a switch and turn yourself off as a writer. I didn't think that it would be possible for you.

VONNEGUT: Well, I've seen it in other people. I mean, Nelson Algren, for instance, who's a friend, said he didn't want to write any more. And this was before I said it about myself. I understood that. He'd written enough. One reason that suicide is very common among American writers, I think, is that a person wants to make his own life a perfect story too, to stop it when it's time to stop it. Hemingway was certainly as deeply sick as my son was. His chemicals were all wrong. But I think he also wanted to end the story at the proper point. And writers don't live very long. Painters live forever. But I've lived much longer than D. H. Lawrence or than Scott Fitzgerald and lots of other writers. And Fitzgerald's life ended perfectly as a Fitzgerald story. And Dorothy Parker provided the perfect last line, as a friend should do. Do you know what it was?

SHORT: No. I don't recall.

VONNEGUT: Well, she looked at his casket out there in Hollywood. And she took a line from *The Great Gatsby:* "You poor son-of-a-bitch!" So Fitzgerald, by dying then—dying before he was fifty-two—was a perfect Fitzgerald story. Algren has probably written enough, has probably completed himself. I think when Orwell died he had finished everything he knew he could do. I don't know how old Dostoevsky was when he died . . . .

SHORT: Hmm, sixty—he'd just turned sixty, I think. [He was within nine months of being sixty.]

VONNEGUT: But there's a very nice wholeness about history. The most influential American writer of my time is J. D. Salinger. I think. It's very strange what he's done—to simply decline to publish.

SHORT: If you actually do become more and more didactic as you go on, does this mean there'll be more and more nonfiction pieces, or will your *fiction* be more didactic?

VONNEGUT: There'll be more and more to complain about in my fiction. People will say it's not fiction any more, it's editorializing. And, you know, the stories are getting sketchier and sketchier and sketchier. But I like stories because they allow you to disgress. I'm not capable of logic, really a paragraph to paragraph logic. And so the story form allows me to just make statements that I know intuitively are true. I can't begin to buttress with arguments.

SHORT: Is "Sourdough, Ltd." still doing well?

VONNEGUT: Oh, we disbanded that. It was very funny. It was myself, a former Hollywood producer, and my lawyer. We were going to produce some plays and were going to make movies, were going to do a lot of things. And the minute we announced we were in business, money started to *pour* in, because we had no track record whatsoever, see? We had no failures. It was a startling demonstration of how the free enterprise system works! But my lawyer decided he'd rather practice law, and I decided I'd rather be a writer, and so we disbanded Sourdough. But we had a *lot* of projects. We even had Duke Ellington working for us for a while.

SHORT: Is that right? Whatever became of the idea to make a musical of *Cat's Cradle?* Is that still a possibility?

VONNEGUT: It's owned outright by a man named Hilly Elkins who produced *Golden Boy* and *The Rothschilds* and things like that, so it's genuinely his property. And whatever happens to it next is up to him. Jacques Levy, who's a theatrical director in New York, and I—we're friends—we worked on a script for it, and were hilarious and thought it was a keen script. And Hilly Elkins, the owner of the property who is also a friend of ours, said we may have been happy when we were writing it, but it was a piece of crap. Probably was! People don't like to see the characters in my books made flesh.

SHORT: Is that right?

VONNEGUT: No. It offends them. I'm less and less interested in movies too. When my children were growing up, I had genuine need for money, and so I *was* interested in the movie business as a way to get money. But I'm just content with the book business now.

SHORT: Yeah. I saw *Slaughterhouse* on television here recently.

VONNEGUT: Oh, it's a good movie! Yeah.

SHORT: Yeah. And when I first saw it, I thought it was tremendous! I couldn't conceive in the first place how they could do a film of *Slaughterhouse,* and so I was *very* pleased when I first saw it. But then after seeing it recently again and rethinking it, it occurs to me that there's *so much* in *Slaughterhouse* that didn't appear in that film that I became sort of disappointed with it. Nothing of Kilgore Trout, and so on. But then, as I *continued* to think about it and talk to people about their reactions to it, it seems to me that the *redemptive* aspect of that film is that it'll pull people into reading the book, where the *real* payoff is, as far as I'm concerned.

VONNEGUT: Oh, it's nice of you to say so. But so much is economics. So much of what is happening to me is *industrial* in nature. I have an extraordinary publisher who keeps me entirely in print. Most books are *junked* now six weeks after publication, absolutely not obtainable. And my publisher maintains *warehouses* with my books in them. So some writers get *frantic* when a movie is made of their books. Because the movie becomes the book—the book itself isn't available. And so the person is *desperate* to have an accurate translation made *to* film. And I don't give a damn because my books are *utterly* available—in bus stations, in drug stores and PX's and everywhere. They're so easy to get. It's unfortunate that way, and that's an industrial freak. But I *am* in print; I'm about the only American author who is. My publisher is Sam Lawrence, who's connected with Dell. He brings out I think seventeen books a year, and he's built a very small stable with me, and there's Richard Brautigan, there's J. P. Donleavy. Brautigan later went to Simon and Schuster. But Sam Lawrence has made it a point of putting all his authors in print. Donleavy's *completely* in print. I'm completely in print. When Brautigan was with Sam Lawrence, *he* was completely in print. Sam is systematically publishing Céline—keeping Céline completely in print. No other publisher's doing this! If you want to start collecting Norman Mailer books, for instance, or Philip Roth books, you're going to have to hang around second-hand bookstalls and church sales and all of that to get 'em all.

SHORT: What about Mark Twain? I sure do see a lot of Mark Twain in your work.

VONNEGUT: Yeah. I *did* read a lot of Mark Twain as a kid. And I just did an introduction to a collection of Mark Twain that a . . .

SHORT: Oh, you did?

VONNEGUT: Yeah. There's a new outfit called Running Press which is down in Philadelphia. And they are bringing out *The Unabridged Mark Twain,* which is a huge book . . . . a paperback book with a very strong spine on the thing so it'll all hold together. But it's almost *all* there. . . . Anyway I did the introduction to this *Unabridged Mark Twain,* and so I've been thinking about him hard recently.

SHORT: I think if I were doing a doctoral dissertation on your work, this is what I'd want to do. I'd want to say that you're sort of an "updated Mark Twain." And I think a good case could be made for that—in a lot of ways. The determinism, the way you use determinism; the way he fashioned "tragedy traps," in a sense, in order to bring people to a deeper realization about things; he used *humor* to form a "tragedy trap," as he put it . . .

VONNEGUT: His judgment turned out to be *awfully* good. In order to write this introduction, I first read a whole lot of stuff over, just really skimmed through the whole output, stopping here and there to refresh myself. And almost nothing he did was dated. There's one thing in the whole collection that is just merely touching, which is his essay on Jews.

SHORT: I've never read that.

VONNEGUT: He tells 'em, in about 1906 or something like that, that he can understand why they'd be so frightened in terms of their past and everything, so mistrustful of their neighbors. But really that's all over now. It's not a patronizing piece at all. That's something Americans have always felt about Jews too, that their time of troubles is over.

SHORT: And he was really writing a lot of science fiction, it seems to me, in a way, some of his pieces.

VONNEGUT: Yeah.

SHORT: I can't recall offhand . . .

VONNEGUT: *Connecticut Yankee* is pure science fiction.

SHORT: Yeah!

VONNEGUT: Time travel. Long before H. G. Wells wrote about time travel.

SHORT: Wells and Orwell and Twain and Huxley—those all seem to enter into the equation pretty strongly.

VONNEGUT: Yeah. Well there's one strong influence on me too—there's one thing I say in the essay: A lot of people claim to be heirs of Twain. If you're truly going to be an heir of Twain, you have to be *extremely* clever with language too. And I thought there was only one person who was as good with language as he was, in this country, which is H. L. Mencken. He controlled it—had absolute command of the language and could pull any word out of his head immediately and play perfectly beautiful games with it. And Mencken was a big influence on me. Such a reactionary old coot that could be so wrong about so many things!

SHORT: Kierkegaard said in his *Journals* that he didn't consider himself an apostle, not having any authority, but he conceived of his task as "making room for God to come." And I've always sort of coupled that statement with your statement in the introduction to *Monkey House,* that you conceive of your work as having a kind of double edge: "cleaning the shit off practically everything" and "no pain"—the "cleaning the shit off practically everything" corresponding with "making room," or "cleaning out"; and "no pain" as your equivalent for his business of putting God in this vacuum. What do you mean, more specifically, about "no pain"? You want to "afflict the comfortable," it seems to me, but also to "comfort the afflicted." And I think this would be another way of paraphrasing what you mean by "no pain." Would that be a fair statement to make, do you think, to "comfort the afflicted"?

VONNEGUT: Oh, sure. I love to do that. Yeah, because I consider it possible. I think it's possible to *say* things to people that will be genuinely comforting, if you think about it—and think it out first. And my son is one generation beyond me—he wants to feed people things that will comfort them, as he himself has been comforted this way, literally feed them.

SHORT: But if it is true that man doesn't live by bread alone, then into this job of comforting people there's got to be a spiritual—a very strong dose of the spiritual dimension—does there not?

VONNEGUT: Yeah, but that's the . . . uh . . . Dostoevsky kiss, it's the touch. You know, I raised three adopted kids, my nephews. When one of them got to be twenty-one, I was trying to make a lot of noise and get him drunk and everything. He said, "You know, you've never hugged me."

SHORT: Is that right?

VONNEGUT: Yeah. And so I *did* hug him. Alyosha answered one of Ivan's most telling arguments with a kiss, which I consider utterly satisfactory. What Zossima said was more preaching, which I really couldn't understand. But I understood the kiss as a total answer. . . . Who was the guy who went to the gas chamber finally out in California, who became famous . . . ?

SHORT: I know who you're talking about. I can't think of his name offhand either.

VONNEGUT: Caryl Chessman.

SHORT: Chessman! Yeah.

VONNEGUT: You know what his last words were?

SHORT: No.

VONNEGUT: Well, this was a man who had not committed murder— he'd committed rape. And because of that the girl had gone to the insane asylum and never recovered. But he'd become a new person. His last words were. "It's all right."

SHORT: "It's all right", Everything's all right?

VONNEGUT: "It's all right." He said that to people who were going to kill him, who must have been as mystified and terrified as he was.

SHORT: You mention in the preface to *Wanda June* that you "live in *chrono syn-* . . ." How do you . . . ?

VONNEGUT: *"Chrono-synclastic infundibulum."*

SHORT: Yes. What did you mean by that?

VONNEGUT: Well, in a *chrono-synclastic infundibulum* everybody's right. I mean, Ronald Reagan and Hubert Humphrey can't both be right. And yet if you bring them in a *chrono-synclastic infundibulum,* of course they're right. It's a sort of "time warp" out there. Everybody *is* right. . . . Somebody said to me one time out in Indianapolis, "How can you stand to listen to your relatives?" Because they're highly intelligent people. Politically they're barbarous! I mean the things they say about black people, and a couple of other things, is *shocking*. These are old people. Thing about it, I realized they didn't listen, really. I loved them and I inhabited a *chrono-synclastic infundibulum.* And I went to a funeral of a friend in Kentucky, and two huge extended families came in there—the husband's family and the wife's family (it was the wife who'd died). And afterward one woman was saying she just couldn't stand her relatives, you know—they embarrassed her when they all came together like that. And everybody jumped on her because relatives aren't there to be liked. They're there to be relatives, you know; they don't have to come up to a certain standard. What's magic about them is they're relatives. Are we talking about what we started to talk about? I forget what it . . .

SHORT: Yeah. Well, I suppose this is related to your feeling that there are no "villains," for one thing. If you have this kind of idea about people, that finally there are no villains, that people do what they *have* to do, then this is part of what goes into making a *"chrono"*—uh—whatchacallit . . .

VONNEGUT: Yeah. *Chrono-synclastic infundibulum.*

SHORT: Thank you!

VONNEGUT: People *can* be instructed. People can take *lessons,* and so they can go *beyond* what they must be. One of my complaints about this country is how little teaching goes on, particularly by the president. I think now that we have television, the president could become an utterly magic teacher. Even Nixon, when he was most despised, could have instructed us if he'd wanted to. He *could* have taught us to conserve energy, and we all would have done it. There *was* a magic time there for a couple of weeks where everybody was driving under fifty-five. I was on the New Jersey turnpike, and some character went barreling by in his Pontiac, and he was honking his horn. And this guy went like this to him [Vonnegut laughs and juts a middle finger into the air] as he went by. They were telling him to slow down and everything. We could have done that indefinitely and saved *billions* of gallons of gas every year. And that all stopped. I was so disappointed. But we could have a president simply deliver a speech on all networks about politeness . . . say, "Look, we're having a hard enough time now, with the depression and there aren't enough jobs and the atmosphere's poisoned by our vehicles and all that. Least we can do is be more polite to each other. Would you please tomorrow try to be more concerned with your neighbors. It's the least we can do."

SHORT: You mention in your essay in *Wampeters*, "Yes, We Have No Nirvanas," the statement that Maharishi made to the effect that all the churches can do is help people "live and die in hope." Immediately following that your comment was that you went out to the front of the hotel and that you "never liked Jesus so much" after you heard him say that. Is this really, do you think, what *ministers* need to concentrate on in the stuff they feed their flocks each week, to give them hope, to not only talk about common decency and manners and so on, but to live in hope?

VONNEGUT: You don't *need* to live in hope. People don't *need* that as much as we assume we do. I mean you ran off this Dostoevskian argument. . . . I've been told that a great contribution Americans have made to civilization, many people feel, is Alcoholics Anonymous, which is living from day to day. You celebrate sobriety and *today,* rather than this wonderful thing that's going to happen to you twenty years from now if you live systematically. So . . . *I* live without hope.

SHORT: Without ultimate hope?

VONNEGUT: Yeah! And that's perfectly all right. I live without . . . uh . . . hope of paradise. I love sleep; so sleep is fine with me.

SHORT: You won't be offended, though, if you die and go to heaven?

VONNEGUT: No. But I . . .

SHORT: . . . would be surprised?

VONNEGUT: You know, you were talking about Mark Twain. In *Captain Stormfield's Visit to Heaven* he describes it, and it's a very tedious place. What Jung resented about dying was to have his awareness mixed with everybody else's, because he'd done so much to refine it, you know. It's almost as though they were going to distribute his bank account to a whole bunch of strangers. His funds are going to be mingled with everybody else's! But I've done *fine* living without hope. One clear hope I had was that I'd be able to—it's a middle-class hope—to give good education to my children. And that I've been able to do. Only when I was about forty-five did I start to have respectable amounts of money. I could suddenly blacktop my driveway, you know; I could suddenly buy a new car. Before that I was making about as much as I would if I were the principal of a junior high school, something like that. It was very modest amounts of money so that the educations I *did* give my kids, with a lot of 'em going to prep schools and stuff like that, resulted from a lot of real scrambling and scrimping and shit-eating, too, with scruffy jobs and vaguely dishonorable activities. [I'm not sure what Vonnegut is referring to here, but I do know that he sold cars for a while.] But once I fulfilled that hope—'cause they all got their educations, they're all out of college now—and I've got a *lot* of money, and there's nothing much I want to do with—there's no hope to fulfill. My father and grandfather were both architects; so I really should build a swell house. They built houses for themselves all the time, you know, architects buy anything they want for themselves in the way of houses. My father designed four houses for himself, and my grandfather designed a couple that I know of. So I should do that, and I find I don't have the courage to.

Notes

Prelude and Dedication

1. Ingmar Bergman, *Scenes from a Marriage,* trans. Alan Blair (New York: Bantam Books, 1974), p. 206.
2. Kurt Vonnegut, *Player Piano* (New York: Avon Books, 1952), p. 140.

Chapter 1

1. Fyodor Dostoevsky, *The Brothers Karamazov,* trans. Andrew R. MacAndrew (New York: Bantam Books, 1970), p. 283.
2. Quoted in *Mark Twain on the Damned Human Race,* ed. Janet Smith (New York: Hill and Wang, 1962), p. xi.
3. George Orwell, "Politics and the English Language," in *The Orwell Reader,* ed. Richard H. Rovere (New York: Harcourt, Brace, Javanovich, 1956), p. 355.
4. Gerhard Ebeling, *Word and Faith,* trans. James W. Leitch (Philadelphia: Fortress Press, 1963), pp. 355, 360–61.
5. Dietrich Bonhoeffer, *Letters and Papers from Prison,* ed. Eberhard Bethge (New York: Macmillan, 1971), pp. 384–85.
6. Dietrich Bonhoeffer, *Ethics,* trans. Neville H. Smith (London: Collins, 1964), p. 207.
7. Edwin Newman, *A Civil Tongue* (Indianapolis/New York: Bobbs-Merrill Co., 1975), p. 131.
8. Quoted in Dietrich Bonhoeffer, *The Cost of Discipleship* (New York: Macmillan, 1963), p. 277.
9. Kurt Vonnegut, *Slaughterhouse-Five* (New York: Dell, 1969), p. 110.
10. "The Awful German Language," *Selected Shorter Writings of Mark Twain,* ed. Walter Blair (Boston: Houghton Mifflin, 1962), p. 178.
11. *Table Talk,* Luther's Works, Vol. 54, ed. and trans. Theodore G. Tappert (Philadelphia: Fortress Press, 1967), pp. 62–63.
12. *Selected Short Stories of Franz Kafka,* trans. Willa and Edwin Muir (New York: Modern Library, 1952), p. 171.
13. Kurt Vonnegut, *God Bless You, Mr. Rosewater* (New York: Dell, 1965), p. 27.
14. Heinz Zahrnt, *What Kind of God?* (Minneapolis: Augsburg, 1971), p. 129.
15. Orwell, "Politics and the English Language," p. 360.
16. John Camper, "Priortizing Maximization: Newman Strikes Again," *Chicago Daily News,* 30–31 October 1976, p. 4.
17. Kurt Vonnegut, *Wampeters, Foma & Granfalloons* (New York: Delacorte/Seymour Lawrence, 1974), p. 200.
18. Quoted in Vonnegut, "On Reading/Writing/Freedom," *Mademoiselle,* August 1977, p. 96.
19. "And/or" is an awkward construction that writers are well advised to avoid. However, in

the case of "Jesus and/or God," I find it a useful and succinct way of expressing something essential about Jesus Christ, which the church has always said in one way or another: This particular man alone was the one, true *God* (hence "God *or* Christ"). At the same time, it was indeed a particular flesh-and-blood, historical *man* who alone was God (and hence "God *and* Christ"). Jesus Christ was *both* fully God and fully a particular, historical man.

20. Dietrich Bonhoeffer, *No Rusty Swords,* trans. Edwin H. Robertson and John Bowden (New York: Harper & Row, 1965), p. 90.
21. Ebeling, *Word and Faith,* pp. 374–75.
22. Roland H. Bainton, *Here I Stand: A Life of Martin Luther* (New York: Mentor Books, 1950), p. 238.
23. Ibid., p. 264.
24. Vonnegut, *Wampeters, Foma & Granfalloons,* pp. 94–95.
25. Herman Melville, *Moby Dick* (New York: Modern Library, 1950), p. 29.
26. *Hamlet,* act 2, sc. 2.
27. Quoted in G. B. Trudeau, *The Doonesbury Chronicles* (New York: Holt, Rinehart and Winston, 1975), inside front cover.
28. "Editorial Cartoons: Capturing the Essence," *Time,* 3 February 1975, p. 62.
29. Bonhoeffer, *No Rusty Swords,* p. 18.
30. Karl Barth, *Deliverance to the Captives,* trans. Marguerite Wieser (New York: Harper & Brothers, 1961), p. 47.
31. Kurt Vonnegut, "Headshrinker's Hoyle on Games We Play," *Life,* 11 June 1965, pp. 15, 17.
32. I realize that calling Bonhoeffer a "Barthian" could get the goats of a lot of theological novices as well as a good number of old hands who should know better. But for my money this is the only way to put together all the pieces of the Bonhoeffer puzzle, including his controversial *Letters and Papers from Prison.* I agree with Eberhard Bethge, Bonhoeffer's closest friend and confidant and the person for whom most of the "letters and papers" were written: "Whatever the implications of Bonhoeffer's earlier or later criticisms of Barth may be, in all four phases [of Bonhoeffer's life] he wanted them to be regarded as coming from inside and not outside the Barthian movement" (Bethge, *Dietrich Bonhoeffer* [New York: Harper & Row, 1970], p. 134).

Chapter 2

1. Quoted in Helmut Thielicke, *Death and Life,* trans. Edward H. Schroeder (Philadelphia: Fortress Press, 1970), p. iii.
2. Karl Barth, *Against the Stream,* trans. Ronald Gregor Smith (New York: Philosophical Library, 1954), p. 141.
3. Karl Barth, *The Faith of the Church,* trans. Gabriel Vahanian (New York: Meridian Books, 1958), pp. 173–74.
4. D. P. Walker, *The Decline of Hell* (Chicago: University of Chicago Press, 1964), p. 67.

5. Mark Twain, *Letters from the Earth,* ed. Bernard DeVoto (New York: Fawcett Crest, 1962), pp. 46–47.

6. Hans Schwarz, *On the Way to the Future* (Minneapolis: Augsburg, 1972), pp. 30–33.

7. Søren Kierkegaard, *The Sickness unto Death,* trans. Walker Lowrie (Princeton: Princeton University Press, 1951), p. 14.

8. Kurt Vonnegut, *Slaughterhouse-Five* (New York: Dell, 1969), p. 73.

9. *Martin Luther: Selections from His Writings,* ed. John Dillenberger (New York: Garden City, 1961), p. 170.

10. *Pascal's Pensées,* trans. W. F. Trotter (New York: E. P. Dutton, 1958), Fragment 547, p. 147.

11. Barth, *The Faith of the Church,* p. 95.

12. Kurt Vonnegut, *The Sirens of Titan* (New York: Dell, 1959), p. 91.

13. Karl Barth, *The Epistle to the Romans,* trans. Edwyn C. Hoskyns (London: Oxford University Press, 1933), p. 259.

14. See William J. Wolf's excellent book *Lincoln's Religion* (Philadelphia: Pilgrim Press, 1970), especially pp. 103–108 and p. 193.

15. Emperor Henry IV before Pope Gregory VII (Hildebrand), in 1077, at Canossa.

16. Quoted in Roland H. Bainton, *Here I Stand: A Life of Martin Luther* (New York: Mentor Books, 1950), p. 60.

17. *Martin Luther: Selections from His Writings, op. cit.,* p. 199.

18. John Calvin, *Institutes of the Christian Religion,* vol. 2, ed. John T. McNeill (Philadelphia: Westminster Press, 1960), p. 955.

19. Karl Barth, *Church Dogmatics,* I/2, Authorised Translation (Edinburgh: T. & T. Clark, 1956), pp. 325 ff.

20. Ibid., II/2, 1957, p. 182.

21. Reinhold Niebuhr, *Faith and History* (New York: Charles Scribner's Sons, 1951), p. 53.

22. Kurt Vonnegut, *The Sirens of Titan* (New York: Dell, 1959), p. 222.

Chapter 3

1. Albert Camus, *The Rebel,* trans. Anthony Bower (New York: Vintage Books, 1956), p. 235.

2. Gerhard Ebeling, *Word and Faith,* trans. James W. Leitch (Philadelphia: Fortress Press, 1963), pp. 355, 360–61. The last part of Ebeling's final sentence is itself muddled in the translation and apparently also in the original German. Therefore, I have recast this part of the sentence in order to make his obvious meaning clearer.

3. Amos Wilder, *Modern Poetry and the Christian Tradition: A Study in the Relation of Christianity to Culture* (New York: Charles Scribner's Sons, 1952), p. xii.

4. John Updike, "All's Well in Skyscraper National Park," *New Yorker,* 25 October 1976, p. 186.

5. Ebeling, *Word and Faith,* pp. 342–43.

6. Fyodor Dostoevsky, *Letters of Fyodor Dostoevsky to His Family and Friends,* trans. Ethel Colburn Mayne (New York: McGraw-Hill, 1964), p. 257.

7. Mark Twain, "The Mysterious Stranger," in Bernard DeVoto, ed., *The Portable Mark Twain* (New York: Viking Press, 1946), p. 743.

8. CBS News transcript of "60 Minutes," 15 September 1970, p. 14.

9. Benjamin DeMott, "Vonnegut's Otherworldly Laughter," *Saturday Review,* 1 May 1971, p. 38.

10. From author's personal interview with Kurt Vonnegut. See appendix.

11. DeMott, "Vonnegut's Otherwordly Laughter," p. 30.

12. Kurt Vonnegut, *Wampeters, Foma & Granfalloons* (New York: Delacorte/Seymour Lawrence, 1974), p. 238.

13. Kurt Vonnegut, *Breakfast of Champions* (New York: Dell, 1973), p. 15.

14. From the Author's personal interview with Vonnegut. See appendix.

15. Conversation of the Author with Vonnegut in Chicago, April 2, 1977.

16. Konstantin Mochulsky, *Dostoevsky: His Life and Work,* trans. Michael A. Minihan (Princeton: Princeton University Press, 1967), p. 563.

17. Edward Wasiolek, ed., *Dostoevsky: The Notebooks for the Possessed,* trans. Victor Terras (Chicago: University of Chicago Press, 1968), p. 2.

18. Kurt Vonnegut, *Slaughterhouse-Five* (New York: Dell, 1969), p. 101.

19. Jürgen Moltmann, *The Experiment Hope,* trans. M. Douglas Meeks (Philadelphia: Fortress Press, 1975), p. 87.

20. S. Paul Schilling, *God in an Age of Atheism* (Nashville: Abingdon, 1969), p. 90.

21. Ebeling, *Word and Faith,* pp. 342–43.

22. Kurt Vonnegut, *Cat's Cradle* (New York: Dell, 1963), p. 59.

23. Kurt Vonnegut, *Player Piano* (New York: Avon, 1952), p. 140.

24. Kurt Vonnegut, *Welcome to the Monkey House* (New York: Delacorte/Seymour Lawrence, 1968), p. ix–x.

25. Vonnegut, *God Bless You, Mr. Rosewater,* p. 77.

26. Quoted in Caroline T. Harnsberger, *Mark Twain's Views of Religion* (Evanston: Schori Press, 1961), p. 17.

27. Vonnegut, *Sirens of Titan,* p. 124.

28. Thomas Hardy, "In Tenebris," in *A Little Treasury of Modern Poetry,* rev. ed., ed. Oscar Williams (New York: Charles Scribner's Sons, 1952), p. 15.

29. Peter J. Reed, *Kurt Vonnegut, Jr.* (New York: Warner Paperback Library, 1972), pp. 205–6.

30. Dietrich Bonhoeffer, *Ethics,* trans. Neville H. Smith (London: Collins, 1964), p. 207.

31. Richard Schickel, "Black Comedy with Purifying Laughter," *Harper's,* May 1966, p. 106.

32. Vonnegut, *Wampeters, Foma & Granfallons,* p. 240.

33. James C. Livingston, *Modern Christian Thought from the Enlightenment to Vatican II* (New York: Macmillan, 1971), p. 9.

34. Kurt Vonnegut, *God Bless You, Mr. Rosewater* (New York: Dell, 1965), pp. 133–34.

35. Kurt Vonnegut, *The Sirens of Titan* (New York: Dell, 1959), p. 215.

36. Vonnegut, *Slaughterhouse-Five, op. cit.,* p. 108.

37. Vonnegut, *Mother Night* (New York: Dell, 1966), p. vii.

38. *What Luther Says: An Anthology,* ed. Ewald M. Plass, Vol. III (St. Louis: Concordia Publishing House, 1959), p. 4074.

39. Vonnegut, *God Bless You, Mr. Rosewater, op. cit.,* p. 42.

40. Vonnegut, *Mother Night, op. cit.,* p. 181.

41. *Playboy,* July, 1968, p. 47.

42. Barth, *The Faith of the Church, op. cit.,* p. 69.

43. Barth, *Church Dogmatics,* II/2, *op. cit.,* p. 147.

44. Mark Twain, *Roughing It* (New York: New American Library, 1962), pp. 345–46.

45. Vonnegut, *Cat's Cradle,* p. 143.

46. Mark Twain, *What Is Man?* ed. Paul Baender (Berkeley: University of California Press, 1973), p. 399.

47. Vonnegut, *Wampeters, Foma & Granfalloons,* pp. 161–62.

48. Dietrich Bonhoeffer, *Letters and Papers from Prison,* ed. Eberhard Bethge (New York: Macmillan, 1971), pp. 384–85.

49. Quoted in Antonina Vallentin, *The Drama of Albert Einstein,* trans. Maura Budberg (Garden City, N.Y.: Doubleday, 1954), pp. 290–91.

50. Quoted in Charles I. Glicksberg, *The Literature of Nihilism* (Lewisburg: Bucknell University Press, 1975), p. 227.

51. Kurt Vonnegut, *Mother Night* (New York: Dell, 1966), p. 84.

52. Kurt Vonnegut, *Slaughterhouse-Five* (New York: Dell, 1969), p. 21.

53. Martin Heidegger, *The Question of Being,* trans. Wm. Kluback and Jean T. Wilde (New York: T. Wayne, 1958), p. 47.

54. Dietrich Bonhoeffer, "The First Table of the Ten Commandments," in John D. Godsey, *Preface to Bonhoeffer* (Philadelphia: Fortress Press, 1965), p. 57.

55. Dietrich Bonhoeffer, *Letters and Papers from Prison,* ed. Eberhard Bethge (New York: Macmillan, 1971), p. 185.

56. Albert Einstein, *Out of My Later Years* (New York: Philosophical Library, 1950), p. 113.

57. A. Boyce Gibson, *The Religion of Dostoevsky* (Philadelphia: Westminster Press, 1973), pp. 180–82, 201.

58. Fyodor Dostoevsky, *The Diary of a Writer,* trans. Boris Brasol (New York: George Braziller, 1954), pp. 538–42.

59. Fyodor Dostoevsky, *The Brothers Karamazov,* trans. Andrew R. MacAndrew (New York: Bantam Books, 1970), p. 283.

60. Ibid., pp. 80–81.

61. Dietrich Bonhoeffer, *Ethics,* trans. Neville H. Smith (London: Collins, 1964), p. 103.

62. *Selected Essays of T. S. Eliot* (New York: Harcourt, Brace & Co., 1950), p. 433. Italics mine.

63. Kurt Vonnegut, *God Bless You, Mr. Rosewater* (New York: Dell, 1965), p. 21.

64. Ibid., p. 183.

65. Kurt Vonnegut, *Breakfast of Champions* (New York: Dell, 1973), pp. 219–20.

66. Ibid., p. 221.

67. Vonnegut, *God Bless You, Mr. Rosewater,* p. 49.

68. Bonhoeffer, *Letters and Papers from Prison,* p. 380.

69. Karl Barth, "Jesus Christ and the Movement for Social Justice," in ed. and trans. George Hunsinger, *Karl Barth and Radical Politics* (Philadelphia: Westminster Press, 1976), p. 36.

70. Vonnegut, *God Bless You, Mr. Rosewater,* p. 183.

71. Bonhoeffer, *Ethics,* pp. 163–64.

72. What Sally Brown says here about wanting "all I can get before . . . the sun has dimmed, and the stars have fallen, and the birds are silent" should be compared to the famous "Allegory of Old Age" of Ecclesiastes 12:2–6. No doubt this is what Schulz is alluding to here.

73. Vonnegut, *Mother Night,* p. vii.

74. Vonnegut, *Breakfast of Champions,* p. 78.

75. Kurt Vonnegut, *The Sirens of Titan* (New York: Dell, 1959), p. 305.

76. The similarities between the views of Ecclesiastes and Kurt Vonnegut are nothing short of amazing. Unfortunately, I stumbled across Vonnegut's work after I completed my book on Ecclesiastes. Otherwise, Vonnegut might have furnished a useful modern-day counterpart to this very "modern" Old Testament writer.

77. Karl Barth, *The Epistle to the Romans,* trans. Edwyn C. Hoskyns (London: Oxford University Press, 1933), p. 43.

78. Vonnegut, *Slaughterhouse-Five,* p. 91.

79. Ibid., pp. 76–77.

80. Vonnegut, *God Bless You, Mr. Rosewater,* p. 93.

81. Bonhoeffer, *Ethics,* p. 74.

82. Karl Barth, *The Faith of the Church,* trans. Gabriel Vahanian (New York: Meridian Books, 1958), p. 32.

83. Fyodor Dostoevsky, *The Brothers Karamazov,* trans. Constance Garnett (New York: The Modern Library, 1950), p. 721.

84. Fyodor Dostoevsky, *The Brothers Karamazov,* trans. Andrew R. MacAndrew, *op. cit.,* pp. 712–713.

85. Kurt Vonnegut, "Nashville," *Vogue,* June, 1975, p. 103.

86. Dostoevsky, *The Brothers Karamazov,* trans. Andrew R. MacAndrew, *op. cit.,* p. 354.

87. Ibid., p. 159.

88. Karl Barth, *The Humanity of God,* trans. J. N. Thomas and Thomas Wieser (Richmond: John Knox Press, 1960), pp. 58–59.

89. Quoted in *Decision,* June 1966, p. 1.

90. Quoted in Caroline T. Harnsberger, *Mark Twain's Views of Religion* (Evanston: Schori Press, 1961), p. 22.

91. Kurt Vonnegut, *Wampeters, Foma & Granfalloons* (New York: Delacorte/Seymour Lawrence, 1974), p. 246.

92. Conversation of the Author with Vonnegut in Chicago, April 4, 1977.

93. Albert Camus, *Resistance, Rebellion, and Death,* trans. Justin O'Brien (New York: Alfred Knopf, 1961), p. 59.

94. Kurt Vonnegut, *Cat's Cradle* (New York: Dell, 1963), p. 59.

95. Albert Camus, *The Rebel,* trans. Anthony Bower (New York: Vintage Books, 1956), p. 305.

96. Albert Camus, *The Myth of Sisyphus and Other Essays,* trans. Justin O'Brien (New York: Vintage Books, 1955), pp. 1–91.

97. Mark Twain, "Jim Baker's Bluejay Yarn," in Bernard De-Voto, ed., *The Portable Mark Twain* (New York: Viking Press, 1946), pp. 43–48.

98. Mark Twain, *What Is Man?* ed. Paul Paender (Berkeley: University of California Press, 1973), p. 13.

99. Vonnegut, *Slaughterhouse-Five,* p. 198; *Cat's Cradle,* p. 178.

100. Twain, *What Is Man?* p. 128.

101. Vonnegut, *Slaughterhouse-Five,* p. 154.

102. Quoted in Gladys Carmen Bellamy, *Mark Twain As a Literary Artist* (Norman, Okla.: University of Oklahoma Press, 1950), p. 306.

103. Vonnegut, *Slaughterhouse-Five,* pp. 8, 164.

104. Ibid., p. 86.

105. Karl Barth, *The Word of God and the Word of Man* (New York: Harper & Brothers, 1957), pp. 28 ff.

106. From record album introduction to *Slaughterhouse-Five,* abridged by Marianne Mantell, Caedmon Records, Inc., 1973.

107. Vonnegut, *Cat's Cradle,* p. 128 and *Slaughterhouse Five,* p. 77.

108. The best literary illustration I know of the self-interested necessity out of which Christians obey is Kafka's short story "A Hunger Artist." At the conclusion of the story the hunger artist tells us: "You shouldn't admire [my fasting]. . . . I have to fast, I can't help it. . . . because I couldn't find the food I liked. If I had found it, believe me, I should have made no fuss and stuffed myself like you or anyone else" (*Selected Short Stories of Franz Kafka,* trans. Willa and Edwin Muir [New York: Modern Library, 1952], p. 200). Christians say the same thing about their obedience to God.

109. Kurt Vonnegut, *Mother Night* (New York: Dell, 1966), pp. 171–72.

110. Vonnegut, *Wampeters, Foma & Granfalloons,* p. 174.

111. Fyodor Dostoevsky, *The Brothers Karamazov,* trans. Andrew R. MacAndrew (New York: Bantam Books, 1970), pp. 707–8.

112. Charles Neider, ed., *The Autobiography of Mark Twain* (New York: Harper & Brothers, 1959), p. 191.

113. Kurt Vonnegut, "Introduction," Louis-Ferdinand Céline, *Rigadoon,* trans. Ralph Manheim (New York: Penguin Books, 1975), p. xvii.

114. Fyodor Dostoevsky, *The Possessed,* trans. Constance Garnett (New York: Modern Library, 1936), p. 409.

115. Vonnegut, *Cat's Cradle,* p. 114.

116. Ibid.

117. Ibid., p. 4.

118. Ibid., p. 17.

119. Ibid., p. 90.

120. Kurt Vonnegut, *Slapstick* (New York: Delacourte/Seymour Lawrence, 1976), p. 230.

121. Vonnegut, *Cat's Cradle,* p. 189.

122. Mark Twain, "The Mysterious Stranger," in Bernard DeVoto, ed., *The Portable Mark Twain* (New York: Viking Press, 1946), p. 742.

123. Vonnegut, *Wampeters, Foma & Granfalloons,* p. 228.

124. Twain, "The Mysterious Stranger," pp. 736–37.

125. Vonnegut, *Cat's Cradle,* p. 134.

126. Quoted in W. H. Auden, *The Dyer's Hand* (New York: Vintage Books, 1968), p. ix.

127. Vonnegut, *Wampeters, Foma & Granfalloons,* pp. 164–65.

128. Vonnegut, *Mother Night,* p. 21.

129. George Steiner, *In Bluebeard's Castle* (New Haven: Yale University Press, 1971), pp. 78–79.

130. Ibid., p. 77.

131. Kurt Vonnegut, *God Bless You, Mr. Rosewater* (New York: Dell, 1965), p. 65.

132. Vonnegut, *Wampeters, Foma & Granfalloons,* pp. 163–64.

133. Twain, *What Is Man?* p. 57.

134. Quoted in Harnsberger, *Mark Twain's Views of Religion,* p. 41.

135. Cleanth Brooks, "Christianity, Myth, and the Symbolism of Poetry," in *Christian Faith and the Contemporary Arts,* ed. Finley Eversole (New York: Abingdon, 1962), pp. 105–6. I am grateful to Prof. John Paul Vincent of Asbury College in Kentucky for calling my attention to this essay.

136. Vonnegut, *Wampeters, Foma & Granfalloons,* p. 239.

137. *Pascal's Pensees,* trans. W. F. Trotter (New York: E. P. Dutton, 1958), Fragment 561, p. 155.

138. *Selected Essays of T. S. Eliot* (New York: Harcourt, Brace & Co., 1950), p. 342.

139. Dostoevsky, *Brothers Karamazov,* p. 205.

140. Dietrich Bonhoeffer, "The First Table of the Ten Commandments," in John D. Godsey, *Preface to Bonhoeffer* (Philadelphia: Fortress Press, 1965), p. 57.

Chapter 4

1. Gerhard Ebeling, *Word and Faith,* trans, James W. Leitch (Philadelphia: Fortress Press, 1963), pp. 341–42.

2. Margaret Mead, "The Occult: On the Edge of the Unknown," *Redbook Magazine,* March 1977, pp. 68, 71.

3. Fyodor Dostoevsky, *The Diary of a Writer,* trans. Boris Brasol (New York: George Braziller, 1954), pp. 543–44.
4. Andrew R. MacAndrew, "Introduction" to Dostoevsky's *The Adolescent,* trans. Andrew R. MacAndrew (Garden City, N.Y.: Anchor Books, 1972), pp. v, xxii.
5. Karl Barth, *The Faith of the Church,* trans. Gabriel Vahanian (New York: Meridian Books, 1958), pp. 104–5.
6. Dietrich Bonhoeffer, *No Rusty Swords,* trans. Edwin H. Robertson and John Bowden (New York: Harper & Row, 1965), p. 147. Italics mine.
7. Ibid., p. 142.
8. Quoted in Konstantin Mochulsky, *Dostoevsky: His Life and Works,* trans. Michael A. Minihan (Princeton: Princeton University Press, 1967), pp. 538–39.
9. Karl Barth, *Church Dogmatics,* Authorised Translation (Edinburgh: T. & T. Clark, 1956), I/2, pp. 325 ff.
10. From record album introduction to *Slaughterhouse-Five,* abridged by Marianne Mantell, Caedmon Records, Inc., 1973.
11. Kurt Vonnegut, *Wampeters, Foma & Granfalloons* (New York: Delacourte/Seymour Lawrence, 1974), p. xxiv.
12. Kurt Vonnegut, *Player Piano* (New York: Avon Books, 1952), p. 140.
13. Quoted in Caroline Harnsberger, *Mark Twain's View of Religion* (Evanston: Schori Press, 1961), p. 17.
14. Quoted in René Fueloep-Miller, *Fyodor Dostoevsky,* trans. Richard and Clara Winston (New York: Charles Scribner's Sons, 1950), p. 51.
15. Quoted in Jürgen Moltmann, *The Crucified God* (New York: Harper & Row, 1974), p. 283.
16. William Peter Blatty, *The Exorcist* (New York: Bantam Books, 1971), pp. 37–8.
17. Wolfhart Pannenberg, *Jesus— God and Man,* trans. Lewis Wilkins and Duane Priebe (Philadelphia: Westminster Press, 1968), p. 84.
18. Paul Tillich, *The New Being* (New York: Charles Scribner's Sons, 1955), p. 44.
19. Bonhoeffer, *No Rusty Swords,* p. 291.
20. Ibid., p. 143.
21. Fyodor Dostoevsky, *The Brothers Karamazov,* trans. Andrew R. MacAndrew (New York: Bantam Books, 1970), p. 786.
22. Henry Ansgar Kelly, *The Devil, Demonology and Witchcraft,* rev. ed. (Garden City: Doubleday, 1974), pp. 18–19. As anyone might guess, most of the literature on the devil and demonology is sheer junk. Kelly's book, however, is a sane and scholarly exception. In it, Kelly also challenges William Peter Blatty's facts of the alleged possession in 1949 on which *The Exorcist* is supposedly based.
23. Tillich, *The New Being,* pp. 36–38.
24. Dostoevsky, *The Brothers Karamazov, op. cit.,* p. 786.

25. *William Peter Blatty on* The Exorcist *From Novel to Film* (New York: Bantam Books, 1974), p. 6.
26. Dostoevsky, *Brothers Karamazov,* p. 765.
27. *William Peter Blatty on* The Exorcist, p. 37.
28. Dostoevsky, *Brothers Karamazov,* p. 780.
29. Archibald McLeish, *J. B.* (Boston: Houghton Mifflin, 1958), p. 11.
30. Barth, *The Faith of the Church,* p. 47.
31. Quoted in Harnsberger, *Mark Twain's Views of Religion,* p. 21.
32. Barth, *Church Dogmatics,* Authorised Translation (Edinburgh: T. & T. Clark, 1956), III/3, p. 530. I am indebted to Prof. Donald Bloesch of Dubuque Theological Seminary for helping me track down this statement of Barth's.
33. Quoted in Edward Wagenknecht, *Mark Twain: The Man and His Work,* 3d ed. (Norman, Okla.: University of Oklahoma Press, 1967), p. 187.
34. Dietrich Bonhoeffer, *Ethics,* trans. Neville H. Smith (London: Collins, 1964), pp. 204–6.
35. Quoted in Helmut Thielicke, *Death and Life,* trans. Edward H. Schroeder (Philadelphia: Fortress Press, 1970), p. 176.
36. *Pascal's Pensees,* trans. W. F. Trotter (New York: E. P. Dutton, 1958), Fragments 277, 278, p. 78.
37. Bonhoeffer, *Ethics,* p. 206.
38. Dietrich Bonhoeffer, *Life Together,* trans. John Doberstein (New York: Harper & Row, 1954), p. 36.
39. Dietrich Bonhoeffer, *Letters and Papers from Prison,* ed. Eberhard Bethge (New York: Macmillan, 1971), pp. 310–11.
40. Ibid., p. 392.
41. This "revolution" also accounts for much of the appeal that Protestant Bonhoeffer has had for Roman Catholics.
42. Bonhoeffer, *Letters and Papers from Prison,* p. 300.
43. Ibid., pp. 382–3.
44. Dostoevsky, *Brothers Karamazov,* p. 309.
45. It is well known that Bonhoeffer believed the world is "moving towards a completely religionless time; people as they are now simply cannot be religious any more" (*Letters and Papers from Prison,* p. 279). Does this mean that "the return of religion," as we have described it in this chapter, disproves this prediction of Bonhoeffer's? Not at all. The upsurge that we are witnessing today of new religions and old religiosity is rather the exception that proves Bonhoeffer's rule. As Ebeling says of the "mythical," the present-day revival of "religion" can only be understood "against the background of an *atheism* which governs our spiritual situation to an extent that church and theology as a rule do not even come anywhere near to adequately realizing." Or, to say the same thing in terms closer to Bon-

hoeffer, it is the deep *godlessness* of "the world come of age" that makes this world so desperate in its search for God. "The world that has come of age is more godless, and perhaps for that very reason nearer to God, than the world before its coming of age" (*Letters and Papers from Prison,* p. 362). Therefore, it is highly doubtful if Bonhoeffer would have been even a little surprised by all of today's religious humbug. Indeed, while in prison he became fascinated by "how superstition thrives in unsettled times" (*Letters and Papers from Prison,* p. 153).

46. Blatty, *The Exorcist,* p. 55.

Chapter 5

1. Dietrich Bonhoeffer, *Ethics,* trans. Neville H. Smith (London: Collins, 1964), p. 206.
2. Karl Barth, *A Shorter Commentary on Romans,* trans. D. H. van Daalen (London: ScM Press Ltd., 1959), p. 147.
3. Dietrich Bonhoeffer, *Letters and Papers from Prison,* ed. Eberhard Bethge (New York: Macmillan, 1971), p. 391.
4. Helmut Thielicke, *Death and Life,* trans. Edward H. Schroeder (Philadelphia: Fortress Press, 1970), p. 11.
5. Fyodor Dostoevsky, *The Brothers Karamazov,* trans. Andrew R. MacAndrew (New York: Bantam Books, 1970), pp. 306–7.
6. Ibid., p. 306.
7. Kurt Vonnegut, *Happy Birthday, Wanda June* (New York: Dell, 1971), p. ix.
8. Kurt Vonnegut, *Wampeters, Foma & Granfalloons* (New York: Delacorte/Seymour Lawrence, 1974), p. 239.
9. Ibid., p. 31.
10. Bonhoeffer, *Ethics,* pp. 211, 213.
11. Quoted in Andre Gide, *Dostoevsky,* trans. Louise Varèse (New York: New Directions Books, 1961), p. 41.
12. Bonhoeffer, *Ethics,* p. 69–70.
13. Quoted in *Newsweek* 25 October 1971, p. 85.
14. *Jesus Christ Superstar,* words by Tim Rice, music by Andrew Lloyd Webber. Copyright © 1969–1970 by Leeds Music, Ltd. Used by permission. All rights reserved.
15. *Newsweek,* 25 October 1971, p. 84–85; *Time,* 9 November 1970, p. 47; *Presbyterian Life,* 1 March 1971, pp. 20–21, 36.
16. *Newsweek,* 25 October 1971, p. 85.
17. *Time,* 9 November 1970, p. 47.
18. Kurt Vonnegut at American Booksellers Association press conference, Chicago, 8 June 1976.
19. Kurt Vonnegut, *Slaughterhouse-Five* (New York: Dell, 1969, p. 108.
20. Barth, *The Faith of the Church,* trans. Gabriel Vahanian (New York: Meridian Books, 1958), p. 63.
21. Bonhoeffer, *Letters and Papers from Prison,* p. 383.
22. Vonnegut, *Slaughterhouse-Five,* p. 109.

23. "Carols for Christmas, 1969," *New York Times Magazine,* 21 December 1969, p. 5.

24. Edwin Miller, "Rock Gets Religion," *Seventeen,* March 1971, p. 168.

25. Edward Wasiolek, ed., *Dostoevsky: The Notebooks for the Possessed,* trans. Victor Terras (Chicago: University of Chicago Press, 1968), p. 252–53.

26. Kurt Vonnegut, *Breakfast of Champions* (New York: Dell, 1973), p. 167.

27. Vonnegut, *Wampeters, Foma & Granfalloons,* p. 205.

28. Soren Kierkegaard, *The Journals of Soren Kierkegaard,* trans. Alexander Dru (London: Oxford University Press, 1938), p. 413.

29. Dietrich Bonhoeffer, *The Cost of Discipleship* (New York: Macmillan, 1963), p. 99.

30. Bonhoeffer, *Ethics,* p. 52. Italics mine.

31. Quoted in Karl Barth, *Evangelical Theology,* trans. Grover Foley (New York: Holt, Rinehart and Winston, 1963), p. 18.

32. Kurt Vonnegut, Player Piano (New York: Avon Books, 1952), p. 96.

33. Mark Twain, *What Is Man?* ed. Paul Baender (Berkeley: University of California Press, 1973), pp. 487–88.

34. D. P. Walker, *The Decline of Hell* (Chicago: University of Chicago Press, 1964), pp. 3–4.

35. Twain, *What Is Man?* p. 483.

36. Karl Barth, *The Humanity of God,* trans. J. N. Thomas and Thomas Waser (Richmond: John Knox Press, 1960), pp. 61–62.

37. Quoted in *Mark Twain and the Three R's,* ed. Maxwell Geismar (Indianapolis: Bobbs-Merrill Co., 1973), p. 154.

38. Karl Barth, *Deliverance to the Captives,* trans. Marguerite Wieser (New York: Harper & Brothers, 1961), pp. 149–50.

39. Quoted in Twain, *What Is Man?* pp. 6–7.

40. Walker, *Decline of Hell,* pp. 29 ff.

41. Quoted in *The World Treasure of Religious Quotations,* ed. Ralph L. Woods (New York: Hawthorn Books, 1966), p. 429.

42. Walker, *Decline of Hell,* p. 262.

43. Quoted in Harnsberger, *Mark Twain's Views of Religion,* p. 46.

44. *Karl Barth's Table Talk,* ed. John Godsey (Richmond, Va.: John Knox Press, 1962), p. 15.

45. Twain, *What Is Man?* pp. 56–57.

46. Ibid., p. 479.

47. From the author's personal interview with Kurt Vonnegut. See appendix.

48. Barth, *Deliverance to the Captives,* p. 86.

49. Karl Barth, *Church Cogmatics,* Authorised Translation (Edinburgh: T. & T. Clark, 1956), II/2, p. 458.

50. Kurt Vonnegut, *The Sirens of Titan* (New York: Dell, 1959), pp. 26, 287.

51. Vonnegut, *Slaughterhouse-Five,* p. 2.

52. Barth, *Church Dogmatics,* II/2, p. 476.
53. Ibid., pp. 477, 497.
54. Albert Camus, *Resistance, Rebellion, and Death,* trans. Justin O'Brien (New York: Alfred Knopf, 1961), p. 59.
55. Vonnegut, *Wampeters, Foma & Granfalloons,* p. 205.
56. Gerhard Ebeling, *Word and Faith,* trans. James W. Leitch (Philadelphia: Fortress Press, 1963), p. 375.
57. Barth, *Church Dogmatics,* II/2, pp. 13–14.
58. Walker, *Decline of Hell,* p. 41.
59. Barth, *Humanity of God,* p. 62.
60. Quoted in Walker, *Decline of Hell,* p. 244.
61. Barth, *Church Dogmatics,* II/2, p. 315.
62. Karl Barth, *God Here and Now,* trans. Paul M. van Buren (New York: Harper & Row, 1964), p. 34.
63. Barth, *Evangelical Theology,* p. 136.
64. Quoted in Hans Schwarz, *On the Way to the Future* (Minneapolis: Augsburg, 1972), p. 217.
65. Quoted in Eberhard Busch, *Karl Barth,* trans. John Bowden (Philadelphia: Fortress Press, 1976), p. 394. Italics mine.
66. *Karl Barth's Table Talk,* p. 87.
67. CBS News transcript of "60 Minutes," 15 September 1970, p. 14.
68. From the author's personal interview with Kurt Vonnegut. See appendix.
69. Barth, *Church Dogmatics,* II/2, pp. 12–13.
70. Ibid., p. 159.
71. See Dean M. Kelly's important recent book *Why Conservative Churches Are Growing* (New York: Harper & Row, 1972).